# THE CATHARS
# AND THE
# ALBIGENSIAN CRUSADE

# THE CATHARS
# AND THE
# ALBIGENSIAN CRUSADE

MICHAEL COSTEN

MANCHESTER UNIVERSITY PRESS
Manchester and New York

distributed exclusively in the USA by St. Martin's Press

Published by Manchester University Press
Oxford Road, Manchester M13 9NR, UK
and Room 400, 175 Fifth Avenue, New York, NY 10010, USA

Distributed exclusively in the USA by
St. Martin's Press, Inc., 175 Fifth Avenue, New York,
NY 10010, USA

Distributed exclusively in Canada by
UBC Press, University of British Columbia, 6344 Memorial Road,
Vancouver, BC, Canada V6T 1Z2

British Library Cataloguing-in-Publication Data
A catalogue record for this book is available from the British Library

Library of Congress Cataloging-in-Publication Data
Costen, M. D.
    The Cathars and the Albigensian Crusade / Michael Costen.
        p.    cm.
    Includes bibliographical references.
    ISBN 0–7190–4331–X (hardcover). — ISBN 0–7190–4332–8 (pbk.)
        1. Albigenses.    2.Heresies, Christian—France—Languedoc—
History—Middle Ages. 600–1500.    3. France—Church
history—987–1515.    I. Title.    II. Series.
    BX4891.2.C67    1997
    272'.3—dc21                                                    97–6133

ISBN 0 7190 4331 X hardback
      0 7190 4332 8 paperback

First published 1997

01 00 99 98 97    10 9 8 7 6 5 4 3 2 1

Photoset in Joanna
by Northern Phototypesetting Co. Ltd, Bolton
Printed in Great Britain
by Bell & Bain Ltd, Glasgow

For Charles Wesley Costen and Nellie Annie Costen

# Contents

# List of figures

# Preface and acknowledgements

My first sight of the *cité* of Carcassonne, its towers gleaming in the sunshine, took me back immediately to the line drawings and water-coloured plates in the books of my childhood. Here was the original of the turreted castles and towns of fairy stories. Even more intriguing were the ruined castles which stood on forbidding hilltops all across the Corbières Mountains. Why were there so many ruined castles here? I soon began to discover more about the people who had built these places and, as someone brought up as a nonconformist, I became more and more interested in the Cathars and the catastrophic consequences of their rejection of orthodoxy. In happier times I was able to share this interest with others by taking groups of students to visit the region. Now the opportunity to write about the Languedoc has been seized as a labour of love.

This book deals with a time and place in which the personal names used were different from those in use in English today. I do not favour the French habit of ruthlessly translating them all into a modern (French) form, which gives the impression that this was how they were written and spoken at the time. Neither can I anglicise them. I have therefore tried to keep to the spellings which were used at the time in Occitan, the Langue d'Oc. I have also tried to avoid inconsistencies, but contemporaries could be very cavalier about spelling.

Place name spellings are those of the official *Cartes Nationales*. The term 'Languedoc' is used to mean that area from Montpellier westwards as far as the western borders of the County of Toulouse, and from the northern edge of Roussillon as far as the Auvergne, north of Rodez. The 'Midi' extends rather further, including Roussillon and as far east as the Rhône. 'Provence' is the region east of the Rhône, south of Lyon all the way to the Mediterranean; it was part of the Holy Roman Empire.

I have tried to use the term 'Gaul' for the whole of the old Roman Empire between the Rhine and the Atlantic, and from the Channel to the Pyrenees, in the period up to about AD 1000. Thereafter, as the old Carolingian Empire disintegrated into the princely dukedoms and counties – Burgundy, Aquitaine and Normandy, Anjou, Toulouse and Champagne – I have called the area nominally under the suzerainty of the kings of the Franks, 'Francia'; though it should be noted that the counts of Barcelona never acknowledged the kings of the Franks. Only as the conquests of Philippe II Auguste started to make royal power a reality can we begin to talk of 'France'.

I was very fortunate that my Department gave me a term's leave from teaching in the autumn of 1994 which enabled me to supplement my pictures of the region and to do much other work towards the project. My colleagues, Dr Joseph Bettey, Dr Rowena Fowler and Professor Michael Aston, read most of the earlier drafts of this book and helped me enormously with their constructive criticism. Dr Frank Thorn and Caroline Thorn gave me helpful advice over translations of Latin text. The Continuing Education classes who have heard me talk on this subject have helped too, by making me think about how to express what I wanted to say.

I am grateful to Dr J. Gordon for permission to use his unpublished thesis. I thank the staff of the University Library at Bristol for their help and also the staff of the University of Birmingham Library. My especial thanks go to Mrs Chris Mossman, who turned the crude maps I drew into the finished articles. Finally I offer my thanks to my colleague, Dr Elizabeth Bird, Head of the Department for Continuing Education at Bristol University, for the Department's support throughout the project.

Just as I was completing this book Janet Shirley very kindly sent me a copy of her new translation, from the Occitan into English, of the *Chanson de la Croisade Albigeoise* (1996). I much regret not being able at this late stage to use this first translation into English.

Michael Costen
Axbridge, Somerset

# 1

## Introduction

The Languedoc is a part of the modern Languedoc–Roussillon region, which encompasses the area bounded by the Pyrenean border with Spain to the south, the Auvergne to the north, the Mediterranean to the south-east, as far as the Rhône delta, and Toulouse to the west. In the twelfth and thirteenth centuries the term meant something more than merely a geographical region. It applied particularly to the language and to the culture of the south of Francia. The sense of being something apart and special, a sense of identity as a people, emerged most strongly from the Crusade against the Cathars, just at the time when that culture was overwhelmed by the military power and political skill of the French.

The people of the whole of southern France, excluding Gascony to the west, spoke Occitan, the Langue d'Oc (using *oc* rather than *oui* to mean 'yes'). Among its speakers this language was known as Romans and like other Romance languages it had developed from the Latin of the late Roman world to which the region belonged. The bounds of the area within which the language was spoken in the twelfth and thirteenth centuries ran from the mouth of the Dordogne, north-east past Angoulême to enclose most of what is now the département of La Creuse before running down towards Clermont-Ferrand and then south-east to cross the Rhone between Vienne and Valence. It then passed south of Grenoble to meet the Alps (Bec 1973; Anglade 1921: 11; Hill and Bergin 1973). The region within which the Crusade was to take place was not as extensive as the linguistic area. Nevertheless, it ran from Agen in the west to Avignon in the east and from the Pyrenees to Cahors in the north-west (figure 1).

The early history of the region is marked by the progressive loss of cohesion which was evident elsewhere in Frankish society. First the imperial counts became *de facto* hereditary rulers as the Frankish kings lost control. Then in the tenth century the counts saw their power diminish and many new noble families emerged, claiming authority in

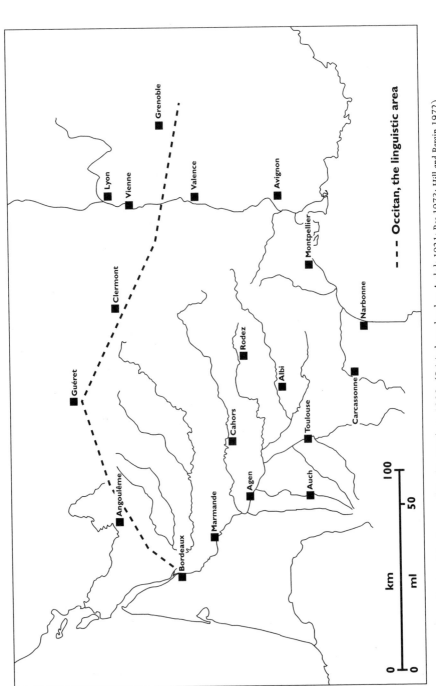

Figure 1 Northern limits of the League d'Oc (Occitan), c. 1200. (Original map based on Anglade 1921; Bec 1973; Hill and Bergin 1972)

- - - Occitan, the linguistic area

more limited areas. The response to loss of central rule was a progressive militarisation of the countryside, marked by the building of castles and the recruiting of knights.

The Church, which had been an instrument of Frankish imperial rule, lost the protection of the distant kings and struggled against the tendency of the new local rulers to dominate it. Church property fell under lay control; monasteries and cathedrals ceased to function; bishops were often replaced by noblemen or not replaced at all. The long fight to maintain the Church as a distinctive ritual component of society was aided by the monastic revival of the tenth and the eleventh centuries and by the growing cohesion of the Church throughout western Europe as the reformers inside the Papacy and the revitalised monastic orders sought to purify its life. Their intellectual and moral leadership of society made the Church a much more powerful institution in the society of southern Gaul by the end of the eleventh century than it had been in the tenth century.

In other parts of Francia the eleventh century saw the emergence of counts and dukes as powerful rulers, who used the new militarised society to build up a web of personal obligations and ties through which they created principalities. In the Languedoc that process was not as thoroughly carried through as in the north. In particular, the counts of Toulouse emerged as the greatest of the new local rulers, but were not able to create the powerful network of obligation which would enable them to master the lesser nobility and link them into a 'state'. In addition, the growth of several minor principalities, Narbonne, Montpellier, Foix and Béziers–Carcassonne, made it possible for the powerful southern county of Barcelona to gain a hold as a political force in the Languedoc and make dominance by Toulouse an impossibility.

Contrasted with the fragmented political world was the world of the towns, which had never entirely lost their urban qualities and which grew again in the eleventh century as trade and manufacturing centres, based initially on the expanding local commerce and a growing agriculture. The expansion of the economy provided the wealth which supported the militarised nobility and helped to make warfare endemic. The Languedoc at the end of the eleventh century was a region of enormous vitality and energy which was displayed through a vigorous culture, but it had a precarious political balance which the twelfth century was to make worse.

## The decline of public power

When Charlemagne died in 814 his empire stretched from Saxony to Barcelona. The region which was to become the Languedoc, centred on the lands of the counts of Toulouse, was divided between the kingdom of Aquitaine, Septimania and the Spanish March, later the County of Barcelona (Hallam 1980: 1–6). The area had been conquered at great cost to Charlemagne in 801 and it provided a buffer between the heartlands of the Franks to the north and the Moslems of Iberia to the south. Under Charles the Bald (838–77) this division continued to exist with the eastern part of the Languedoc, including the bishoprics of Albi, Carcassonne, Béziers and Agde and the archbishopric of Narbonne, forming part of Septimania. The towns of the Rhone delta and valley and the bishopric of Uzés in Provence were part of the eastern Empire after 843, while in the west, Toulouse lay in Aquitaine.

Early in the reign of Charles the Bald, Aquitaine became a centre of resistance to his authority under Pippin II, the grandson of Charlemagne and son of Pippin I, king of Aquitaine. Although Pippin had lost support by 848, it was not until 864 that he was captured. In the intervening period he remained as a focus of rebellion and resistance, operating in the Spanish March (Nelson 1992). His attempted independence was fed by support from among the nobility of the south, who were a mixture of Gallo-Roman, Visigothic and Frankish aristocracy. One of the major supporters of Pippin's cause was Bernard, Count of Barcelona (executed by Charles the Bald in 844) while the city of Toulouse appeared as a centre of resistance. One way to solve the problem of continuous rebellion was to give the Aquitanians a king of their own from the royal family and in 855 the young Charles, second son of Charles the Bald, became king of Aquitaine. After his death in 866 Louis the Stammerer took his place as king and enabled his father to maintain control of the south.

Charles the Bald ruled his vast kingdom by balancing and exploiting the rivalries of his great magnates and by granting and withholding offices and benefices. By the time of his grandson Charles the Simple, who became king of all the West Franks in 898, that system had broken down. The king could no longer travel throughout his realm and restricted himself to the Frankish heartlands, in the valleys of the Oise and the Seine. More importantly he ceased to control the great *honores* of his kingdom. These came to pass within a family in a manner which can be seen as straightforwardly hereditary. Instead of a system whereby the great aristocracy received lands and honours from the king and had them taken away if they offended, now they became essentially autonomous. In effect the king ceased to have any control in the south and west of his kingdom, as his access to its lands ceased and the great men of the region ceased to attend his court. The counts of the south were independent rulers by the beginning of the tenth century (Nelson 1992: 259–60).

The king's loss of power did not stop at the level of the counts. He had had many vassals throughout the provinces commended to him, but since he was no longer an effective power, these men transferred their allegiance to local magnates, partly because they were constrained to do so, partly because it became the necessary way of advancement. The appearance of power among these great families was in some ways illusory, for the reality was that the loss of influence of the kings of the Franks was followed by the loss of power by these families also. The viscounts and other minor officials – who, like the counts, had been appointed officials in Charlemagne's time and in the ninth century – also made themselves secure by appropriation of the fisc used for their support and they too, emerged as hereditary and semi-independent nobility (Wolff 1967: 132).

In 900 viscounts existed in Nîmes, Béziers, Narbonne, Carcassonne, Toulouse, Roussillon, Catalonia, Albi and the Limousin. By 975 the independent noble families in the Languedoc numbered at least 150, all claiming their titles and power by hereditary right (Lewis 1965: 196). While the families at the top of the tree had not increased in numbers, those below them, claiming rights and powers over other men, had increased enormously.

The loss of power was in part caused by the habit of dividing lands among children, so that great patrimonies were divided into petty units. There was nothing revolutionary about this practice, which had been the norm for centuries. What was different was that the custom was now being applied to territories and powers which had previously been the preserve of the king and had been part of the public domain. Now counties, previously administrative regions, together with all the public powers within them, were also being divided. The state itself was being parcelled out as private property and public powers divided among heirs.

## The new principalities

By the early tenth century there was a small number of great families in the region, descended from the counts appointed by Charlemagne and his successors, who had established themselves as powerful hereditary rulers. The family of the counts of Toulouse was descended from Fredelon, appointed by Charles the Bald in 849. By the early years of the tenth century they claimed control of the Auvergne and the Limousin to the north and Carcassonne, Narbonne and the Razès to the south-east. In the north this produced enmity with the family of the counts of Poitou and in the south conflict with the heirs of Oliba, Count of Carcassonne. This family sought to control the southern part of Septimania, while allies and relatives controlled Barcelona to the south (Lewis 1965: 179–85).

The counts of Toulouse were adept at building political power through marriage alliances from the tenth century onwards. The marriage of Eudes, Count of Toulouse (879–918) to Garsinde brought the Albigeois into their hands. Later in the tenth century Guilhem III Taillefer (950–c. 1037) married in 990 Emma, the daughter of Rotbold, Count of Provence who brought the family her right to the county (Debax 1988). This strategy was to continue during the eleventh century and into the twelfth and provided a counterbalance to the dispersal of lands and powers as cadets inherited.

During the eleventh century the counts of Toulouse continued to divide their inheritance. When Guilhem, Count of Toulouse died in about 1037, his sons Bernard and Pons divided the county between them. The lands in the east were ruled from St-Gilles. When Pons died in 1061 the new count, Guilhem IV, again divided power with his brother Raimon of St-Gilles. It was not until Raimon of St-Gilles succeeded as Raimon IV in 1088 that all the lands of the House of Toulouse were finally united, but not territorially unified (figure 2).

The counts of Carcassonne in the tenth century were members of the family which also ruled in Barcelona. Roger the Old, who died in 1002 bequeathed his lands to his three sons. His daughter married into the House of Barcelona. One son founded the County of Foix and the other, Raimon-Roger, took Carcassonne itself. In 1067 the County of Carcassonne collapsed as a result of the death of Roger III. The title fell to his sister Ermengarde who had married Raimon Trencavel of Nîmes and Albi; but not all the rights connected with Carcassonne and the Razès went with the title (Dunbabin 1985: 170). Along the coast the viscounty of Narbonne had become effectively independent of Carcassonne. The viscount ruled half the city and a coastal strip which reached nearly to Perpignan in the south. This independence was to last throughout the twelfth century. At Montpellier in 985, the Bishop of Maguelonne, the lord of the district, granted territory to a nobleman called Guilhem, who became the viscount of Montpellier. The act was ratified by the Count of Melgueil who thus gained a vassal. Because the immediate lords were relatively weak the family founded by Guilhem was able to develop and maintain its real independence, enhancing this position in 1085 when the Count of Melgueil placed his lands under papal protection (Montpellier 1884–6).

Thus the viscounts of Montpellier, the viscounts of Béziers and Carcassonne and the viscounts of Narbonne made themselves virtually independent rulers. Since the middle of the tenth century they had been

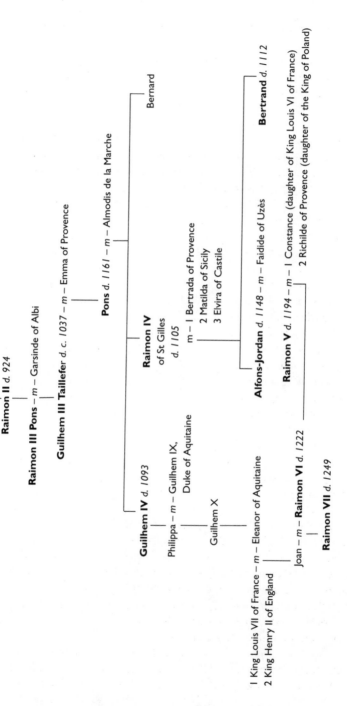

Figure 2   The counts of Toulouse (names in **bold**)

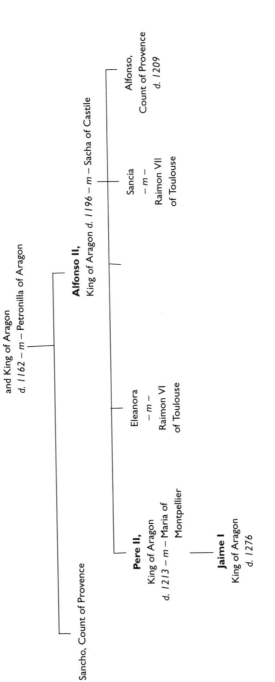

Figure 3  The counts of Barcelona (names in **bold**)

gaining power and independence at the expense of the counts of Toulouse. By the late tenth century the real power of the counts of Toulouse was limited to the regions around Toulouse, Albi and Rodez and the Rhone valley (Lewis 1984: V 252), and despite the wars of the eleventh century they could not regain control of the rest of the region.

The other important force in the region was the count of Barcelona. The county had been founded as a marcher lordship by Charlemagne and by the early eleventh century it was so far from the king of the Franks that the counts never acknowledged him. Raimon-Berenger I of Barcelona had married as his third wife Almodis de la Marche – she had been married first to Hugues de Lusignan, and had left her second husband Pons, Count of Toulouse in 1053 or 1054, for Raimon-Berenger (Hill and Hill 1959: 5) (figure 3). She bore him twin sons, Raimon-Berenger II and Berenger-Raimon II. Their father decided to provide for his younger children by increasing his share of the County of Carcassonne and in 1068 set out to buy up the rights which Ermengarde of Carcassonne had inherited in the previous year. This he did with the aid of some 5,000 oz (140 kg) of gold, probably the spoils of his successful aggression against the Moors to the south of Barcelona, so that he came to possess an allod in Carcassonne (Valdeon 1980: 216).

His eldest son Pere-Raimon, heir to Barcelona, murdered Almodis his step-mother in 1071 and disappeared. Raimon-Berenger I himself died in 1076 and was succeeded by his twin sons, who ruled the County of Barcelona jointly. In 1082 Berenger-Raimon 'El Fratricida', murdered his twin and seized sole power. Because of the turmoil caused by this violent act he was unable to assert his rights over Carcassonne and Bernard Aton, the son of Ermengarde of Carcassonne and Raimon Trencavel, seized Carcassonne and its territory and retained it. However the claims of the House of Barcelona continued to exist and became a general claim to overlordship which provided the counts of Barcelona with their interest in the region in the twelfth and thirteenth centuries. By 1150 the Trencavels acknowledged the overlordship of Barcelona and received formal recognition as Viscounts of Carcassonne (Abadal i de Vinyals 1964) (figure 4).

The House of Toulouse failed to take advantage of the weakness in Carcassonne, despite a political interest in the county. By the late eleventh century there was a block of territory, stretching from Albi to Béziers in the north, down the coast to the south of Narbonne and from the sea to Carcassonne, which was outside their control. This territory lay across the natural lines of communication between Toulouse and the Rhône valley and covered the coastal route into the County of Barcelona

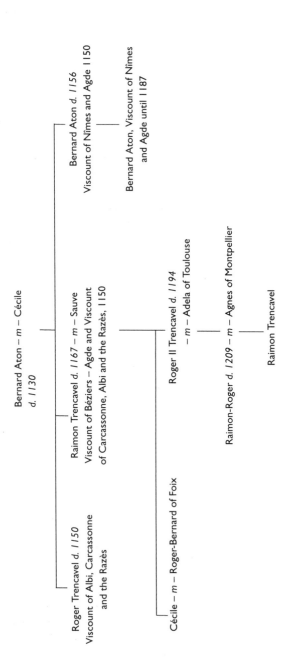

Bernard Aton – *m* – Cécile
*d. 1130*

Roger Trencavel *d. 1150*
Viscount of Albi, Carcassonne
and the Razès

Raimon Trencavel *d. 1167* – *m* – Sauve
Viscount of Béziers – Agde and Viscount
of Carcassonne, Albi and the Razès, 1150

Bernard Aton *d. 1156*
Viscount of Nîmes and Agde 1150

Bernard Aton, Viscount of Nîmes
and Agde until 1187

Cécile – *m* – Roger-Bernard of Foix

Roger II Trencavel *d. 1194*
– *m* – Adela of Toulouse

Raimon-Roger *d. 1209* – *m* – Agnes of Montpellier

Raimon Trencavel

Figure 4  The House of Trencavel

so the counts of Barcelona provided a counterbalance which enabled the smaller principalities to maintain their independence.

The county of Toulouse was ruled from St-Gilles, which had become a rich trading centre, but the most effective political power lay in the west around Toulouse. Like other great men of his day, Raimon IV of St-Gilles was deeply affected by the call to the First Crusade and went off to become one of the leaders of the army which captured Jerusalem in July 1099 (Hill and Hill 1959; Runciman 1951). He became deeply preoccupied by the Holy Land and in 1105 he was killed while conquering the County of Tripoli, leaving an infant son, Alfons-Jordan (he had been baptised in the River Jordan). At home Raimon's lands were ruled by his illegitimate son Bertrand, who could not inherit. In 1098 Raimon IV's daughter, Philippa, had married Guilhem IX, Duke of Aquitaine, who proceeded to seize Toulouse in Raimon IV's absence. Only excommunication by the Pope in 1100 persuaded him to hand back the city and its lands. Bertrand then departed for the East where he became the ruler of his father's County of Tripoli. Thus the lands in the Languedoc were left with no effective ruler and Guilhem IX reoccupied them. It was some years before Alfons-Jordan could intervene. Meanwhile in 1112 Raimon-Berenger III of Barcelona took as his third wife Douce, the daughter and heiress of the Guibert, Count of Provence, who had died in 1110 (Valdeon 1980: 217). Now the counts of Barcelona had a foothold on the eastern side of the Rhône and it became inevitable that the houses of Barcelona and Toulouse would intensify the struggle for control of the coastal strip between the Rhône and the Pyrenees.

### The militarised society: castles

The result of the fragmentation of power was the tendency towards the militarisation of society and this was manifest in the rapid spread of castles throughout the area. Some of these castles were entirely the property of the families who constructed them and lived in them; others were granted as fiefs to the castellan, while others were simply granted to a castellan on limited terms (Lewis 1984: V 254).

There had been stone fortifications in use in the Languedoc for many centuries, but in the middle of the tenth century, as the power of lesser lords grew, castles began to appear and they multiplied, particularly in the early years of the eleventh century. A Bull of Pope John XV of 986 confirmed to the Abbey of Cuxa *in comitatu Fenoliotensi ecclesiam sanctae Crucis cum castello et omnibus rebus ad se pertinenes* (quoted in Quèhen et Dieltiens 1983: 31). By 1011 the castle of Puilaurens was in existence, while the castle at Rennes-le-Chateau existed by 1002. Throughout the Cor-

bières Mountains other castles were certainly in existence in the early
years of the eleventh century. Peyrepertuse was first mentioned in 1020
and the castle of Auriac in 1028 (Quèhens and Dieltiens 1983: 32–5).
In most cases the earliest surviving masonry at these castles dates from
the early eleventh century also. This is certainly the case at Peyrepertuse
and at Puilaurens (Salch 1977).

The dangerous nature of the countryside, at least for local rulers,
was expressed by the early construction of castles and it is interesting to
notice the number of very early castles in the region to the west of Montpellier and Béziers. So many early castles suggests that the district was
rich enough and well enough organised to have surpluses which could
be used for the expensive business of castle building (figures 5 and 6).
The other region with very early castles was in the eastern Pyrenees, in
an area which was difficult to control because of the terrain and where
the fragmentation of power was extreme.

### The knights

Castles needed soldiers to make them useful, and parallel with their
appearance came the milites, the knights, men of often humble social origins who formed the garrisons of the castles, working for wages. In the
Carolingian kingdom, military power had been exercised by the king
and his magnates who formed an army at the king's command. Each
magnate brought along his dependants and the king summoned his own
vassals to serve in his army, their responsibility in return for the
benefices they held. By the tenth century that system had been taken over
by the new aristocracy, who now granted benefices to their followers in
return for military support, so that the new private armies were composed partly of soldiers who were paid money wages and partly of followers who had received a gift of land in return for their support. These
fees became hereditary and enabled the new aristocracy to build up
around themselves a class of military retainer who formed the under-
pinning for their social group and among whom the nobility themselves
came to be subsumed as soldiers.

So the men who owned the castles and recruited the soldiers came
to see themselves as firstly military men. As that happened the whole
social structure of the Languedoc became militarised. So it is not surprising that the owners of castles began to demand contributions from
the local population. A variety of taxes were raised under the names of
alberga or recepta in addition to the customary cens paid by tenants to
landowners. By the end of the tenth century the district within which a
particular castle might demand these taxes was becoming well defined
and the militarisation of the landscape was well advanced also. This ten-

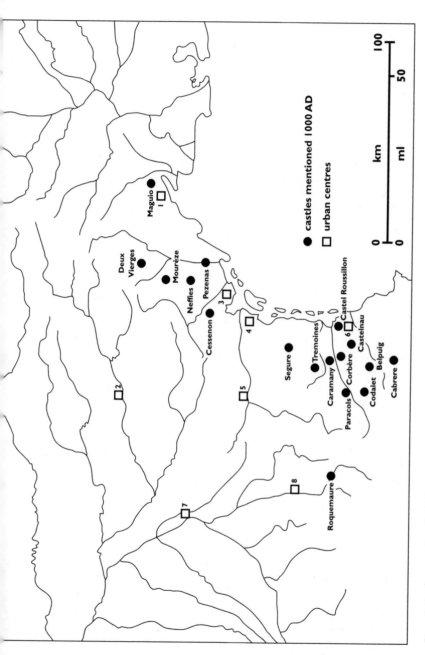

Figure 5 Castles mentioned 1000 AD

● castles mentioned 1000 AD
□ urban centres

Maguio
Deux Vierges
Mourèze
Neffies
Pezenas
Cessenon
Segure
Tremoines
Caramany
Corbère
Paracols
Codalet
Belpuig
Cabrere
Castel Roussillon
Castelnau
Roquemaure

km
ml

0          50          100

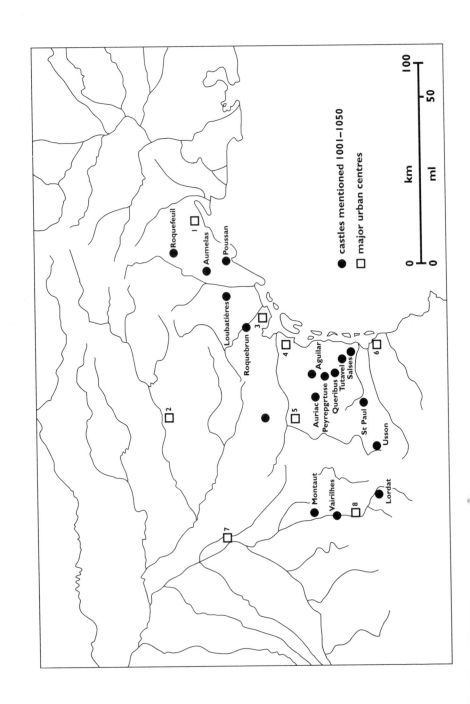

● castles mentioned 1001–1050
□ major urban centres

Roquefeuil
Aumelas
Poussan
Loubatières
Roquebrun
Auriac
Aguilar
Peyrepgrtuse
Queribus
Tutavel
Salses
St Paul
Usson
Montaut
Vairilhes
Lordat

km
ml

0    50    100

dency became even more marked in the first half of the eleventh century as castles multiplied and the status of the *miles* began to rise.

Where the counts of Toulouse and other local rulers failed was in not being able to bind these military rulers to themselves with oaths of loyalty and with gifts of land. Instead the local aristocracy retained their allods as the most important parts of their lands and thus did not find themselves placed in positions of dependence upon great rulers. This failure to link the aristocracy of the Languedoc into a tight web of 'feudal' alliances meant that the relationships which matured in the twelfth century were looser, and the minor nobility retained more political control and independence of action than was the case in northern France.

### The countryside and the peasants

In the Languedoc the peasant community of the tenth and the eleventh centuries contained few slaves, but some bondmen and alloidal landowners. Furthermore, in the south the Carolingian estate system, with its unified territories and its large demesnes, had never taken root. Most estates consisted of scattered holdings with no demesne, so that lords took money rents and dues in kind rather than labour services, and their relationships with their tenants were more distant and less personal than in the north (Poly and Bournazel 1991: 253). Some estates, *casales disruptos*, consisted of little more than a dwelling and a few dispersed fields and vineyards, others formed *manses*, larger areas of ground which might be exploited by a single peasant farmer, or by a group, often related to one another. Such holdings were evidently substantial in size and the owners relatively well-to-do. Monastic land might often consist of individual *manses*, each farmed by a peasant who owed cash rents to the monastery, or might owe fixed labour services.

Some peasants lived on *apendariae*. These were smaller holdings, evidently carved out of former waste lands, often as dependencies of named *manses*. Other peasants were the proprietors of *bordaria*, which consisted of little more than a cottage (Magnou-Nortier 1974: 130–4). Those peasants who lived on their allods were the *boni homines* of contemporary documents, members of families which were often to form the new minor gentry of the feudalised countryside of the thirteenth century. All seem to have paid taxes or tolls of some sort by the middle of the eleventh century. These often included the obligation to provide for the support of soldiers for a period each year. In this way the militarised owners of castles supported their troops. The local *vicars*, secular officials, often castle owners, held the rights to levy the corvée – labour services – on many *manses*. They had taken over what had once been public rights to labour service which were exercised over lands which had once belonged to the royal fisc.

The majority of peasants were not alloidal owners. They were tied to their lands in the manner of the late Roman colonate, from whom they were descended (Ourliac, 1990: 133). When property was sold they went with the land and this state continued in the eleventh century, although it was somewhat tempered by the possibility of escape to one of the new *sauvétés* (see below). Extension of the lord's power to the control of utilities, such as mills and waste land, and to demands for taxes and dues was a natural result of the growth in power of the rulers of the countryside. Many alloidal peasants also came to do homage to local lords as a form of self-protection and many others were drawn into the power of the local lord in the eleventh century. The lords' control was exercised through the right to take dues and taxes from the peasantry rather than in the exaction of labour. This exercise of banal lordship was the way in which the new militarised class in the south was able to extract part of the surplus labour of the peasantry. Particularly in the eleventh century, the peasantry were becoming increasingly dependent upon the lords, although the division of society into free, noble and militarised on the one hand and servile, dependants on the other never became as clear-cut in the Languedoc as it did in northern France.

There is some evidence that despite the instability of the tenth century the population began to increase; and this increase was to accelerate in the eleventh century (Duby 1975: 397). Up to the mid-tenth century and possibly beyond, the countryside was still organised on the basis of the old Roman system of *villae* (Bourin 1990). Peasantry lived in scattered farmsteads and hamlets on lands which retained boundaries which had descended from the late Empire of the fifth century. It seems that the development of villages is a phenomenon of the later tenth and the eleventh centuries. At Montaigut and St-Jean-le-Froid, both in Tarn, the two deserted villages were both tenth-century foundations according to the excavators (Hensel and Nadolski 1965; Hensel and Dabrowski 1965).

A further sign of growing population was the appearance of *sauvétés*. A development of the eleventh century, they were nearly always at first on church lands and were essentially villages built close to or around a church or monastery and to which the church extended a special protection. The *sauvété* of Vieux-en-Albigeois was founded c. 1035 on the lands of the church. The village was the work of Bishop Amiel of Albi and Pons of Toulouse, both of whom had been involved in the 'Peace' movement at Limoges and Bourges in 1031. The charter of the *sauvété* laid down that anyone breaking the peace of the *vicus* inside a laid-down perimeter would be excommunicated and banished from the county (Biget 1990). Many other fortified villages also began to appear in the later tenth and eleventh centuries as peasants gathered together in one place and found security behind walls which had hitherto been rare. Considering the growth of castral *sauvétés* in the twelfth century it seems likely that this revolution which swept the peasantry into villages was something which happened under the pressure of the militarisation of southern society and which was propelled by the lords rather than initiated by the peasantry. It was part of the process by which the peasantry was made dependent.

Some of the new villages only gathered the pre-existing population together in one place, but in other cases they were genuinely new settlements which opened new land up to cultivation. Here again the Church was active as an institution. Cluniac monasteries needed increased incomes to fund their lavish building programmes and to maintain the rich monastic lifestyle which had developed. The Abbey of Moissac was active in the eleventh century in the foundation of both villages and towns, as for instance Villeneuve d'Aveyron (Bousquet 1963: 517).

## The towns
The Languedoc was an area of ancient towns. Narbonne could trace its foundation to the Greeks, and many others were the product of the early Roman Empire. Toulouse had been a great Roman city and the Rhone Valley was still full of the monuments of that empire in places such as Arles and Nîmes. These places survived, usually behind their walls, and it was not until the late tenth and early eleventh centuries that the appearance of *bourgs*, additional parts of the town where commerce was carried on, signalled the beginnings of growth. Narbonne had a *bourg* by 978 and by 1000 the *bourg* of Besalu was in existence. Albi and Nîmes had their *bourgs* by the mid-eleventh century Toulouse by 1077, and Béziers, Nîmes and Carcassonne by the end of the century (Le Goff 1980: 61–7). The slightly later development of the *bourgs* here as compared with more northerly parts of France was probably due to the lack of any real central authority. The growth of towns was caused by the need of the new elites to control trade for their own benefit. Because of the weakness of so many secular lords it often fell to bishops and other ecclesiastics to undertake development and control (Hodges 1982: 196–7). So at Albi in 1042, it was the bishop of Albi and the bishop of Nîmes, together with his brother Bernard Aton, Count of Albi, who initiated the construction of the first bridge across the Tarn (Le Goff 1980: 111).

By the early eleventh century trade with the world outside the Languedoc certainly existed. Money was in wide circulation and the accumulation of treasure by churches and by individuals has been documented. Some of the gold in use undoubtedly came from Moslem Spain, either as booty or as wages paid to the *milites* of the Languedoc who served as mercenaries in the armies of the Moslem rulers (Bonassie 1978: 286–8). This gold was used to placate the saints with gifts to their altars and to pay ransoms, but some of it must have passed into trade. In the eleventh century the growth of towns was still essentially a local phenomenon and seems to have owed relatively little to international trade, and this is perhaps a measure of the extent to which this region was isolated from the rest of Francia. Mediterranean trade, while it existed, was not of great importance. However, the towns were well placed to participate in the twelfth-century expansion, both as manufacturing centres and as sites for the accumulation of the capital necessary to carry on long-distance trade. Their connections with the Church became increasingly important as the bishops took a more active interest in politics and as they rebuilt cathedrals and church organisations. It was in the towns also that the government of eleventh-century rulers was situated, so that Narbonne, Toulouse, Albi, Béziers, Perpignan and Carcassonne were places to which men looked for authority.

## The Church

### The ancient Church

In Charlemagne's time the Church had been part of the machinery which the emperor nurtured to enable him to control his vast empire. In the Languedoc both bishoprics and abbeys were ancient. Some of the bishops, such as those of Toulouse and Narbonne, could trace their predecessors back to the earliest days of Christianity in the Midi, in the third century. Saint Saturninus of Toulouse was martyred in the mid-third century and became the centre of a cult which has lasted until the present day. Gregory of Tours claimed that Saturninus and his companion Paul, the apostle of Narbonne, were among seven missionaries sent to the Midi in the mid-third century (Thorpe 1974: 87). Whatever the truth of the story, there can be no doubt that the cult began at a very early date in the region. Saint Benoit founded his monastery of Aniane in 782. Saint Attilio founded St-Thibéry in the diocese of Agde, and Nebridius founded Lagrasse soon afterwards in 788, while Guilhem of Toulouse founded his monastery at Gellone – later St-Guilhem-le-Desert – in 806 (Wolff 1967: 126–7). The abbeys of Caunes, St-Laurent, St-Hilaire and St-Polycarpe all date from the same period.

## The monastic revival

The Languedoc was affected by the monastic revival of the early tenth century. St-Pons-de-Thomière was founded by Count Raimon Pons of Toulouse in 936 (Lewis 1965: 243) and the monastery of Lezat was founded c. 940 by the Viscount of Lautrec (Lewis 1965: 244). New foundations such as St-Michel-de-Cuxa (see figure 7), founded 975 (Verrassel 1992: 337), St-Sauveur-de-la-Font (beside the sacred spring of Nemausus at Nîmes) founded in 990 and St-Martin-du-Canigou, founded in 1009 (Verrassel 1992: 335) continued to appear through the tenth century. The impetus to reform and to the expansion of the property of the Church continued right through the tenth century, so that ancient foundations, such as St-Hilaire, Aniane and St-Guilhem, as well as cathedrals such as Béziers, Narbonne and Elne, were able to expand their lands substantially.

The new reform movement was a genuine response to a newly felt spiritual need. That much is clear from the way in which so many members of the nobility helped to found monasteries and gave generous donations of lands and men, and of course also provided the monks who entered the new monasteries. The south was affected by the same movement which had swept across the rest of western Europe. Inevitably it increased tensions between laity and Church, since it developed in parallel with the growth of the newly militarised aristocracy.

The revival and growth of monasticism, together with the resumption of lost lands and its access to surpluses through new lands donated by powerful noble families, made the Church an especially attractive target for the new militarised local aristocracy. One method of control was to make sure that lay members of their families served as *custodes* or *praepositores*, that is 'guardians', of the monasteries. As monasteries and cathedrals developed their resources, they were pressed by the local nobility who sought to gain actual control of Church lands and men by using their new castles to overawe both the churchmen and their tenants. Thus in the County of Commignes the Cluniac abbey of Lezat suffered such depredation by laymen between 980 and 1020 that it had to place itself under the protection of the local Marquis Raimon-Guilhem, since *sicut fuerunt multi donatores etiam adfuerunt multi persecutores*; both laymen and clerics had extorted property from the monks (Ourliac 1990: 134). At first the efforts of the laity to control this new Church wealth were probably quite successful but by the middle of the eleventh century that trend had been reversed and by 1050 the Church held about thirty-five per cent of the land in the south – an increase of about seven per cent in the century (Herlihy 1958: 92).

By the middle of the eleventh century the reform movement was strengthened by the spread of affiliation to Cluny. The monastery of

Figure 7  The abbey of St-Michel-de-Cuxa

Arles-sur-Tech, which was rebuilt and probably refounded in 1048, affiliated in 1078 (Cottineau 1935–7 and 1971). Auch had affiliated in 1066 and Moissac, a very ancient foundation, in 1053 (Racinet 1988). With it went many small priories which were its dependencies (Racinet 1988: 117–18). The monastery of Lezat had been given to Cluny at its foundation but had left the influence of the order, only to come under its influence again by 1073 (Evans 1938). With it went as many as fourteen dependent houses. Layrac was founded in 1072 by the abbot of Moissac as part of the Order (Evans 1938). In 1096, when Pope Urban II was staying at Toulouse, he issued a Bull in which he insisted that the bishops of Cahors, Agen, Toulouse and Lectoure, should grant Moissac about forty churches. By 1100 Moissac was the most powerful Cluniac abbey in the Languedoc (Capelle 1981: 81). Altogether somewhere over 160 monasteries, some large, others tiny, but all belonging to the Cluniac Order, existed in the Province of Gascony by the early twelfth century (Evans 1938).

The affiliation helped to remove the local monastery from the formal influence of surrounding magnates and placed oversight of the abbey's internal and external relations in the hands of Cluny, which itself was under papal protection. Joining the Cluniacs was thus a way of reforming the spiritual life of the house and of simultaneously reducing the influence of laymen on estates and in important matters of policy such as the choice of prior. The Gregorian Reforms thus found early and very practical expression.

The rebuilding of so many churches, here as elsewhere in Gaul, testifies to the vitality of Church life in monasteries throughout the region throughout the later tenth century and into the eleventh and twelfth. As the new popular devotion to pilgrimage spread, the Languedoc became caught up in the movement and many of its churches became a part of the great route which led to Santiago de Compostela. Thus the pilgrims coming from Italy commonly passed from Arles to St-Guilhem-le-Desert, to venerate the fragment of the True Cross kept there, before moving on to St-Sernin at Toulouse and thence westward to the Pyrenees and Spain (Vielliard 1963). Other routes led the pilgrims from the north into the west of the Languedoc, passing through Conques and Moissac. The surviving Romanesque monuments at these sites point to the wealth of the monastic communities as well as to their spiritual vitality (Schapiro 1985).

## The bishops
The great ecclesiastics of the region, bishops and abbots, behaved as independent princes as the old system of patronage of the Church

became increasingly attenuated. This was especially noticeable in Narbonne, where the archbishop ruled half the city. More serious was the domination of great offices in the Church, the bishoprics, archbishoprics and abbacies, by the local noble families. The archbishopric of Narbonne was purchased by the family of the counts of Cerdanya–Besalu c. 1016, while the counts of Carcassonne controlled the abbacies of St-Hilaire and Montolieu. The Viscount of Béziers owned the office of bishop and could leave it in his will as a piece of family property (Lewis 1947: 322–3) and did just that in 990 when he left both Béziers and Agde together with their bishoprics to his wife and daughter (Vidal 1951). At Toulouse the three great churches of St-Sernin, La Daurade and St-Etienne were all neglected, with lands in the hands of laymen and services not performed.

However, the Gregorian reforms were instituted in Toulouse by Bishop Izarn who succeeded to the diocese in 1071. Under his influence the cathedral was rebuilt and a new chapter of canons installed. With great difficulty the reform was then spread to St-Sernin and the construction of the present building commenced (Magnou 1958). The reform of Albi cathedral c. 1072–3, by its bishop, involved the construction of a cloister as well as the reform of the life of the canons, who were exhorted by their bishop, Frotaire, to lead a communal life and to perform the offices. Other cathedrals, along the coast and in Roussillon, seem to have been revived and reformed at about the same time (Magnou-Nortier 1974: 481–6). There can be little doubt that the spread of building at this time, whether it was the rebuilding of cathedral churches or of monasteries, reflects the changing spirit and the desire for reform within the Church. Although great church offices continued to be dominated by great local families throughout the eleventh century, the growth of the corporate spirit within the Church which the reformers sought to encourage did develop within the Languedoc and is probably best exemplified by the 'Peace of God' movement.

### The Peace of God

The idea that the Church might be able to apply spiritual sanctions to military men, to stop or at least regulate their warfare, was possible because the Church had for so long condemned warfare among Christians.

> We plunder our brothers and therefore the heathens justly rob us and our property ... and how shall we be able to conquer our enemies when the blood of our brothers drips from our mouth and our hands are full of blood and our shoulders are burdened with the weight of misery and plunder.

Thus spoke Carloman, the son of Louis the Stammerer (quoted in Rosenwein 1971: 150). Even in the early eleventh century, churchmen still demanded that soldiers should do penance for the men they killed in battle. The constant propaganda particularly affected the *milites* as their status began to rise and so the Church was able to play on their feelings of guilt about the part they played in war. Because as a military class they were now increasingly separated by their activity and position from other groups in society, such as the clergy themselves, the peasantry and the new town dwellers, merchants and craftsmen, who were none of them involved in warfare, except as victims, it was possible for the Church to organise an alliance against the *milites* and their masters.

The rise of the concept of the 'Peace of God' owed much to the needs of the Church for escape from the domination of powerful lay-men, perceived by local churchmen as a bellicose and uncontrollable soldiery. Guy, Bishop of Le Puy, summoned a group of other bishops, including Fulcran of Lodève and Raimon of Toulouse, to a conference in 975. Together with some local nobles they issued a code of practice in the form of canons to be adopted by local military leaders. These forbade theft, the requisition of property and forced labour on castle building:

> Henceforth in the bishoprics and counties, let no man break into churches; let no man carry off horses, foals, oxen, cattle, asses, she-asses with their burden, sheep, goats or swine. Let no man lead others to build or besiege a castle except people dwelling on his own land, allod or beneficium; let no man harm monks or their companions who travel without arms; or stop any peasant, man or woman, and compel them to pay a ransom. (Braudel 1991: 133)

Nearly forty years later the Council of Toulouges in Roussillon (1027) introduced the 'Truce of God' with its ruling that 'it is forbidden to every man to assail his enemy from the ninth hour on Saturday until the first hour on Monday so that each man can render God His due on the Lord's day' (Wolff 1967: 140–1).

In the Council of Narbonne held in 1054, it was laid down that 'no Christian should kill another Christian, for whoever kills a Christian undoubtedly sheds the blood of Christ' (quoted in Cowdrey 1970: 53). The Peace obtained was normally reinforced by the taking of oaths upon relics, thus bringing the sanctions of the saints themselves to bear, to back up the spiritual threats of the clergy. This was a very powerful threat to aim at the new class of knights as they emerged into semi-respectability. As this idea spread it became more formalised, as a series of ceremonies at which laymen and clerics took oaths to keep the peace and to aid one another against wrongdoers. Clerics were able to get the support

of laymen because the associations were patronised by the most important of the local nobility and thus gave lustre to the lesser men. By the
middle of the eleventh century, the system had spread across the Languedoc. The existence and continuance of the movement points to the
weakness of the formal authority of rulers all across the region and also
suggests the determination of the Church to contain and control unruly
elements in civil society which threatened the functions of the Church
at a day-to-day level.

In the north the Peace movement was adopted and sustained by
increasingly powerful rulers who were able to adapt and secularise the
system so that it provided a prop to the spread of their jurisdictions
(Cowdrey 1970: 60–1), giving a moral authority to their courts which
other men's lacked. In the south it seems that the local rulers were not
able to take advantage of the Peace movement in the same way. This may
well be because the courts of the counts of Toulouse were not powerful
enough to make use of the Peace. Once more we return to the point that
the counts of Toulouse failed to establish a centralised county which
could impose order on society, or to develop social structures which
would bind the warlike together in stable relationships which would
minimise the opportunity for armed conflict.

The Peace of God and the Truce of God were responses to the great
crisis in society in Gaul and must have created great tensions inside the
new military class as its aspirations to rule by force of arms clashed with
the ideology of the Church which tried to limit the exercise of force
(Poly and Bournazel 1991: 141–62). In the North, secular rulers were
beginning to tame the knights, but in the south the control exercised by
rulers was less, so spiritual sanctions were correspondingly more important. Perhaps this is why the nobility of the Languedoc were so power-
fully affected by the call to the First Crusade, providing as it did a sudden
release of conscience for the military class. The concept of the Peace was
not lost to the Church in the south, despite its eclipse in the north of
France, and was to re-emerge in the twelfth century, when it was to form
a powerful part of the ideological warfare used against the heretics.

# 2

# The Languedoc in the twelfth century

## The princes

During the twelfth century the princes of western Europe were able to use the new framework of feudal relationships to organise their political relationships with one another. By extending the network of obligations, they were able to temper the anarchy which might otherwise have existed. Each sought to make himself as secure as possible within his own territory and to expand his dominions at the expense of his neighbours, using warfare and marriage relationships. Territory and power became concentrated in fewer and fewer hands and by the end of the century the kings of France, England and Aragon dominated political life in Francia.

The city of Toulouse and its surrounding territory, the Toulousain, seemed vulnerable to such entrepreneurial rulers in the early twelfth century. The counts of Toulouse had become deeply involved first with the crusades and then with the creation of new Christian principalities in the eastern Mediterranean. In 1098, after Raimon IV of Toulouse departed for the First Crusade, leaving his son Bertrand in charge, Guilhem IX of Aquitaine seized the town, using his wife Philippa's claim as the pretext. In 1100 he gave up the city because the Pope threatened him with excommunication (Wolff 1961: 76), but in 1114 he retook it (Limouzin-Lamothe 1932), driving out Alfons-Jordan, the new count, who was only eleven years old.

Alfons-Jordan withdrew to his lands in the Rhone delta where he faced a threat from the counts of Barcelona. In 1112 Raimon-Berenger III of Barcelona had married Douce, the heiress to the county of Provence, and thus gained extensive territories on the east bank of the Rhone and along the Mediterranean coast, including the city of Marseille. The young count was soon embroiled in a war with the Catalans and in 1119 it was the citizens of Toulouse who rescued the count by first expelling Guilhem IX from their city and then relieving the siege of Orange where Alfons was trapped.

As Alfons became old enough to take an active role in politics he was able to ignore the threat from Aquitaine for a few years, turning his attention to the Rhone Valley and Languedoc. By 1125 he had won agreement from Raimon-Berenger that Alfons should have the northern half of Provence. In 1130 Bernard Aton of Béziers and Carcassonne died and his sons divided their lands. In 1131 Raimon-Berenger III of Barcelona died and his second son took Provence. Finally, in 1134 Aymeric II, the Viscount of Narbonne was killed at Fraga by the Moslems, leaving his young daughter Ermengarde as heiress. As Duke of Narbonne, Alfons-Jordan was her superior lord and her feudal guardian. He proposed to marry her himself (Caille 1985: 231).

Neither Berenger, Ermengarde's uncle, who was Abbot of Lagrasse, nor Raimon-Berenger IV, Count of Barcelona, wanted to see this extension of the power of Toulouse. In the ensuing war Alfons encouraged the Montpellians to revolt against their lord, an ally of Barcelona. With the aid of the Count of Barcelona the revolt in Montpellier was suppressed and Alfons-Jordan captured in battle. To make matters worse Louis VII of France, now married to Eleanor of Aquitaine, exerted his rights over Toulouse, inherited along with Aquitaine from Eleanor's grandmother Philippa. In 1141 he besieged the city but failed to make any headway.

Alfons-Jordan lost the war and had to surrender Narbonne in 1143, and by 1147 he had been defeated by Raimon-Berenger IV in the fighting in the Rhone valley. Disgusted with his bad fortune he retired to Tripoli where he was killed in 1148. Over the next few years the lords of the principalities along the Mediterranean coast all did homage to Raimon-Berenger. As the power of the Count of Toulouse declined, the importance of the Count of Barcelona grew. In 1137 he became ruler of Aragon through his marriage to the heiress Petronilla. She was a child at the time, but when she was old enough to consummate the marriage he was able to become king, and the county and the kingdom remained afterwards united through their common ruler, though they continued to be administered separately (Vilar 1987).

Raimon V was fourteen years old when he became Count of Toulouse in 1148 and he found himself in a weak position. In 1149 Raimon Trencavel II of Béziers reunited Béziers and Carcassonne when he succeeded his brother and in 1150 he did homage for his lands to Raimon-Berenger IV (Vilar 1987). In the same year Guilhem VI of Montpellier retired to the monastery of Grandselve and the new viscount, Guilhem VII, received the homage of the lords of Castries, Clermont l'Hérault, and Santeyrargues and also took over the profits of the mint of

Melgueil (Wolff 1967). He too was an ally of the King of Aragon. The block of land along the Mediterranean coast and territories as far inland as Albi had escaped completely from the control of the counts of Toulouse.

Raimon V's response was to seek an alliance with the King of France. During the second Crusade he had met Louis VII and he married the king's sister Constance, the widow of Eustace, King Stephen's son, in 1154. She was to bear him four children (figure 8). This marriage to the sister of a king marked a new departure for the counts. Many of the wives of Raimon V and his son were drawn from royal houses, a sign that the feudal game had higher stakes than before and that the House of Raimon was increasingly embroiled in the dangerous political world of Henry II Plantagenet and the kings of France. Some modern historians have seen this as a sign of ambition on the part of Raimon V, but it seems more likely that these marriage alliances were forced by the need for more and more powerful protectors and were a sign of growing relative weakness (Debax 1988).

Eleanor of Aquitaine had taken her claim to Toulouse to Henry II of England when she married him in 1152, and in 1159 he took advantage of the continuing hostility between the counts of Toulouse and the King of Aragon to launch an attack on Toulouse. The city was probably saved from capture by the presence there of King Louis himself. Henry was said to be reluctant to attack his overlord and, after devastating the land around the town, withdrew in September as winter came on and sickness among his troops became a problem. He had taken Quercy and left a garrison in the region, even after withdrawing from the Toulousain (Warren 1973).

This pattern of alliances continued for some years, but was complicated by the deteriorating relationship between the Count of Toulouse and his wife. From 1164 onwards she complained to her brother of Raimon's treatment of her and in August 1165 abandoned her husband and fled to her brother's court (Debax 1988: 227). In 1162 and again in 1164 the citizens of Toulouse had called on King Louis for aid but in 1166 Raimon obtained an annulment of his marriage to Constance through his support for the anti-pope Pascal III and the Emperor Frederick. He then married Richilde, the widow of the Count of Provence and the niece of the German Emperor. In the fighting which followed, Raimon was once again at war with the princes of the coastal strip and encouraged the citizens of Nîmes and Béziers to revolt against their lords. Raimon Trencavel was hanged by his subjects at Béziers. His son Roger II did homage to Alfonso II, King of Aragon, but he was unable to resist Raimon V and was forced to sign a peace treaty and marry Rai-

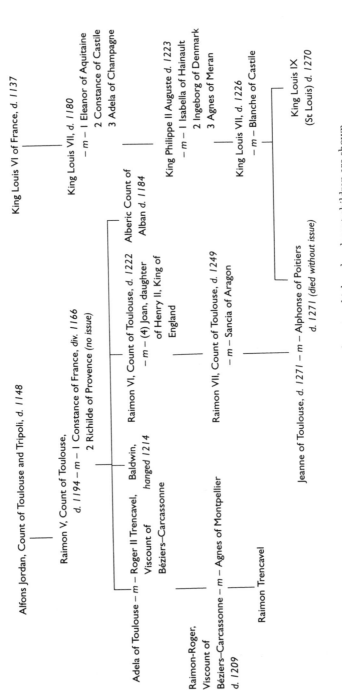

Figure 8 The kings of France and the counts of Toulouse: an outline genealogy in which only relevant children are shown

mon's daughter Adela. Since he could no longer rely on the King of France as an ally, Raimon was forced to turn to his rival and in 1173 he met Henry II at Limoges and did homage to him for Toulouse. Two years later Alfonso II launched an attack against Toulouse, but in the following year Raimon made peace with Alfonso and the two confirmed the division of Provence which had taken place in 1125 (Wolff 1967).

No permanent peace was possible, probably because Raimon V still hoped to achieve some major advance in Languedoc. In 1179 King Philippe of France was crowned and a new phase in the struggle between the two great powers in Francia began. Richard of England's attack upon Toulouse in 1186 had to be countered by an appeal to the king and Richard retained Quercy until Raimon VI, who succeeded in 1194, married Richard's sister Joan in 1196 (Debax 1988). This same year also saw the death of Alfonso II and finally, in 1198, Raimon VI reached a settlement in the Treaty of Perpignan, in which he ceded his rights over Montpellier, Narbonne, Roussillon, Bearn and Bigorre. The counts of Toulouse had finally to recognise, that after a century of warfare, they had lost control of the lands around Carcassonne, Albi, Nîmes and Béziers and that the King of Aragon was the most powerful force in the region (figure 9).

Striking confirmation of the political failure of the House of Raimon comes from examination of the movements of population into the towns in the twelfth century. Most migrants moved into the nearest town and the catchment area from which they were drawn shows the zone of influence of the city. The zones of influence of Narbonne and Toulouse met near Carcassonne, with Montpellier and Béziers within the Narbonne area. The boundary between the lands of the Trencavels on the east and the House of Raimon to the west is clearly delineated by the migration patterns. Political success for the counts of Toulouse would surely have led to an overlap between Toulouse and Narbonne (Higounet 1953).

The House of Raimon stood uneasily in the new pattern of politics, in which the number of rulers who could operate without an overlord was shrinking. The Duke of Aquitaine, the King of France, the Emperor and the King of Aragon were visible expressions of a world in which the agglomeration of power into the hands of a few great rulers, made possible by the application of primogeniture and exogamy, placed smaller rulers at a grave disadvantage. Independence could only be preserved by accepting the protection and support of great rulers and by trying to balance the influence thus granted by alliances with others. The situation was inherently precarious and the counts of Toulouse were extremely vulnerable.

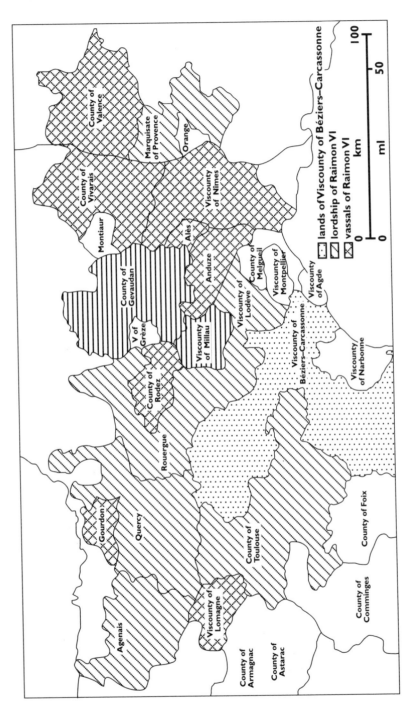

Figure 9  Lands of Raimon VI in 1209

The position of lesser rulers was not necessarily any more comfortable. At Narbonne we have already seen that it was only the accident of Alfons-Jordan's capture by Raimon Trencavel which stopped him taking over Narbonne with its young countess Ermengarde. She married a Castilian, who held property from the Count of Barcelona, but herself ruled the city of Narbonne and its territories, keeping an allegiance to the counts of Barcelona throughout the wars of the second half of the century (Caille 1985). Her independence was guaranteed by the Count of Barcelona, who had the added advantage of being a somewhat distant overlord. Ermengarde could not have survived without his support. On his side the Count of Barcelona gained a close ally in a sensitive area.

## Towns and trade

During the twelfth century the expansion of agriculture and of the towns finally filled up the landscape and by 1200 it was difficult to find large areas of waste suitable for intensive exploitation. The money which made the wars of the twelfth century possible came from the expansion of the economy of the Languedoc and the towns were the most conspicuous source for the revenues of the Count of Toulouse and of the other rulers in the region. However, the towns were not necessarily obedient to the will of the lord and during the twelfth century, as wealth grew, so did the desire for freedom of action and independent government.

The towns of the twelfth century were not neat entities, each under the control of a lord (figure 10). Most of them were subject to several jurisdictions. At Toulouse the bishop exercised power in the cité. At Narbonne the archbishop was the lord of half the town and at Montpellier the bishop of Maguelonne had a court, as did the viscount and his official, the viguier (Lewis 1947: 55–6). This division of jurisdiction mirrored the general political structure of the region, where the rights of lords often overlapped and even the greatest might claim pre-eminence but not obedience. The citizens of Toulouse had a common council running the town by 1152. In part at least this was because the count was too weak to direct the government himself. In 1119 it was the citizens who expelled Guilhem IX's government, although his officers held on to the Chateau Narbonnais, the castle on the outskirts of the city, until 1123 (Limouzin-Lamothe 1932: 112–16). For the townsmen the motivating consideration was probably that their trade was with the south and the east, rather than with Bordeaux, although that too was important. Alfons-Jordan offered the town concessions to keep its allegiance and between 1120 and 1140 founded a salvetat (or sauvété) which included a

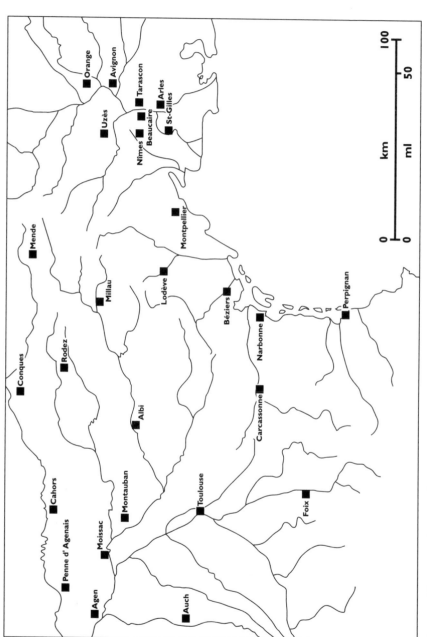

Figure 10 The principal towns of the Midi in the twelfth century

part of the cité within its bounds and which was intended to encourage immigration.

By 1140 the whole of the bourg and the cité were surrounded by a new city wall and the townspeople were granted concessions over local comital taxes and military service (Wolff 1961: 63). During the second half of the century Raimon V, like his predecessors, lived mostly at St-Gilles and so the attacks by Henry II, Richard I and later by the King of Aragon had largely to be met by the citizens themselves and from their own resources. As we have seen above, in 1159 it was the presence of King Louis in the town which deterred Henry II from a full-scale attack and when he threatened the town again between 1162 and 1164 the citizens appealed to King Louis for protection (Warren 1973). These years of difficulty seem to have given the citizens the opportunity to establish and to refine the institutions of self-government. By the 1170s their judges had expanded their jurisdiction into areas previously controlled by the Count and began to issue legislation for their city, calling themselves consuls (Mundy 1954: 55–7).

By the time of the visit to Toulouse by the papal legates, Peter of Pavia and Henry of Clairvaux, in 1178, the leading families of the city formed a consulate which provided all the functions of government. This patrician class was largely composed of urban knights and landowners who mostly lived on their rural rents and upon moneylending (Hilton 1992: 89). It was this group which provided the capital needed to fund the trading and manufacturing activities of the towns. Banking was an essential part of the life of the towns, but provided a ready source of discontent from among those who needed to borrow. Loans were made at anything from 12 to 40 per cent, reflecting the relative scarcity of capital and the risks in lending, but presenting the borrowers with great danger and hardship (Wolff 1961: 71).

This urban oligarchy developed a self-confidence and a financial solidity which made them formidable opponents. Raimon V made attempts during the 1180s to regain influence but he seems not to have been very successful. Using the fighting between King Richard I and Raimon V in 1188 the citizens revolted against the count (Mundy 1954: 60). By 1189 the city administration was powerful enough to have its own common seal, to enforce registration of property transactions with the town authorities and to have built itself a 'town hall', the Capitol. Between then and the outbreak of the Crusade the town began to build itself a 'patria tolosa' – territory directly dependent upon the town – by means of wars and treaties with towns and villages nearby. During this period twenty-three rural lords and communities were attacked in an area which ran from Auch to the Lauragais (Mundy 1954: 68). The citizens were seeking the sort of autonomy which had been gained by some great Italian cities or which, closer to home, existed at Avignon.

Similar developments occurred in other towns throughout the Languedoc. Consuls existed in Béziers by 1131, in Narbonne by 1132, and at Nîmes by 1144. The same process of grants of freedom from taxes occurred in these towns too. At Nîmes in 1124 the viscount, Bernard Aton, abandoned the tolte, though not without a cash payment from the citizens (Chedeville 1980: 178). At Albi the Trencavels became the chief lords of the town when Raimon V ceded authority in 1163. But the bishops also remained powerful lords and since they were on the spot had more real influence than the Trencavels. During the twelfth century the town grew rapidly and a new wall was built c. 1190. About 270 merchants and knights formed an oligarchy which dominated the commercial life of the town (Biget 1983). Montpellier grew from being a town of around 5,000–6,000 people in the middle of the century to one of 12,000–15,000 by the year 1200 (Russell 1962). The autonomy sought by the capitouls of Toulouse and other cities was possible because the counts of Toulouse and the viscounts of Béziers were relatively weak rulers. Absence, and the pressure from other lords, combined to make it relatively easy to extend the immunities of the towns. But the power to raise and maintain a militia, as at Toulouse, depended on the town's wealth.

Although towns were often difficult to control they represented a new source of revenue for rulers. New towns, with more traders, brought more wealth to the countryside and so rulers with the necessary political power founded new towns. Alfons-Jordan founded the town of Montauban and granted it a charter by 1144. The town was intended to secure the interests of the count in the west of the Toulousain, controlling the road into Quercy and access to the central parts of Aquitaine. In this it succeeded admirably and the town quickly grew wealthy on the trade it attracted (Lavedan and Hugueney 1974: 69). By the end of the century there were nearly eighty towns in the Languedoc, including the great centres such as Toulouse and Narbonne. Although most were very small the concentration of urban centres gave the Languedoc a character more similar to parts of Italy than it was to other parts of France (figure 11).

The growth of wealth and the expansion of the urban moneyed classes is well demonstrated by the example of the mills of Toulouse. By the mid-twelfth century the town had sixty floating mills. These watermills were mounted on boats and drew their power from the rush of water past the moored hull. Individually none of these mills was very large and they were very vulnerable to the violent floods of the Garonne

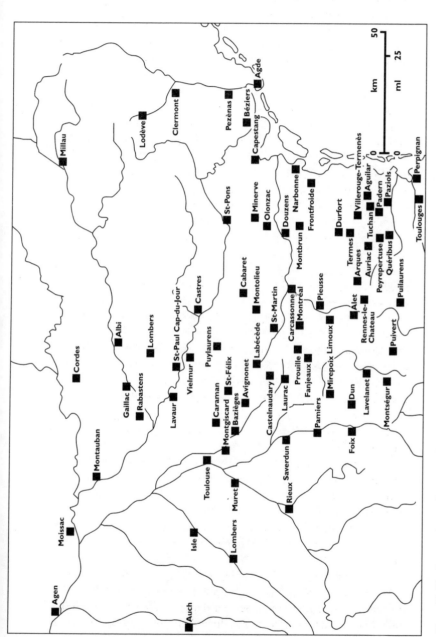

Figure 11 The Languedoc at the time of the Crusade

in winter and spring. As the city grew, the demand for flour increased and the building of new floating mills was probably not a solution. Instead, c. 1177, the owners of the mills got together to build three dams across the river which raised the water levels far enough to allow a series of mills to be built along the banks. Forty-three new mills replaced the old floating mills. They were owned in shares by the three groups which had built the dams. Shares were of course saleable – something which was taken for granted because of the tendency towards the division of property at death – and thus three milling companies emerged, with appointed managers and paying dividends. If success can be measured by longevity it should be noted that, in an amalgamated form, the companies survived as businesses into the twentieth century (Gimpel 1988: 17).

Throughout the region, wealth was based upon the manufacture of cloth and leather and other goods and on trade with Mediterranean cities, with the growing kingdoms in Spain, as well as the immediate locality. Cloth was produced in all the towns and cities (Wolff 1978). Many Cathars were to be found among the weavers (Duvernoy 1963). The trade of the towns was built on two pillars, the expansion of settlement and agriculture and the growth in international trade.

Toulouse and other towns in the Toulousain benefited from overland trading routes between the Mediterranean and the west coast of France, from where much trade passed northwards to Britain. It was not until the late thirteenth century that shipping began to use the Straits of Gibraltar. During the earlier part of the twelfth century the Languedoc saw the establishment of many fairs which catered for the growing part of the trade which was based on long-distance movement of goods. By 1109 the Count of Toulouse had granted special privileges to Genoese merchants in return for their help in the establishment of the county of Tripoli. During the century Narbonne signed at least three peace agreements with other cities, aimed at ensuring easy access for merchants and traders. In 1148 Raimon-Berenger of Barcelona granted the inhabitants of Narbonne the right to trade with Tortosa without paying the usual duties. In 1166 the archbishop, the countess and the citizens joined to negotiate a five-year peace and trade treaty with the consuls of Genoa and in 1174 Ermengarde concluded a very similar pact with the community of Pisa (Narbonne 1994).

The fair at St-Gilles was established in the early years of the century with the aid of the Count of Toulouse (Lewis 1980: 66). At Nîmes two fairs are mentioned in 1151. At Moissac the charter for the fair dates its foundation to 1125, and in 1158 Carcassonne gained the right to hold two fairs (Combes 1958). The fair at Nîmes later emerged as a major centre for the sale of cloth and the region came to have many Italian merchants who brought in spices, sugar, alum, silk, carpets, perfumes and dyestuffs and exported the cloth and leather goods (DeSoigne 1976). The great fair at Beaucaire emerged after 1150, and since the town was under the control of the counts of Toulouse, whose castle still dominates the fair-ground, it provided a source of wealth for the family.

It was through the merchants who frequented the fairs that contact with the eastern Mediterranean was established and maintained. The links with the Italian cities were particularly important. The arrival of Papa Nichetas at St-Felix might well be ascribed, in general terms, to the contacts between the Languedoc and the northern Italian cities built up in the twelfth century. Relations were so close that it was to the Cathars of Italy that many persecuted Albigensians fled in the mid-thirteenth century. By the end of the century merchants from the towns on the Mediterranean were to be found trading as far as North Africa, Romania, Egypt and the Holy Land, selling cloth and bringing back the high-value goods, such as spices, sugar and dyes which made money locally but could also be exported onwards into northern France (Lewis 1980).

The existence of many families with names connected with Toulouse and the other great towns of the Languedoc suggests that trade connections were particularly strong between the Toulousain and the neighbouring territories of eastern Gascony, Quercy and Aragon and Navarre. In the east there was a flow from Carcassonne, Narbonne and other Mediterranean towns towards Barcelona. Movement from Barcelona northwards is also noticeable. The movements were mostly due to the expansion of commercial contacts, although the expansion of Christian Spain southwards also drew settlers (Higounet 1953).

Increasing wealth led to a growing sophistication of society. By the end of the century students of the Arts and of Law were present in Montpellier, well before the foundation of the University (Russell 1962), and the town had a reputation for medical skills by the middle of the century. The Jews, particularly, had a reputation as doctors, founded on their knowledge of the medical traditions passed through the Moslem world, particularly in Spain. Jewish communities, often very large, existed in all the larger towns of the Languedoc. We must suppose that they grew by natural increase, as well as by immigration from other parts of the Mediterranean, since there had always been Jewish families in the towns of the region from early in the Roman period (Lunel 1975: 7–11). In the twelfth century there were synagogues in Béziers, Lodève, Lunel, Mende, Montpellier, Nîmes, Pamiers, Pèzenas, Posquières, Toulouse and St-Gilles, and Narbonne had some three hundred Jewish families in the second half of the century, suggesting a population of 1,200–1,500 people (Lunel 1975: 14–15).

In both Narbonne and Montpellier the Jewish communities were wealthy enough to be able to run Talmudic schools (Blumenkranz 1972: 51–2) and the Jews of Narbonne were sufficiently famous, even as far away as England, to figure in the sulphurous creation, by Thomas of Monmouth in 1150, of the story of Saint William of Norwich (Langmuir 1984: 4–5). It would be wrong to imagine that Jews lived without prejudice in the towns of the south. In the eleventh century, ritual attacks upon Jews in Holy Week had been a regular feature of life in Béziers and Toulouse. In the twelfth century the practice ceased, but only because payments were made (Moore 1987). In the Toulousain, as elsewhere, the Jews were vulnerable to the rising tide of organised anti-Semitism which sprang from the views of the Church reformers of the eleventh and twelfth centuries and which was taken up by rulers (Moore 1992). As in most parts of western Europe, by the late twelfth century the Jews, despite the fact that they were descended from the native inhabitants of the country, were regarded as an alien minority, under the protection of the lord of the town and often closely linked to him because of their prominence as moneylenders and because they often acted as government officials.

In Toulouse the Jews all lived in a special district of the city at Jouxt-Aigues. Here they had their synagogues and lived under their own laws. They were protected by the count, but subject to a special tax (Wolff 1961: 73). In 1193 Roger, Viscount of Béziers and Carcassonne, was known to be taxing the Jews of Alet, the Razès and Carcassonne and no doubt he did the same for the Jews in the rest of his lands (Nahon 1977: 55). They were 'his' Jews and their status closely resembled that of their co-religionists in the north of France. Legal authorities regarded the Jews as the bondmen of the ruler (Gilles 1977) and this status, which was only slowly recognised by the lawyers of the thirteenth century, reflected the real position of weakness experienced by the Jews as the opposition to them hardened in the twelfth century. They suffered in the same way as heretical groups, as the Church defined itself more fully against the rest of the world. Prejudice against Jews was common, but in the south persecution was not. Organised and official persecution of the Jews became a normal feature of life in the south only after the Crusade because it was only then that the Church became powerful enough to insist on the application of positive measures of discrimination. Until then the Jews were tolerated as a specialised minority who mixed well in the urban societies of the south, took part in the growth of local self-government and who prospered as urban society prospered.

The towns of the Languedoc developed an urban manufacturing class providing the goods which were exported to pay for the import of luxuries and which met the needs of rural customers. The basic cloth industry provided work for weavers, dyers, fullers and tuckers and many workmen who were concerned with the manufacture of items of dress. Shoe- and clog-makers, hatmakers, tailors and dressmakers now found employment. The growth of the urban environment provided employment for building workers on a much larger scale than before, so that masons, carpenters and the ancillary trades became full-time workers in a stable urban setting. By the middle of the century most towns in the Languedoc had trade associations for manufacturing artisans and for traders (Gouron 1958). Trade associations of this kind regulated the numbers in the trade and controlled prices. Eventually they were to provide a vehicle for political power for their richer members in many places, but at this period they probably provided some security and control over working conditions for groups who were not rich or powerful. These groups formed an urban proletariat which was vulnerable to famines and the dislocation caused by wars and which borrowed capital, rather than lending it.

In the towns a very distinct hierarchy had emerged as wealth grew. At the top were the great nobles who were often resident in the town, along with the bishop and other senior clergy. Often at loggerheads with them were the knights, and trading and banking families, who controlled the capital of the town and formed its government. Below them came the mass of smaller manufacturers and traders, together with their apprentices and servants, and in the case of smaller towns, the farmers and the labourers. In many parts of northern France and in England the expansion of urban self-government and most importantly independence from princes, was checked in the 1180s. In the south the relative weakness and division of the princely class enabled that independence to continue until the collapse of the Languedoc in the face of northern royal power.

## The countryside

The agriculture of the lowlands concentrated on grain and wine. The increasing population needed bread, and extension of agriculture was profitable. In the countryside the work of the Hospitallers, who were granted much land in the region to the south-west of Toulouse, led to the foundation of new villages. Around Toulouse they founded the villages of St-Clar, Alan, Poucharramet, Fonsorbes and Larramet; and, near Montauban in 1120, Fronton. The Templars also used grants of land to found *sauvétés*, at Villedieu in the County of Foix in 1136 and another place of the same name near Montauban in 1144 or 1154

(Lavedan and Hugueney 1974: 67–8). At the beginning of the century the Hospitallers founded some forty *sauvétés* along the left bank of the Garonne in the lower Comminges (Higounet 1953).

Other monastic orders had been active in this same way in the later part of the eleventh century, especially in the regions to the west of Toulouse, where the Abbey of Moissac and the Abbey of Conques were particularly active. It seems likely that monasteries such as Moissac did not feel the need to found villages in the twelfth century. They had established their estates in earlier centuries and did not need to do more than exploit what they already held. Moissac seems to have founded only one village during the century, St-Nicholas-de-la-Grave in 1135, its last effort. Although a *sauvété* with plots of land around it was laid out, there were *manses* in the area and so it seems that the new *sauvété* was not on waste land, or land which had never been exploited, but was a reorganisation of existing land (Higounet 1963). In this *sauvété*, by the middle of the century, there was a castle, built by the viscount, Odon de Lomagne, who held the property as a vassal of the abbey and in effect was the beneficiary of its existence.

By the middle of the twelfth century it is likely that there were few large areas of wilderness left to exploit and that the expansion of agriculture came from intensified exploitation, rationalisation of holdings and estates, and better capitalisation. Of the Cistercian monasteries in the dioceses of Albi, Toulouse, Rodez, Narbonne, Nîmes, Agde, Cahors and Carcassonne, nineteen were founded before 1150 (figure 12 shows the position at the end of the twelfth century). It is clear that little of the land they were granted was unsettled. Almost everything which they received was already exploited, tenanted and subject to tithe, and in order to achieve their ideal of living without dependants the monks of all the new houses spent much time and energy on the purchase of rights and the removal of peasantry to create their 'wilderness'. Often the monks obtained land and rights which were so fragmented by division among heirs and by sale as to be almost useless. Consolidation under one owner made profitable exploitation possible once more (Berman 1986: 11–30).

By the end of the century the Cistercians had accumulated substantial savings from their form of agriculture. In its first phase, when peasants donated their land to the order and then continued to work on it as lay brothers, *conversi*, for their house, monasteries had a substantial advantage over peasant farmers because there were no families to support. By the end of the century new grants by new lay brothers had declined sharply and surviving *conversi* were elderly, so that arable farming lost some of its competitive edge, but the advantages of economies of scale and capital investment, particularly in sheep, remained.

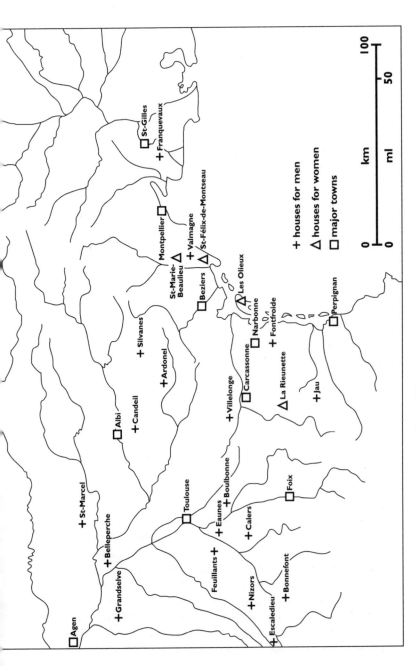

Figure 12  The Cistercians in the Languedoc before 1200

Pastoralism and the practice of transhumance had been a feature of life in the Languedoc from time immemorial. Villages in the Pyrenees, for example, seem to have lived almost exclusively from animal husbandry and the life of the peasants depicted much later, at the end of the thirteenth century, suggests that animal farming, with long-distance movement of sheep, was normal. It has been suggested that large areas of grazing were comparatively underexploited at the time when the Cistercians first entered the economy of the region. They and other monastic groups were able to invest in large flocks of sheep – normally about a thousand animals per monastery – and take advantage of the growing market for their wool. By the end of the century they seem to have filled up the pastures, no doubt competing with laymen, and in the next century disputes with local lay landlords became common (Berman 1986: 100–1).

Written agreements concerning transhumance appear in the south for the first time towards the end of the century, showing that the practice had become so common that regulation was needed (Duby 1968: 147). Big institutions were able to use their power and influence to get rights of passage so that transhumance expanded as the numbers of sheep increased. Although the Cistercians, and to a lesser extent other monastic groups, were able to make high returns on their sheep as a result of their privileges, there is nothing to suggest that laymen also could not profit from the rapid expansion of pastoral husbandry. The capital to enable peasants to run flocks often came from nobility or town merchants who put up the cash in exchange for a fifty per cent share of the profits of wool and milk (Paterson 1993: 127).

The twelfth century saw an expansion, not only in wealth and in population, but also in poverty. The rapid growth of the twelfth-century economy gave plenty of opportunity for the poor to multiply as new lands were exploited and towns grew, but the nature of medieval society meant that many people existed on the edge of survival. As a result a bad harvest was always likely to cause a famine and the twelfth century naturally had its share of such problems. There was, for instance, a widespread famine during the 1140s in almost the whole of western Europe north of the Alps and in Aquitaine in 1162–3, while in 1197 the failure of the harvests induced famines practically everywhere (Mollat 1986: 61–2). One traditional remedy for such eventualities was that the monasteries should feed the poor and this they did, but there are signs that this was becoming a problem for them by the end of the century. Such problems were inevitably seen in religious terms and expressed in the preaching of men such as Saint Norbert of Xanten and Saint Bernard. While Churchmen called for pity for the poor, others were anxious to make it clear that this did not mean that they could riot or demand a change in social structure. If they were poor, it was because of sin (Mollat 1967). The rapid expansion of both town and countryside, while increasing wealth for some, also encouraged social instability by multiplying the numbers of poor.

## Nobility and the *castra*

The nobility of the Languedoc lived both in the country and in the towns. For most of them income was already drawn chiefly from rents and dues rather than from direct exploitation of estates. Although they were rural landowners, almost all their land was let to tenants and the large demesne farms typical of northern France seem to have been absent, except from the estates of the Cistercians. The custom of dividing inheritances among sons continued among the nobility of the Languedoc in the twelfth century. This may explain why in 1159 the town of Mirepoix had eleven co-seigneurs, all owing fealty to Roger-Bernard I, Count of Foix, and also why there were thirty-five co-seigneurs by 1207 (Pasquier 1921). There clearly were a great many people who could see themselves as 'noble' by the late twelfth century.

One measure of the numbers of nobility must be the presence of castles and fortified villages. During the twelfth century their numbers grew considerably. In the modern departements of Hérault and Aude there are thirty-six castles which were mentioned for the first time in the twelfth century and it is likely that this is an underestimate of the total number then existing (Salch 1977) (figure 13). Cheyette mapped sixty-seven fortified villages between Carcassonne and Béziers for the same period (Cheyette 1976). In the Hautes Corbières there is evidence that every village had some sort of fortification, often a castle (Quèhen et Dieltiens 1983). Villages such as Tuchan and Olonzac still have at their hearts a circular street with a continuous line of building, marking the ancient heart of the settlement, even where walls have disappeared. The habit of building circular villages is widespread in the Languedoc and it has been suggested that many of them first appeared in the early eleventh century, usually clustered around a castle or a church. However, it was in the twelfth century that most of them seem to have been fortified for the first time, usually with a ditch and then later with walls (Pawlowski 1987).

By the second half of the century, *castra* – the fortified villages – seem to have been the norm and the word *castrum* was applied as a matter of course to every village. There is no doubt that the creation of *castra* was linked to the seigniorial class. Their building on church lands is clearly

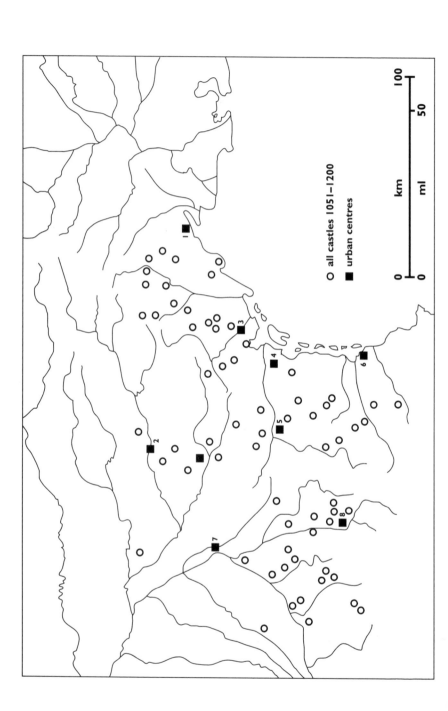

O all castles 1051–1200

■ urban centres

km

ml

0    50    100

connected with the creation by the Church of fiefs for laymen (Gramain
1980: 128–33). The circular villages have been linked with the political
ambitions of Bernard-Aton IV of Béziers (d. 1129) and it has been suggested that the creation of these fortified towns and villages was part of
a regular policy by the Trencavels to strengthen their grip over the region
against the counts of Toulouse (Pawlowski 1987: 421). Although there
were many agreements – *convenentiae* – between the Trencavels and their
subordinates, aimed at preventing the fortification of these sites against
the viscounts, in practice they point to the relative independence of such
lords. In an area where there was no real concept of over-riding jurisdiction many lords were free to hold property from more than one overlord and in effect lived independently.

In any case the whole concept of obligation as a result of enfeoff-
ment was alien to the nobility of the region. A 'feudal' obligation would
have meant little to these men. For example the Lord of Termes, in the
Corbières mountains, held his château from the viscount, who in turn
held from the Abbey of Lagrasse. Many of the villages which made up
the Termenès were held in the same way, but some were held from the
Archbishop of Narbonne. The influence of both superiors was negligi-
ble. In the second half of the twelfth century the family further extended
its authority, so that by 1163 they also held the castle of Durfort and the
property that went with it. In 1125 the castle of Arques (figure 14) and
the eight villages which it commanded were granted to the family by
Viscount Bernard Aton of Carcassonne. Unlike most of their landowning neighbours, the family seems to have had a limited number of children and to have avoided the practice of dividing the property among
heirs as well as grouping their lands together into a compact territory
(Langlois 1991). Raimon, Lord of Termes at the time of the Crusade,
was described by Pierre des Vaux-de-Cernay as a man 'who feared neither God nor man. He had such confidence in his fortress that he fought
sometimes with the Count of Toulouse and sometimes with his own
overlord, the Viscount of Béziers' (Guébin et Maisonneuve 1951:
71–2). The lords of Montréal, Minerve and Cabaret were no different
(Barber 1990). Each of these men in turn had men who were their vassals, but who were not necessarily easy to control either.

There is much evidence which suggests that the nobility did not
always see themselves as primarily soldiers. Although the twelfth century saw a rapid spread of the fief as a method for the holding of land,
there were also many money fiefs created. Most fiefs seem to have been
hereditary and many, perhaps most, do not seem to have been created
with a definite military obligation as their purpose (Gramain 1980). The
term 'knight' was not used to distinguish warrior–gentlemen and the

Figure 14  The castle of Arques

simple link between nobility and the practice of warfare did not exist in the Languedoc. The knight in the Languedoc was simply a professional soldier, who might also be a nobleman. Many knights were not noblemen and, although the occupation was prestigious, it was an occupation rather than a distinction or a badge of rank (Paterson 1993: 63). As Maurice Keen has shown, chivalry as an *ordo* seems to have developed after 1180 (Keen 1984). It was essentially a northern French and English invention and seems hardly to have affected the south. The tournament, one of the distinguishing features of the military society of the north which developed along with the concept of nobility, was not a feature of southern life (Paterson 1993: 77) and its absence may point to a deficiency in the training of knights for equestrian warfare.

Nevertheless, it would clearly be perverse to imagine that the Languedoc was not a highly militarised society. The presence of so many castles and fortified villages demonstrates the overwhelming need to protect lands and people against attack, as well as to assert control of people and lands. The maintenance of so many fortifications implies the presence of many soldiers. When the Crusade began, the defenders could quickly provide garrisons capable of manning both towns and castles, although many were composed of mercenary soldiers. When the castle of Termes fell, many of the garrison who fled were described as Aragonese, Catalonians or men of Roussillon (Martin-Chabot 1973–89 vol. 1: 135–41). It does seem likely, in these circumstances, that there were in southern society many young men of noble birth who were not highly skilled as warriors and this helps to explain why the *routiers*, mercenary soldiers often from Spain, were so common a feature of military life in the Languedoc.

## The courtly culture

The gentility and sophistication of southern courts has often been remarked. Since each lord aspired to independence, each held a real court. Those of the greatest lords led by example, each seeking to outdo their rivals by munificent display and refinement. This was not something especial to the Languedoc; all royal households sought to make a show, since kings and princes knew that a dazzling court was a powerful way to gain prestige. In the Languedoc the desire to ape such manners spread far down through the ranks of the nobility, although most nobles were not very rich. It was in such circumstances that the patronage of the troubadours developed.

Few groups of medieval people are as well known now as the troubadours. Exponents of a specialised poetic genre first made fashionable by Guilhem IX of Aquitaine, over a long period the troubadours developed as the mouthpieces of a courtly ethic which revolved around the sublimation of the sexual and social tensions inevitable in such households. The troubadours themselves were highly regarded for their poetic skills, so that a humble background was not an obstacle to success. Their poetry provided the literary vehicle which made a convention of love between men and women one of the driving forces inside noble society. Often using the language of feudalism, they redirected the structure of aristocratic male society to describe the relationships between men and women. The troubadour Marcabru, a man of very lowly social origins, was a moralist who believed that love could be used as a stabilising force in society and for the individual (Topsfield 1975). He worked at many courts, including Toulouse, Barcelona, Castile and Portugal, so that his ideas were widely disseminated.

After c. 1180 the style and content of the poetry changed to become more concerned with the social conventions than with the interior life. At their best the troubadours advocated a way of life controlled by moderation and courtesy, refined behaviour and an abstracted love which is rarely physically expressed. All the counts of Toulouse were patrons of the troubadours and Raimon Miraval (flourished 1191–1229) was a close friend of Raimon VI of Toulouse for over twenty years. In the late twelfth century the courts of Foix, Comminges, Béziers, Toulouse and Narbonne all patronised the troubadours, and as a result lesser noble men were anxious to grace their own halls with such men. Raimon de Miraval recommended the castles of the Carcassès as a happy hunting ground for patronage. Such men were privileged by their art, so that although they were rarely a part of the noble society within which they moved, they were treated as members of the group (Loeb 1983).

No doubt the ideal and the reality often overlapped rather than being congruous. It is difficult to imagine a poetry of longing which is never informed by a certain amount of satisfied desire. A complete suppression of the physical expression of sexual love would have meant the death of the ideal also. And as so many have noted before, this was adulterous love and therefore dangerous and all the more exciting for that. The refinement of the expression of love between men and women undoubtedly signalled a change in the relationships between the sexes. The romantic literature which was popular at courts, but which spread throughout society by the early thirteenth century, depended upon the consent of the lady to the romantic contract, which she could and did withdraw. Since most poetry was written by men and from a male standpoint the emotional risk described was all male. In real life the emotional cost was shared between the parties.

Such a change in sensibility has been noted as part of the discovery of the individual which was taking place in the twelfth century (Morris 1972: ch. 5). The idea that intention and motivation were of supreme importance led to the view that consent mattered. The new ideas about consent dominated the new doctrine of marriage developed during the century and, since women were normally the weaker party in marriage, that doctrine worked in favour of women (Morris 1989: 327–32). The reality of society and the theories of theologians are, however, often very far apart. That is not to say that such views about the nature of personal relationships did not have a profound impact on the nature of secular as well as religious society – they did – but the weight of secular society and its sheer inertia meant that for most women little changed, except perhaps the perception of the gap between ideal and reality.

In practice in the twelfth century, although there are many instances of great ladies ruling or acting independently, for the great majority of women their lot was one of subordination to fathers, brothers and husbands. The overwhelming social and legal pressures subordinated women to the needs of the family units inside which they lived. It was true that women could and did head households, own their own property and make wills; but they were in practice rarely wealthy enough to exercise choice. In bourgeois and aristocratic families, although there was no legal impediment to stop girls inheriting land, in practice property was passed to sons, and girls were provided with cash payments which were intended to enable them to marry or to enter a monastery, for there was realistically nothing else a girl could do (Mundy 1990: 27–36). There was no other life available to her.

Many women practised trades in towns and. especially among the artisan classes, the skills women brought to the family business made them a powerful force within it and often the driving force once their husbands were dead; but normally families ran businesses and families were controlled by men. A nice indication of this comes from Dr Mundy's study of the personal names in documents from Toulouse. Among the 205 couples studied, there were 35 names available to men, but 89 different names given to women. At a period when the idea of a family name or surname was not yet firmly established, men took a limited range of 'family' names, as modern kings and queens still do, but parents were able to give their imaginations free rein for their daughters, since they were destined to leave their families and become part of another grouping (Mundy 1990: 39ff.,103 & 104).

The same study suggests that the expression of sexuality by women was regarded as dangerous, as at most times in European history. Concubinage existed and was widely condoned and since it was a practice which was initiated and controlled by men, it tells us little about women's attitudes to sex. However the amazing story of the Abbot of Lezat shows that some women entered illicit liaisons with their eyes open and an advantage in view. Over a period of years he had several mistresses and he seems to have supported them and his illegitimate children, in some style. Their status was so well known that one woman was known jokingly as *abbattissa*, 'the lady abbot'. Another mistress was apparently able to provide her mother with a pension and her brother with a horse. Even at this time a public fight between two of his mistresses was considered quite shocking but the ladies clearly felt he was worth battling for (Mundy 1990: 59). It is noteworthy that in Toulouse, although the penalties for adultery were in theory draconian, the practice was so hedged around with provisos that public proof of guilt was extremely hard to provide. By the thirteenth century confession was not accepted as evidence of guilt. According to Alphonse of Poitiers, even finding two people together naked in bed was not proof enough and the town law of Toulouse forbade the arrest of any married person 'for reason of adultery, fornication or coitus in any store or house he or she rented, owned or maintained as a residence' (Mundy 1990: 130). Of course Toulouse was a sophisticated city. What happened in the countryside was probably a good deal more primitive and violent.

The twelfth century was a time when the Church was gradually gaining a hold over the practice as well as the theory of marriage, and although this had some advantages for women, in that it became more difficult for husbands, even wealthy ones, to put away their wives, and in theory at least the Church was anxious to control violence by husbands, in practice the new rigidities which the Church introduced actually bound women more closely to their husbands' families. As their status within marriage rose, inevitably their status outside marriage declined. It may be true that some women in the Languedoc were more autonomous than women in other parts of France, since they could and did own property, but this was not a society in which men and women were equal. Socially, legally and economically, women's roles were subordinate to those of men. On the one hand the language of the troubadours preached an equality in intimate relationships. On the other hand men like Raimon VI, well known as a lecher, married many times over, and begat illegitimate children. Theory and practice were a long way apart.

Inside this aristocratic and bourgeois society there is little evidence of a sense of 'national' identity. That feeling, that the south was different from the north and that the northerners were foreigners, the sense of 'us' and 'them' did not yet exist. Loyalty was to a local lord or to the city which provided a sense of identity. It was the Crusade itself which gave a sense of unity expressed through the word *paratge*. This word expressed the idea of legitimacy of inheritance and therefore of the right to inheritance and to its enjoyment. This was a concept which applied to the whole of society, not just to the nobility (Ghil 1989).

Catharism flourished inside this society which was divided politically, but linked by a common language and by an increasingly important intellectual culture. The influence of the Cathars, especially of the sect's leaders, the *perfecti*, was out of all proportion to their numbers. This of course has been true of other dissident or non-conforming groups which have stood outside mainstream religious practice. In the Languedoc, Catharism was particularly influential among the nobility. The relatively open nature of aristocratic society and its interchange of members and culture over a considerable area, together with the relatively secular nature of noble courts, made transmission of Cathar ideas easy. In the countryside the peasantry were not closely supervised by their lords, since they mostly paid rents. Again it was possible for dissident ideas to spread and the growth of many small towns and the expansion of major urban centres encouraged the spread of ideas along with traded goods. At all levels the Languedoc was a relatively open society.

# 3

# The Cathars

## The beginnings of heresy

Catharism was the most serious and widespread of all the heretical movements which challenged the Catholic Church in the twelfth century and challenged it most severely in the Languedoc. As we shall see, it became a movement with a coherent body of belief and with an organisation which made it into a kind of 'counter-Church'. Perhaps because it did not spring fully fledged from the head of some heresiarch but grew from the elements which came together quite slowly in the first half of the twelfth century, Catharism took a very firm hold in the Languedoc.

Since the eleventh and the twelfth centuries were periods of turmoil within the Church, it is not surprising that divergent opinions should have appeared and that these should have hardened to the point that groups would spring up whose views put them in conflict with the Church. Such groups, often isolated, appeared before the beginnings of the attacks on simony at the synods of Sutri and Rome in 1046 (Tellenbach 1993: 141). The Clerks of Orléans, a group of teachers working at the cathedral, who were burnt to death for their heresy in 1022, were an early and dramatic example of a group of scholars who developed for themselves a theology based upon a belief in the inner promptings of the Holy Spirit. We, 'who have the law written upon the heart by the Holy Spirit', they said, 'recognise nothing but what we have learnt from God, Creator of all' (Wakefield and Evans 1969: 81). They seem to have rejected the Church's teachings on the birth, death and resurrection of Christ (Lambert 1992: 11). Their condemnation owed something to political intrigue at the court of the king of France but the radical nature of their beliefs made them vulnerable (Moore 1987: 15).

Other less well educated dissenters, such as Ramihrdus of Cambrai, burnt to death in 1076, were preaching and reacting against the very weaknesses inside the Church which were officially attacked by the reformers: such prelatical failings as simony and lack of chastity; their wealthy lifestyle; a failure to adhere to the ideals of the apostolic life of the Gospels (Moore 1987: 115). The line between zealous reformer and heretic was often difficult to draw and depended to some extent on the attitude of local bishops. For such preachers, condemnation often came from the growing desire of the Church to define its own position. Producing heretics could be said to be something the Church needed to do, in order to redefine its own limits and make its own theology and practice more coherent.

By the first half of the twelfth century there were wandering preachers of heresy who were able to reach many thousands of ordinary people and convert them to new ways of thinking. This was, in part at least, due to the violent attacks by the official reformers on the ills of the church. Attempts to reform the clergy easily spilled over into a more generalised anti-clericalism. Attacks on unworthy priests soon hardened into a belief that the sacraments administered by a sinful priest were inefficacious. In this the views of many of the reformers were dangerously close to the unorthodox. In 1059 the Pope himself had urged the laity to stay away from the sacraments administered by married and simoniac priests (Morris 1989: 104). This was intended as weapon with which the Pope would use the laity to force reform upon a recalcitrant clergy. But it was a dangerous weapon to use, for from there it was not a long step to dispensing with the priest altogether, as later popes and the canon lawyers of Paris realised (Sayers 1994: 43).

What is extraordinary is the way in which the preachers of such views were able to move around the country for so many years before they were stopped. It was difficult often for contemporaries, even sophisticated clerics, to distinguish between reforming, radical preachers, who might be contained within the Church and those whose zeal drove them to take positions which the Church in the twelfth century found increasingly difficult to accommodate.

One famous example was Peter de Bruis, a village priest from the Alps who preached mostly in the area around Gap and Die and then extended his influence into the Rhone Valley. Working from about 1119 until 1139–40, he preached that the sacrifice of Christ was an act performed only once and not even to be commemorated by symbolic repetition. He also rejected infant baptism and prayers for the dead. His puritanism extended to the rejection of the use of church buildings, of singing in worship and the veneration of the Cross. He made a literal appeal to the Gospels as the source of his views and set aside the traditions of the Church and the doctrines developed by the Church Fathers.

For Peter, the Church was to be seen as a spiritual company of the Faithful (Lambert 1992: 48–9). He rejected the contemporary and near-universal view of the physicality of the link between God and Man which showed so vividly in the popular devotion to relics and which was being reinforced by the definition of the doctrine of the Eucharist, a definition formulated in the eleventh century which emphasised the physical nature of Christ's presence in the communion (Morris 1989: 374–5). Peter died at St-Gilles while trying to burn crucifixes, when the townspeople pushed him on to his own bonfire.

Peter was closely linked with another heretic with a long career, Henry the Petrobrusian. This man, a priest and former monk, appeared as a radical preacher at Le Mans in 1116. Initially he was welcomed by the bishop, Hildebert, who was a supporter of Gregorian reforms. Hildebert then left for Rome but returned to find that Henry's preaching had produced enormous enthusiasm among the laity of the town, who had turned against the clergy who were the dominant force in the city (Lambert 1992: 44–5). It was with difficulty that the bishop restored his authority and had Henry expelled. Thereafter Henry preached at places as far apart as Lausanne and Bordeaux. Called to account at the Council of Pisa in 1133, he agreed to give up his preaching. Up to this point, at least, Henry must have seemed very like men such as Robert of Arbrissel or Norbert of Xanten in his enthusiasm, his ability to stir men by his preaching and his interest in the poor and dispossessed. Like them he was difficult to control.

Henry soon returned to his old habits and seems to have met or been influenced by Peter of Bruis, becoming heretical rather than simply very radical. He had adopted an anti-clerical stance throughout his career. When he adopted the Pelagian view that men were not tainted with original sin from birth, but fell through their own actions in the world, he rejected the need for the clergy and with it went the Catholic view of the sacraments. The clergy were not needed, since it was the personal decision of the individual which fixed his relationship with God. Baptism, the first of all sacraments, became the outward sign of a conscious decision of the adult, not a supernatural gift of Grace from God. The Catholic view of all the other sacraments also fell, as did the new teachings about the nature of marriage, which became solely a matter for consent between the individuals concerned.

Henry's heretical views seem to have inspired a great popular following wherever he went. Much of that success probably sprang from the anti-clerical message, which was clearly recognised by his enemies (Wakefield and Evans 1969: 115–18). His later career was based in and around Toulouse, where he seems to have been protected by the civil

authorities. Peter the Venerable, when he wrote a tract against the heresies of the two men and their followers, clearly thought that they had
attracted many people to their sects and revealed a real fear of the consequences if the heresy were not countered (Fearns 1968: 10–11). In
1145 Pope Eugenius III sent Bernard of Clairvaux, and the bishops God-
frey of Chartres and Alberic of Beauvais, to Toulouse to preach against
Henry.

It has been suggested that Bernard found that Henry had met a pre-
existing group of heretics in Toulouse who shared his anti-clericalism
(Moore 1974). Some commentators have thought that early Cathars
were already present in the city (Manselli 1956; Griffe 1969), but Dr R.
I. Moore has argued against this view very vigorously, suggesting that the
heretics of Toulouse were essentially anti-clericalist, rather than Cathars
(Moore, 1974). Saint Bernard's mission was cut short by the demands
of his abbey, but his prestige was sufficient to bring an end to Henry's
career. He seems to have been captured and imprisoned by the Bishop of
Toulouse. However it is clear that the social circumstances in the city of
Toulouse and the surrounding territory made for fertile ground for dissent and there is nothing to suggest that Saint Bernard's preaching put
an end to heretical belief.

### The Waldensians
Important in accustoming people in the Languedoc to the idea of
organised dissent was the appearance of the Waldensians. They took
their name from Peter Valdes of Lyon, who experienced a sudden conversion in 1173 and abandoned his position as a well-to-do merchant
and moneylender in favour of a life of poverty. He was deeply affected
by the tensions which had arisen during the twelfth century between the
rapidly expanding wealth of the new commercial classes in the towns
and the calls to heed the condition of the poor made by Churchmen
such as Saint Bernard and which built upon the traditional Christian
concern for the poor. Normally one might have expected such a man to
enter one of the new orders, such as the Cistercians, but Peter felt called
to preach and there was no order which could accommodate an 'illiter-
ate' layman with such a calling.

He quickly gathered a group of like minded followers and earned
the mistrust and hatred of the clergy when he first commissioned translations of the Scriptures in the vernacular Occitan and then began to
preach the Gospel (Thouzellier 1969: 16). Peter was a layman and both
*indoctus* and *illiteratus*. His movement was much like that which was to be
founded by Saint Francis a generation later, in its emphasis on the evangelical poverty of the group and on the need to preach the Gospel to the

poor; but it was also anti-clerical, in that its desire to spread the scriptures in the vernacular, and its belief that the conventional training of the priest and the bishop was not as important as the inward call to preach the Gospel, struck hard at the professional monopoly of the clergy.

At the Third Lateran Council in 1179, Alexander III was moved by the example of poverty set by Valdes and his followers but very wary about allowing them to preach or to spread the Bible in the vernacular. In 1180 a provincial synod met at Lyon, presided over by Henry de Marciac, the Pope's legate. Here Valdes made a lengthy and elaborate profession of faith, drawn up for him by the synod. The confession laid great emphasis on many of the points where the Cathars were to disagree with the Church; on the nature of God and his omnipotence as Creator; on the humanity of Christ; on the universal nature of the Catholic Church; on the nature of the sacraments and on the nature of the priesthood (Thouzellier 1969: 27–30).

The Waldensians could not be contained by this profession, for at this stage the differences between them and the Hierarchy were still about the right to preach. Because they would not desist, in 1182 they were excommunicated and driven out of Lyon by the archbishop and his clergy. Freed from local constraints in this way, the Waldensians became widespread and popular in the Languedoc, particularly around Narbonne, and accustomed people to radical wandering preachers who were by no means always shunned by the parish priests. The Languedoc provided an area where there was little effective ecclesiastical control over their activities and the preachers began to develop their doctrines in ways which led them from schism into heresy. The preachers were celibate missionaries, both men and women, who owned nothing and lived entirely on alms. They learnt long tracts from the vernacular Bible by heart and this training formed the basis of preaching which was aimed primarily at calling their hearers to repentance.

The nature of such a group, which was fundamentally Biblicist, meant that there were many opportunities for differences of opinion. Over the years some Waldensians emerged who denied the efficacy of prayers for the dead and the existence of purgatory. Normal among the Waldensians was the belief that oaths were forbidden to Christians and that killing and bloodshed, even judicial bloodshed, were absolutely forbidden (Biller 1983). The divisions in the group were highlighted by the return to orthodoxy in 1208 by a group led by Durand de Huesca, who formed a society called the Poor Catholics (Thouzellier 1969: 217–19). Other Waldensians developed the practice of baptising children themselves, of hearing confessions and even of celebrating the

Eucharist, often because the priests available did not meet with their approval (Lambert 1992: 72–7).

In 1205 a split between the Waldensians of Italy and France led to a permanent division between the two groups. The Italian group survived to become the Waldensians of modern times, while the French group found themselves caught up in the struggle against the Cathars. Their preachers were sometimes known as *perfecti*, like the Cathars adepts, and their followers often as 'believers'. Their break with the Catholic Church was slow in coming and never very clean. An elderly lay witness, giving evidence about the position as he had known it in the 1220s, said;

> The Waldensians pursued the said heretics and he often gave the said Waldensians alms when they sought help for love of God. Because the Church then supported the said Waldensians and because they were in the church singing and reading with the priests he thought them to be good men. (Mundy 1985: 8)

By the mid thirteenth century the Waldensians often existed as well organised and settled groups, with schools, hospices and cemeteries of their own, as seems to have been the case at Montauban (Duvernoy 1994). The theology of many of the Waldensians of the Languedoc did not differ greatly in its fundamentals from the beliefs of their Catholic neighbours. They recognised the sacraments but their preachers seem not to have administered them except for exceptional circumstances. Confession was an important sacrament and practice, but penance did not exist and the remission of sin could come only from God. The Waldensians maintained their fierce opposition to oaths and to killing in all circumstances. In one way however the Waldensians set themselves apart from the Catholic Church. The preaching of the Word of God remained fundamental to their belief and practice.

Viewed from the modern world the Waldensians seem to be much like the more evangelical of Protestant sects in their emphasis on the primacy of scripture, their emphasis on the need to repent and on the primacy of preaching. But to contemporaries they seemed very like the Cathars in their anti-clerical stance and in their insistence on poverty, while their view that sacraments offered by sinful priests were to be avoided, looked back to the controversies and heresies of the early twelfth century. They clearly met a deep need among the laity for instruction in the basic tenets of the Faith and their preaching was often warmly welcomed. As with the Cathars, for most men and women the example set by the actions of the Waldensian preachers was more important than the theological content of their preaching in affecting their lives and their attitudes towards the dissidents.

## The Cathars

Catharism, of the moderate kind, which became widespread in Western Europe, had its roots in the Bogomilism of Bulgaria which had arisen there in the tenth century and which spread to many parts of the Byzantine Empire. This heresy arose about the middle of the tenth century, in a region which then stretched from Macedonia to the Danube and which was sandwiched between hostile forces. The Byzantine Greeks controlled the region in which the resident aristocracy, the Bulgarians, were a group of warrior–incomers. To the north and the east the Magyars and the Russians were a constant threat. In an area which had only recently been penetrated by Byzantine missionaries, and where the Church was seen as a force commanded by the Byzantine Emperor, orthodoxy was difficult to maintain. The sect took its name from its founder, Bogomil, who seems to have been a village priest and a native of the region (Lambert 1992: 55–6).

The early Bogomils were moderate dualists, who displayed most of the practices which were to be followed by the Cathars of the Languedoc. Their doctrines sprang from a strain of Christian thought which, although not orthodox, had very ancient roots in the early centuries of Christian belief and which had existed in the Balkans for many years. These heretical teachings of the Paulicians and the Massalians were joined together by Bogomil to make the doctrines of the sect he founded (Oblensky 1948: 111–20). The initiates avoided all foods which were the products of coition, lived celibate lives and fasted frequently. They believed that the physical world was the work of the Devil and intrinsically evil. Many of their beliefs were the antithesis of the beliefs – and above all the practices – of the Greek Church. They rejected the mass and the Eucharist, miracles, the Old Testament prophets and the Old Testament itself, baptism, marriage and the priesthood. They developed for themselves a rich mythology of the Creation and Fall which acted as a substitute for much of the Bible which they had rejected (Denkova 1990: 70–1). These dualists accepted that matter was the creation of the Good God, but believed that Satan had fashioned the world and the material bodies of men from it, either trapping the spirit of an angel within the material body to form Adam or having the clay animated by the Good God. Thereafter souls were created as children were born (Duvernoy 1994: 42). During the next two centuries their beliefs spread widely, firstly through the Balkans and into Constantinople, and a large literature survives related to the debates their views engendered. By the end of the eleventh century the heresy was so serious and widespread that the Emperor himself led the movement to destroy it and oversaw the burning of its chief proponent in the capital, a doctor called Basil (Duvernoy 1979: 36–9). In 1147 the Patriarch Cosmas was deposed because of his heretical sympathies, but the dualists continued to exist as a flourishing group until the fall of the city to the Latin crusaders in 1204 (Foreville and Rousset de Pina 1953: 331–2).

The evidence of the Cathar Council of St-Felix shows that by the end of the twelfth century there were at least five separate dualist churches in the Eastern Empire, those of Bulgaria (which included much of modern Serbia), Dalmatia, 'Melenguiae',[1] Constantinople and Dragovitsa (Hamilton 1979). The Cathars of the east were anxious to proselytise and the growing contacts between the Eastern Empire and western Europe, particularly those associated with trade, allowed the heresy to spread. A well organised group existed in Cologne by 1143–4. Evervinus, the Prior of Stinfeld, wrote to Saint Bernard about them in 1143, explaining that the group denied the mass and held the papacy and the priesthood to be so corrupt that they could not represent God. They denied all the sacraments except baptism and that was for adults only. Marriage, except between virgins, was the same as adultery; fasting and the aid of the saints were pointless, as were penances for sins. Purgatory did not exist and the souls of the dead went immediately to eternal rest or punishment. The group still existed in 1163, despite burnings. Similar views were held by groups in Flanders and there were more burnings at Vézelay in 1167. Cathar missionaries were also active in Italy by the 1160s, coming, it has been suggested, from the north of France (Lambert 1992: 55–6).

By the time that Cathar views were documented in the Toulouse area it is clear that the heresy was well established, having spread into the Languedoc from the north. In 1165 a public debate was staged at Lombers, about fifteen kilometres (ten miles) south of Albi. A group of very senior churchmen, including the bishops of Albi, Toulouse, Nîmes, Lodève and Agde and the archbishop of Narbonne, were supported by the Countess of Toulouse, who was the daughter of the King of France, and the viscounts of Béziers and of Lavaur, who were intended to add secular weight to the cause and to persuade other local nobility not to support the heretics (Griffe 1969: 62). According to contemporary accounts a great many members of the general public also attended. The heretics present were told that they would not have to take oaths concerning their beliefs (they thus avoided the danger of judicial condemnation for their statements) and on that basis were willing to talk quite freely. The heretics called themselves 'good men'.

---

[1] Identified by Dr Hamilton (1979) as a Slavic tribal group in the Peloponnese.

They were first asked whether they accepted the authority of the Bible. They rejected the Old Testament. They accepted the efficiency of the sacrament of communion, but believed that any good man, lay or cleric might consecrate the host. Confessions might be made to any person and they evidently saw no need for physical penance. On some subjects they were unwilling to make any comment. They refused to discuss baptism and referred to Saint Paul on the subject of marriage. However, they attacked the taking of oaths and the wealth of the clergy. The statement which they then made was almost entirely orthodox:

> We believe in one God, living and true, triune and one, the Father, the Son and the Holy Spirit. The Son of God took on flesh, was baptised in the Jordan, fasted in the wilderness, preached our salvation, suffered, died, and was buried, descended into hell, arose on the third day and ascended into Heaven. At Pentecost, he sent the Spirit, the Paraclete, unto his disciples, and he shall come again on the Day of Judgment to judge the quick and the dead, and all who will rise again. We acknowledge also that what we believe in our hearts we ought to confess with our mouths. We believe that no one shall be saved who does not partake of the body of Christ, and that it is not consecrated except in the Church and also unless by a priest, whether he be good or bad, nor is consecration more effectively done by a good man than by an evil one. We believe also that one is saved only by baptism and that children are saved by baptism. We also believe that husband and wife may be saved, even though they know each other carnally, and that everyone should accept penance by mouth and in heart, and be baptised by a priest in a church. And if there be anything further in the Church that can be shown from the Gospels and the Epistles, that we will accept and confess. (Wakefield and Evans 1969: 193)

The refusal to take an oath was enough to ensure their condemnation as heretics, but if the profession quoted here was true (rather than an attempt to avoid danger), then these men were hardly to be reckoned as Cathars. Their views speak much more of the common anti-clericalism of the day and suggest that Henry's influence lived on. Only a few years later, however, there is evidence that Catharism had not only penetrated the region but was already well organised. The Catharism of the Toulousain owed its existence to influences from the north, and the group in the Toulousain looked to a Cathar bishop in the north as their source of spiritual authority (Wakefield 1974: 30). Sometime between 1174 and 1177 a meeting of Cathars was held at Saint-Felix-de-Caraman in the Lauragais (Hamilton 1979). Here a substantial group of heretics who were already Cathars, but who followed the more moderate doctrines of the Cathars of Bulgaria, were converted to uncompromising dualism by Nichetas, the representative of the 'Dragovitian' Cathar church. Nichetas seems to have come from Constantinople and he came via Lombardy, where Catharism was spreading and where adherents of the Bulgarian branch of the movement already existed. At this same meeting the Cathars of the region decided to reorganise their church. Hitherto there had been only one Cathar bishop, at Albi. Now Nichetas consecrated bishops at Toulouse and Carcassonne, and probably Agen also (Hamilton 1979: 35–6). This conference is recognised as marking the point at which the new heretical church became mature. It now had a spiritual organisation which would enable it to perpetuate itself without reference to authorities outside the Languedoc.

In 1177 Raimon V made a dramatic appeal to the Chapter-General of the Cistercians and to Alexander, the head of the order. His letter was couched in terms which described the spread of heresy as a disease *putrida hæresis tabes prævaluit* (the rotten plague of heresy spreads) and in dramatic language catalogued the difficulties of the Church:

> *et antiqua olimque veneranda ecclesiarum loca inculta jacent, diruta remanent, baptismus negatur, eukaristia abominatur, poenitentia parvi penditur, hominis plasmatio, carnis resurrectio, abnegando respuitur, et omnia ecclesiastica sacramenta annulantur, et, quod dici nefas est, duo etiam principia introducuntur.* (Bouquet 1871: 140)

> (formerly venerated ecclesiastical sites lie neglected, they remain in ruins, baptism is denied, the eucharist is despised, penance is scarcely performed, the creation of man, the physical resurrection, is utterly rejected, and all the sacraments of the Church are set at nought, and what is dreadful to relate, the Two Principles are also taught.)

There can be no doubt, then, that by the end of the 1170s uncompromising Catharist heresy was openly preached in the Languedoc. Raimon V may well have used his letter to the Cistercians as part of a political campaign against his rivals, the Trencavel viscounts of Carcassonne and Béziers, and perhaps against the citizens of Toulouse, but he could not have made the charge if the heresy had not been widespread. The existence of the church organisation of the Cathars which had come into being during the decade shows that the group felt self-confident about the future and that, whatever the absolute numbers of the sect may have been, they were perceived as increasing.

### The beliefs of the Cathars

Catharism as professed by the Albigensians of the Languedoc was founded on the belief that there are two gods at work in the Universe, and that one is good and the other evil. This was a version of the absolute dualism preached by the Dragovitian Church, represented by Nichetas of Constantinople. Alain de Lille, writing in the very last years of the twelfth century, attacked the Cathars of the Languedoc (Thouzellier

1969: 81). The Cathars, he said, believed that there are two gods, one the principle of light from whom come spiritual things, souls and angels, the other the principle of darkness and evil, the opposite of being, a principle of non-being, from whom spring the things of this world. Such a belief was one way of accommodating the gap between the individual's experience of suffering and the explanation offered for that experience by religious thought (Nelson 1972: 66). How could a good God allow the manifest evils of the World to continue? The answer must be that He does not have control over events in the world, which must be governed by some other force. Cathar dualism was a rational response to this problem within the framework of the cosmological and scientific knowledge of the world then available.

Dualism then, was an answer to the problem of evil in the world. For the Cathar the world was mutable and perishable. It was to be explained as the creation of the God of Darkness, Satan, *princeps mundi*, a creation which mocks the work of the good God and which cannot contain life of its own, since that is beyond the powers of the Devil. Nothing good can come of the world. As it says in Matthew 7.18, 'A good tree cannot bring forth evil fruit, neither can a corrupt tree bring forth good fruit' (Thouzellier (ed.), 1973: 163). Cathar mythology, much like orthodoxy, suggested that the evil God had struggled against Heaven and tempted some of the angelic host to sin by rebellion against the good God. Their fall provided the Devil with spirits with which to animate the clay of his world. The principle of non-being could not create life, only trap it; consequently the souls which animated each body came solely from the stock of fallen angels, and none could be created in the world, as some of the less extreme dualists believed. Thus the fallen spirits inhabited a world made by the Devil. They were in hell. For the absolute dualists the Two Principles were equal and opposite and co-eternal.

> dicunt enim Albanenses duos creatores esse sine principio et medio et fine, et semper fuerunt contraria et sunt et erunt, et habent ambo trinitatem et unus quisque habet suam creationem, et filius dei tenebram cum angelis suis in celum ascendit. (Salvo Burce, quoted in Thouzellier 1970: 344)

> (So the Albanensians say that there are two creators who have neither beginning, middle nor end and that they have been, are and always will be opposed to one another and that they both have their Trinity and each has His creation and the Son of the God of Darkness ascended to Heaven with his angels).

The Good God was the God of light and of the unseen world of the spirit. In the early fourteenth century Pierre Maury could say:

*duo erant dii, unus eorum erat 'bonesa' et alter 'malesa' vel malicia, et Deus-bonitas fecerat spiritus et illa que non possunt videri, ita quod bonos angelos et animas et spiritus bonorum hominum fecerat Deus-bonitas, set Deus-malitia fecerat omnia corpora alia et omnia que videri possunt vel aliter sentiri, et etiam omnes demones et animas vel spiritus hominum malorum. Et Deus-bonita regebat et gubernabat celestia, et Deus-malicia istum mundum visibilem et omnia corpora alia. Et Deum-maliciam vocabant Satanam, Deum vero Bonitatem vocabant Deum Claritatis.*

(there were two gods, the one was 'bonesa' and the other 'malesa' or evil, and the Good God made the spirits and that which cannot be seen. In the same way the Good God created the good angels and the souls and spirits of good men but the God of Evil made all other bodies and everything which can be seen or otherwise be experienced as well as all the demons and the souls or spirits of wicked men. The Good God reigns over and governs the heavens, and the God of Evil reigns over and governs this visible world and all other bodies. And the God of Evil they call Satan, the Good God they call The God of Light.) (Duvernoy 1965: vol. 2, 179)

Because of this belief it was obvious that the God of the Old Testament was Satan. There the creation of the world is described. Pierre Garcias of Toulouse, speaking in 1247, remarked that the Law of Moses was nothing but shadow and vanity and that the god who gave it was a murderer and wicked (Douais 1977: 91–2). The God of Light and Life revealed himself in the New Testament, particularly in the Gospel of Saint John. The world was a battleground on which the Good God struggled for the souls of the spirits who fell. They had been seduced by Satan when he climbed up to heaven and a third of the heavenly host fell with him (Thouzellier 1969: 291). Because the souls were in the Devil's world they could either leave for their true home or stay where they were. If they stayed where they were then they would have to suffer reincarnation. Some Cathars believed that there was a limited number of reincarnations available to the lost soul. Pierre de Vaux-de-Cernay thought that the Cathars believed in seven reincarnations and other writers quoted nine. Thereafter the soul was irretrievably lost (Duvernoy 1976b: 94–5).

Many consequential beliefs flowed from these central tenets. For the Cathar the battleground of this world was essentially evil. Nothing in it was made by the Good God. Plants and animals were simply part of the Evil creation. Since men in their fleshly existence were solely the creation of the Devil it followed that human society had no divine sanction behind it. It was simply part of the world, and therefore of no especial value. For the Cathars there was no divine sanction for the structure of the society in which they lived. Indeed, their experience of persecution proved to them the essential wickedness of the world of men.

Human society was not something intrinsically good, willed by God, although corrupted by the sins of men, but something which was essentially evil.

The human body was, of course also worthless and evil. Its needs were to be treated in the most grudging manner. Reproduction was regarded with particular horror, since new bodies were seen as part of the Devil's way of providing for the continuation of the world. Sexual relations were considered to be intrinsically evil. One myth taught that Adam and Eve had no knowledge of sex at first and that the Devil found it necessary to teach Eve the pleasures of sexual intercourse by appearing to her as a serpent! She then introduced Adam to the delights of sex and the dreadful round of procreation then began. This was the Original Sin and a formidable battery of New Testament quotations were assembled to prove the essential worthlessness of marriage (Duvernoy 1976b:178–9).

Since animals were manifestly part of this cycle and might in any case contain the souls of men, to eat them was to encourage their breeding and thus help the devil in his work. The *perfecti*, the innermost members of the sect, neither engaged in sexual relations nor ate meat or any of the by-products of animal reproduction, such as eggs, milk, butter or cheese, although fish, believed to generate spontaneously in water were consumed. To avoid sexual relations and certain foods was not therefore, as in the Catholic world, an act of penance or contrition, intended to make an offering to God as an act of love for the Creator, or intended to gain grace, but a rejection of wrong behaviour, just as for a Catholic, abstinence from murder could hardly be said to be an activity with which one actively sought merit. This was an example of the way in which Catholic and Cathar behaviour often converged, so that Cathar asceticism was familiar and attractive to converts, but where the motives behind the actions were very different.

In any system of Christian theology the teaching on the nature of Christ is central and here also the Cathars were sharply at odds with the Catholic Church. Doctrines seem to have differed somewhat over a period, but most Cathars believed that Christ was either the Son of God, but not his equal, or that he was an angel (Duvernoy 1976b: 81–2). More importantly, Christ, they said, was not truly a man of flesh and blood. This was because the good God could not have co-operated with Satan by assuming a real body. Christ's body was therefore a simulacrum, a representation of a body. His body was only placed inside his mother and did not draw nourishment from her. Pierre Authié, at the beginning of the fourteenth century, said:

*quod non erat dignum cogitare vel credere quod Dei Filius natus est de muliere vel quod in re tam vili, sicut mulier est, Filius Dei se adumbraverit.*

(that it was not fitting to imagine or believe that the Son of God was born of a woman or that the Son of God should show a shadow of himself in such a vile thing as a woman is.) (Duvernoy 1965: vol. 2, 409)

Christ was an angel sent from God with the message of salvation which would release trapped souls from the cycles of the world. His death was not therefore a real death or the Resurrection a real resurrection (Duvernoy 1965: vol. 2, 409). Christ's death was not seen as a sacrifice for the sins of mankind. As a result the sacrament of the Mass could not be real, any more than the Body and Blood of Christ could be real in the Mass, since the sacrifice had never been made. For many Cathars the idea of the Real Presence of Christ in the Mass was profoundly distasteful and some mocked it by suggesting that the body of Christ, even if as big as a mountain, would long since have been consumed (Duvernoy 1965: vol. 2, 410–11). Salvation came through the message which Christ brought, not by his sacrificial death and Resurrection.

Since Catharism was not a religion of sacrifice, there was no concept of a priesthood. Every believer could approach God directly through prayer. Neither was the sacrament of baptism with water used. As a religion of gnosis, understanding and consent was needed, which the child could not give – and in any case the water was merely a material symbol from the world and of no significance. Because there was no separate hell there could not be a purgatory. In 1247 Pierre Garcias said 'that there was not a purgatory, that good works done by the living for the dead were of no use to them and that no one might be saved unless he had done perfect penance before his death. The spirits which could not do penance in one body, if they were to be saved must pass into another body in order to perfect their penance' (Duvernoy 1976b: 94).

Because Catharism insisted on the divorce between the material world and the world of the spirit, oaths were forbidden and the Gospels were cited to justify the point (Matt: 5. 36). Although a dislike of oaths was not unique to Catharism,[2] this stance marked the Cathars out from the people around them, since medieval society was built upon the proposition that God justifies oaths through the agency of relics of Christ and the saints or through the Word of God Himself, in the Bible. Oaths permeated the medieval world and were needed at every turn of daily life, in the courts, when a lord bound a new retainer to himself or when

---

[2] The Humiliati of northern Italy also refused to swear oaths, but their objections were not as fundamental as those of the Cathars, since they were prepared to compromise with Innocent III in 1201 (Sayers 1994: 145).

a steward made a survey of an estate. If a person refused to take an oath, normal activity was severely affected. The fabric of everyday life and of society itself was threatened. By refusing the oath the Cathar rejected courts and much of the structure of the society within which they lived. The *perfecti* also refused to fight or indeed to kill any creature. The refusal to fight was a parallel to the same prohibition which applied to clergy both regular and secular, but the refusal to kill animals was comprehensible to contemporaries only in the context of deviant belief.

The Cathars rejected the need for an elaborately organised Church structure with special buildings for worship, since they were merely part of the material world. Church buildings were associated with the Catholic Church which was seen as an instrument of Satan, in which the piling up of lands and the collection of tithes contrasted sharply with their own beliefs about apostolic poverty. For the Cathars, as for many other later radical sects, the rejection of the world meant that they saw themselves as a small and beleaguered group in a hostile and alien environment. Persecution was therefore to be expected. The *Liber de duobus principiis* devoted a long section to the subject (Thouzellier 1973: 406–55) and cited many scriptural texts, such as 'for I will smite the shepherd, and the sheep of the flock shall be scattered abroad' (Matt: 26. 31) and 'if the world hate you ye know that it hated me before it hated you. If ye were of the world, the world would love his own: but because ye are not of this world, but I have chosen you out of the world, therefore the world hateth you' (John: 15. 18–19). If so many Cathars went into the flames in joy and confidence it was because of the knowledge that this persecution proved the validity of their faith and was a guarantee of their immediate salvation.

The Cathars had no priests, but the sect was sustained and organised by its inner core of committed believers. These were the men and women variously described as 'the perfect ones' (*perfecti*), 'the good men or women' or simply 'Christians'. It was this inner group of believers who committed themselves to the disciplines which would bring salvation. They refrained from sexual relations, ate no meat, took no oaths, did not fight, and spent their lives in prayer and preaching. In their behaviour they were as much spiritual athletes as the religious of the new enclosed orders.

Men and women became *perfecti* by receiving the *consolamentum*. This was the spiritual baptism, believed to be the gift of the Holy Spirit given by Christ to his followers at Pentecost and granted through the laying-on of hands by other *perfecti*. Thus the initiate was made spotless, perfect and without sin. Thereafter assiduous attention to the details of the life of the *perfectus* maintained that status. Any failure led to the immediate

loss of the state of grace, which could only be regained by the re-admin-
istration of the *consolamentum* (Lambert 1992: 108). Thus for the *perfectus*,
life was highly ritualised and constant attention was needed to avoid the
fall from grace. For that reason the *perfecti* normally lived and travelled in
twos, so that when they ate one might be the witness of the probity of
the other. Even the vessels in which their food was cooked had to be
clean of every trace of meat or its products. Special utensils were often
kept in the houses where they stayed and used only for cooking their
food.

To become a *perfectus* was no easy matter. There was a period of a year
or more of training, during which the postulant learnt to fast and follow
the strict rules on oaths, lying and intercourse as well as receiving
instruction. This often took place in a community of *perfecti*. Then the
novice would submit to a solemn ceremony in which the right to say the
Lord's Prayer was conferred and then the ritual laying-on of hands
granted the *consolamentum*. With the *consolamentum* came the duty to follow
the rituals and to pray, using the Lord's Prayer, before eating and at other
times of the day and night (Duvernoy 1976b: 143–58). It seems that the
*perfecti* were marked out from other people by the wearing of a black or
dark blue habit and that the men allowed their hair and beards to grow
(Nelli 1969: 45–6). It was from among this group of people that the
preachers of the sect were drawn.

The *perfecti* were organised into a hierarchy, based primarily on
seniority of consolation. The record of the Council held at St-Felix-de-
Caraman makes it clear that the Cathars were organised in dioceses and
that at the head of each diocese there was a bishop (Hamilton 1979).
Bishops were appointed in the Languedoc for the first time at St-Felix.
By the thirteenth century succession was through supporting offices.
Each bishop had two officials known as the *filius maior* and the *filius minor*
(the senior and junior sons). On the death of the bishop he was succeeded by his 'eldest son'. The eldest's place was taken by the junior and
a new *filius minor* was elected by the *perfecti*. When this pattern emerged is
not clear, but it was probably in response to persecution. More 'biblical'
were the deacons, *perfecti* who had authority in a district, who heard confessions for minor sins and absolved them while imposing penance.
They preached and consoled as well as often running a house in which
travelling *perfecti* might stay (Duvernoy 1976b: 236–7). Altogether they
behaved very like parish priests with a cure of souls.

The major task of the *perfecti* was to preach, both to believers and
unbelievers. The Cathars of the twelfth century were a proselytising
group. Their attacks concentrated on the vices of the Catholic clergy and
they condemned the Church as the harlot of the Apocalypse (Guébin et

Maisonneuve 1951: 6), a role the Catholic Church was to play for other radical groups in European Christianity in later centuries. They aimed to detach the listener by stressing the failings of the Church and its clergy, contrasting the wealth of the clergy with the poverty of Christ and his disciples. Then they might move on to expound their own alternative doctrines. There can have been few adults in the Languedoc at the end of the twelfth century who were not familiar with the main outlines of Cathar belief, the doctrine of the Two Principles.

Most men and women who listened to the Cathars did not seek to become one of the *perfecti*, just as most Catholic laypeople did not aspire to enter the Cistercian Order. For laypeople, known as 'believers', the command was that they should live peaceably, do good to one another, not lie, steal or commit acts of violence or take oaths. They should also accept the authority of the *perfecti*, which they acknowledged by attendance at preaching, acceptance at their hands of bread at meals and by bowing before the *perfecti* at any meeting. Above all the believer sought to receive the *consolamentum* from the *perfecti* as the moment of death approached so as to be certain of salvation (Wakefield 1974: 32). They were not expected to follow the strict dietary and sexual rules of the *perfecti*. Nor were they expected to abstain from warfare. They lived much as did their devout Catholic neighbours. The beliefs of the Cathars were not always as austerely consistent as the exposition here might suggest. There were many fantastic myths current in the Languedoc among the *perfecti* by the early thirteenth century, some of which were mutually inconsistent (Thouzellier 1969: 285–8). For the layperson the example of the life of the *perfecti* was the most important part of the message.

### The sociology of the Cathars

The establishment of the dioceses at the Council of St-Felix gives important evidence about the relative strength of the region. Albi, Toulouse, Carcassonne and possibly Agen were the centre of dioceses (Hamilton 1979: 34–6), although the Cathar bishops usually resided at other centres, probably because they would have felt vulnerable close to the seat of an orthodox bishop (figure 15). The vast jurisdiction of the Cathar bishops, in the case of the bishop of Carcassonne including the whole of Catalonia, suggests that the total numbers of believers was not great throughout the region, but that nevertheless some few did exist, even as far away as Barcelona – and later accounts show this to have been true. Clearly, though, the concentration of the faithful was greatest in the regions close to where the bishops had their seats. Mapping the incidence of deacons (Delaruelle 1968: 27), of bishops (Hamilton 1979), of known burial grounds (Duvernoy 1976b: 25fn. 4) and convents

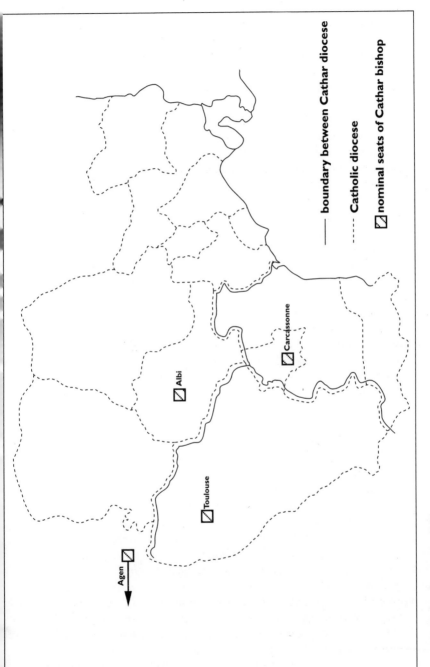

Figure 15  Cathar dioceses in 1209

(Griffe 1969: 148) shows clearly that at the end of the twelfth century organised Catharism was concentrated in the central area between Toulouse and Carcassonne, although much anecdotal evidence shows that it was also widespread in the Catholic diocese of Carcassone, and south into Foix. The Toulouse diocese had at one time at least fifty deacons working within it, showing that here above all the heresy was concentrated (figure 16).

Contemporary commentators noted how widespread support for Catharism was among people in authority, particularly the nobility. This was in marked contrast to heretical movements at an earlier date in Northern France, where most adherents seem to have been anonymous peasants or artisans. One needs to treat with caution the comments of the twelfth- and thirteenth-century writers, since any adherents who were notable were likely to be remarked upon, even if they were not actually prominent in the movement. Such heretics were likely to be all the more hated for having betrayed the group to which they and most senior churchmen belonged. The sense that men of high rank should stand at one with the clergy, and that the heretics could be easily comprehended and controlled if they sprang from peasant or even bourgeois stock, was normal. Guilhem de Puylaurens remarked that 'even the nobles, scorning authority and of their own accord and without any opposition, followed one or other of the heretics' (Duvernoy 1976b: 25). Pierre des Vaux-de-Cernay, a northerner and a violent partisan of the crusaders, said 'the lords of the Languedoc almost all protected and harboured the heretics, showing them an excessive love and defending them against God and the Church' (Guébin et Maisonneuve 1951: 5).

The lords of Laurac lived in the heart of the region particularly affected by Catharism. Vassals of the Trencavel lords of Carcassonne and Béziers, their influence extended into the Albigeois to the north, and south-east into the Carcassès. Blanca, the wife of Sicard II, lord towards the end of the twelfth century, was a Cathar and one of her daughters, Mabila, became a *perfecta* while another, Geralda, married the lord of Lavaur and was killed when the town fell to Simon de Montfort's forces. Yet another daughter, Esclarmonde, married the lord of Niort, the head of a noble family which was notorious for its heresy, and with her children was condemned as a heretic in 1237 (Griffe 1969: 156–7). Further south, the Count of Foix, Raimon-Roger, was certainly a sympathiser with the Cathars and his sister was consoled at Fanjeaux in the presence of a great gathering of local nobility c. 1204 (Griffe 1969: 159). The count appointed his wife as the head of the Cathar convent he founded at Dun and his sister, Esclarmonde, as leader of his convent at Pamiers. Of 1,190 named *perfecti* mentioned in sources between 1190

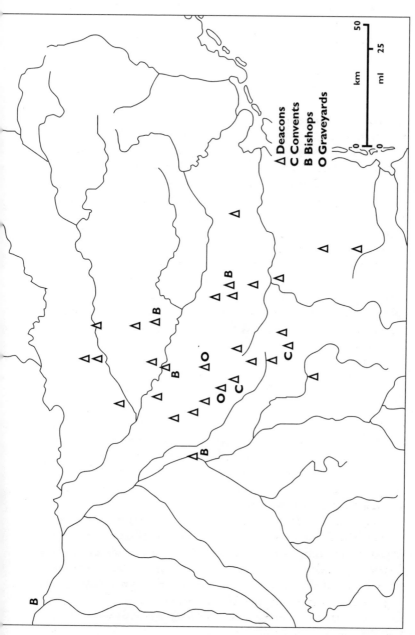

Figure 16 Catharism c. 1210: deacons, convents and bishops in the Lauragais, Albigeois and Carcassonnais

and 1250, 172 were members of the nobility. Such a figure certainly suggests that there were many adherents among that group, but they were probably disproportionately represented among the *perfecti* where they took leading roles, much as they did in the orthodox Church. That so many members of the nobility were involved was of the first importance, since their political weight and economic power provided protection as well as financial support for the movement. No organisation, however well run and however close it remained to its ideal of holy poverty, could hope to expand or even survive in the long term without such patronage.

As a group the nobility of the region were independent enough to be able to think for themselves on matters of personal belief. But economic reasons for the anti-clericalism which helped to fuel their dissident beliefs were also strong. Division of property among heirs continually reduced the incomes available, and consequently the ownership of churches and of their tithes was of great importance. The insistence that the ownership of spiritual property and revenues was a mortal sin for laymen, which had been preached assiduously since the mideleventh century, was therefore deeply unwelcome (Biget 1972). Pressure to return spiritualities to the Church was intense and many lay owners of tithes and churches must have felt inclined towards Catharism, since it did not ask for tithes and attacked the church for its materialism.

With so many of the nobility at least sympathetic towards Catharism it was possible for the heresy to spread in the countryside among the peasantry. Very little is known about the frequency of dissident beliefs among this group in the twelfth century. The detailed revelations of the registers of Jacques Fournier deal with peasant society over one hundred years later. But the line dividing town and country was very thin and it seems likely that the heresy spread in the countryside at this early date, as it certainly did later. More information about the spread of Catharism in the towns is available. In 1178 when Henry de Marciac, Peter of St-Chrysogonus and the bishops of Bath and of Poitiers visited Toulouse to preach against the heretics, they met Pierre Maurand, the leader of a group of dualists who was persuaded to recant, perhaps because of the presence of Raimon V in the city. As part of his punishment he was condemned, amongst other penalties, to have his fortified houses pulled down and to repay the interest he had taken on loans (Stubbs 1867: 218). Clearly he was an important man in the city.

The chroniclers were clear that Toulouse was an important centre of Catharism. Pierre des Vaux-de-Cernay called the city 'the principal source of the poison of heresy' (Guébin et Maisonneuve 1951: 3). By the time the Crusade began there were members of several prominent families among the heretics, including the Maurands, the Carabordes and the Embrys. There were also many artisans, particularly weavers (Wolff 1961: 89). Catharism was clearly well established in other towns in the Languedoc. Many of these places were relatively small, but the seat of a deacon seems usually to have been in a town of some importance. Thus towns such as Mirepoix, Montréal and Fanjeaux had deacons, but so did many small settlements, such as Termes and Puivert (Duvernoy 1979: 230–5). Both these places were primarily castle sites and it would not be too fanciful to see their deacons as akin to orthodox chaplains to the noble families.

Inside the towns it is evident that many members of the bourgeoisie were prominent in the new cult. It is unlikely that Catharism could have flourished for long in the urban environment if that had not been so, since it was this group that controlled town government almost everywhere. Among the merchants and traders of the towns the twelfth century saw an intensification of the theological problems presented by the process of business. The Church in the twelfth century had increasingly preached against usury, as credit became necessary to facilitate trade. A dilemma of conscience arose, as social pressure from the Church competed with the need to make profits. Some merchants solved this problem by abandoning trade and their wealth and by accepting 'conversion' in a more or less orthodox way. Fulk of Marseille dramatically ended his career as a merchant – and his family line – when he entered the Cistercians along with his wife and son. Peter Valdes did much the same, but stepped outside the line of orthodoxy. An alternative was to become a Cathar, since Catharism did not preach against usury.

Among the Cathars women were often prominent, but it would be wrong to imagine that it appealed especially to them. There is no evidence to suggest that more women than men were Cathars (Abels and Harrison 1979). The relative lack of a hierarchy enabled women to play a more prominent and active part and there was no doctrinal reason why women should not, as *perfectae*, preach and administer the *consolamentum*. This they certainly did on occasions, but it seems to have been chiefly in emergencies (Abels and Harrison 1979: 227, n.61). They probably preached more often, but even so Abels and Harrison record only 12 instances among 318 mentions of *perfectae* (Abels and Harrison 1979: 228). Esclarmonde of Foix was an unusual example of a female Cathar who took part in religious debate. In 1207 she was admonished during a debate at Pamiers to 'go to your spinning, Madame. It is not proper for you to speak in a debate of this sort.' Probably what she had to say made the Catholic clerics uncomfortable (Duvernoy 1976b: 49). But the case of such a high-ranking and elderly aristocratic lady was very unusual. Ladies of her rank were allowed actions which would not have been tolerated from women of lower social standing.

The prejudices and assumptions of a masculine world were strong among the Cathars also and in addition the dangers for an unprotected or unsupported woman were the same whether she was a Cathar or a Catholic, making independent action among women without powerful social connections very difficult. Women do not appear among the deacons or among the other officers who assisted the bishops (Mundy 1987: 117). However, they were active in the formation of convents and there were many houses in which female *perfectae* gathered together, scattered across the central part of the Languedoc. The wife of Guilhem-Roger of Mirepoix left her husband to join just such a house of *perfectae* and then persuaded her daughter to join her (Griffe 1971). There were relatively few Catholic houses available to women in the Languedoc; certainly they were much less densely distributed than in northern France. The province of Auch offered only one convent for women and the province of Narbonne, within which Toulouse stood, only seven (Verdon 1976).

It seems likely that Cathar houses filled a need for women who no longer felt at home in marriage or did not wish to marry. The relatively greater freedom to own real property and thus to act independently probably helped women to set up such ventures for themselves. Furthermore, since unsupported women were at much greater risk of molestation or exploitation than solitary men they had perforce to group together and to live stable lives, rather than wandering from one place to another. Without churches much Cathar proselytising was carried on in houses and it was the *domus* which was the particular domain of the wife in Langedoc society. As the heresy became widely established over a long period, children were born into the faith and raised as Cathars. Thus it is likely that much of their early instruction came from the women of the house. There are examples of little girls, as young as nine years old, being placed by their parents in the convents of *perfectae* and receiving the *consolamentum* while still very young. This seems to have been often because the family were too poor to marry off their daughters according to their social position. Some girls placed in this situation subsequently abandoned the convent to marry of their own volition (Abels and Harrison 1979: 233).

The *perfecti* included many women as well as men, perhaps as many as one third, but it would be too easy to assume that the Cathars regarded men and women as equals. The belief that (female) *perfectae* became male, or more probably sexless along with men, when they finally gained salvation suggests that the Cathars rationalised the subordinate position of women in medieval society, just as the Catholic world did. However, in doctrinal terms, there was no reason why women could not exercise exactly the same spiritual functions as men and we have seen that they sometimes did. This fitted well with the relatively freer position of women in Languedocian society as compared with the French of the north.

For both sexes yet another reason for the attraction of Catharism may have lain in its paradoxically relaxed attitude to sex and marriage. Marriage was and is a major determinant of the structure of society and Dr Goody has shown convincingly that the structure of Western European society has been profoundly influenced and determined by the way in which the Church sought to gain control of marriage and by degrees came to dominate that area of human activity (Goody 1983). In particular, the wide extension of the prohibited degrees under the late Empire and their reinforcement in the twelfth century, together with enforcement of serial monogamy and the banning of divorce, led to the normal practice of exogamy. This resulted in the break up of close knit family groups and the dispersal of property as well as laying the inner workings of the family open to the scrutiny and regulation of the Church (Morris 1989: 331). The very wide prohibited degrees, in particular, made it easy for the hierarchy to interfere in the family and sexual lives of the faithful. This interference undoubtedly helped the Church to gain control of property by legacy, particularly when it led to the failure of male heirs.

For the *perfecti* marriage was an essentially sinful state and so Cathar theology had little to say about it and was largely indifferent to its form. Furthermore the Cathar Church had as yet little interest in enforcing or extending the prohibited degrees, unlike the Catholic Church. So at a time when the official Church was controlling the private lives of the faithful more and more closely, Catharism offered a return to a more relaxed attitude to marriage. Particularly for the poor in rural areas, prohibited degrees made finding a partner difficult. In this Catharism took up a theme which had been common to other heretical groups, particularly the followers of Henry the Petrobrusian. He had claimed marriage as a rite belonging to the community at large, rejecting the new theology of marriage by which the orthodox Church was gaining control of the institution, and rejecting the tightening of prohibited degrees (Moore 1977: 91).

The question of how many Cathars there were is almost impossible to answer. Fifteen hundred has been suggested as the approximate number of *perfecti* in the Languedoc at the end of the twelfth century (Mundy 1954: 70) and it is difficult to imagine that the numbers of believers can ever have amounted to more than ten times that number. Experience shows that the importance of dissident groups rarely depends upon their absolute numbers. The fact of their existence, especially when they are a vociferous minority, gives importance far beyond numbers, especially for the established order which is threatened.

To be a Cathar was to be a nonconformist, to stand outside the official religious life of the community and such action has always meant a positive step on the part of adherents. As in so many other examples of nonconformity in European society, it can be seen as a response to the instability of life, here in the Languedoc of the twelfth century. The social and economic pressures on the minor aristocracy, the insecurity of the new urban proletariat, uncertainties about the morality of the practice of the new merchant class, all reflected an unprecedented fluidity in society. Catharism was a response to the need to reassert control by ordinary people over their surroundings, to re-orientate themselves in a community. Solidarity was achieved inside the group, with new rituals and new norms of conduct which reasserted the value of communal action. A coherent world view in place in the interior life of the believer gave security and comfort in an uncertain world.

Catharism affected people from all walks of life in the society of the Languedoc, although the clergy do not seem to be well represented. For the laity of the Languedoc the Cathars offered a characteristically 'nonconformist' message. They demanded purity of life and conformity to the Gospels, especially among their spiritual leaders. They wanted to turn away from the world at large to find support and comfort in a group of the elect. They wished to reconcile their experience of a harsh and changing world with their wish for certainty and control over their own destinies. They wished to be able to participate in religious practice. They needed their religion to reinforce and support those elements of their personal lives which were most important to them, family and community relationships, and they wanted the cost of their religious practices to be contained within what they could afford and to be recirculated within their own world. They wished to wrest control of their spiritual lives from the clergy who were discredited by their attempts to elevate their status and by the dichotomy between rhetoric and practice. In a milieu where political and religious authority were distant and relatively undemanding all this was possible. Like most nonconformist movements, Catharism was a statement against the established Church. Its preaching, which portrayed the Catholic Church as the whore of Babylon and the Church of the Devil, emphasised that part of its agenda; but it was also a positive movement and to its adherents it offered new relationships between individuals and a new message of hope from God to Man.

# 4

# The Catholic Church in the Languedoc

## Dioceses and bishops

The organisation of the Church in the Languedoc was untidy. The distribution of dioceses and the responsibilities of metropolitans reflected the ancient organisation of the south, and the jurisdictions often crossed political boundaries. The Archbishop of Narbonne, with his seat in the ancient Roman capital of Gallia Narbonensis, controlled Elne (in Roussillon, a dependency of the counts of Barcelona), Carcassonne, Béziers and Agde in the lands of the viscounts of Carcassonne and Béziers, Maguelonne, the bishopric for Montpellier and Lodève, Nîmes and Uzès, which were all in lands controlled in some way by the counts of Toulouse. In the west the Bishop of Toulouse also owed him obedience and the territory of that bishop also covered the independent County of Foix. Within the lands of the counts of Toulouse, Cahors and Rodez to the north owed allegiance to the Archbishop of Bourges. At Albi, within Trencavel territory, the bishop also owed allegiance to Bourges. In the far west Agen belonged to the archbishopric of Bordeaux. In the Rhone delta and valley the lands were subject to the Archbishop of Arles (figure 17).

One result of the Gregorian reforms, at least in the later eleventh and early twelfth centuries, was to loosen the grip of the nobility upon great Church offices. The gradual regularisation of elections, so that in the twelfth century it became accepted that an election by the chapter of the Cathedral was the normal way of selecting a bishop, did provide some guarantee of his suitability. However, the nobility of the Languedoc soon came to understand the new system and, as the century went on, their grip on high office was reasserted. That in itself did not matter if the incumbent was willing to perform his office conscientiously, but in practice it meant that bishoprics with extensive temporalities were the most attractive to powerful noble families, while poorer sees were left to men of lesser social rank, with less local prestige.

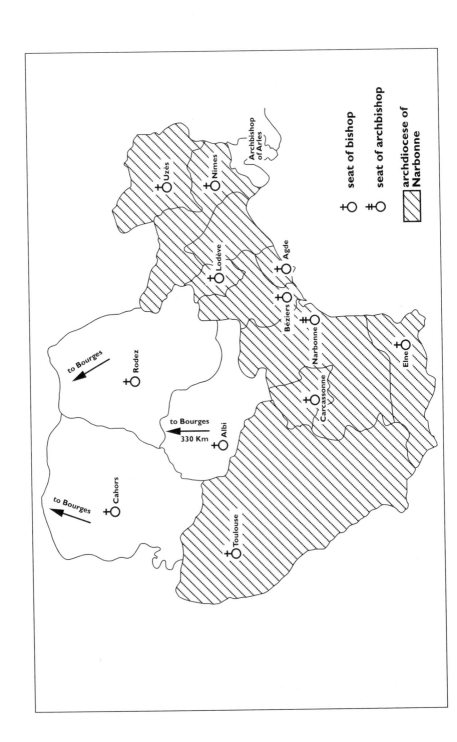

seat of bishop

seat of archbishop

archdiocese of Narbonne

Uzès

Nîmes

Archbishop of Arles

Lodève

Agde

Béziers

Narbonne

Elne

to Bourges

Rodez

to Bourges

330 Km

Albi

Carcassonne

to Bourges

Cahors

Toulouse

During the twelfth century the bishops of the region, much condemned by Pope Innocent III at the time of the Crusade, varied
immensely in their quality. The archbishopric of Narbonne had as
incumbents men of quite varied social backgrounds during the course
of the century. Richard (1106–21) was the son of the Count of Millau
and was the great-uncle of Douce of Provence, wife of Raimon-Berenger
II of Barcelona. Arnald (1121–49) was the son of the count of Lèvezon.
Peire (1149–56) was the son of the lord of Andouze and brother-in-law
of the Viscountess of Narbonne. His successor, Berenger I (1156–62)
was the son of the Viscount of Narbonne and the uncle of the Viscountess Ermengarde. He was also the uterine half-brother of Count Raimon-
Berenger III of Barcelona. After two more archbishops of comparatively
humble background the seat fell to Berenger II (1191–1212), the illegitimate son of Raimon-Berenger IV of Barcelona and half-brother to
King Alfons II of Aragon and uncle of King Pere II. He had formerly been
the abbot of Mont-Aragon, near Tarragona, and then Bishop of Lerida.
He was still abbot of the monastery in 1203 and was supposed never to
have visited either his diocese of Lerida or his archdiocese (Dossat
1944).

The bishops of Albi were not men of the first rank during the early
years of the century. During the schism of Anacletus II (1130–8) the
bishop supported the anti-pope, while the chapter supported Innocent
II. In so far as Innocent II represented the more reformist wing of the
curia the bishop found himself ranged against figures such as Bernard of
Clairvaux. However, at Albi the bishop was far from his metropolitan
and was chiefly concerned with his relationship with the secular lords of
the town and the viscounty. Although the counts of Toulouse had ceded
their powers in Albi to the Trencavels the new rulers exercised relatively
little power. In 1132 Roger I Trencavel had become the effective patron
of the bishopric, but by the end of the century the bishop had emerged
as the most powerful figure in the town. His fiscal powers gave him a
source of wealth which enabled him to pay knights as well as ensuring
his judicial control of part of the town (Biget 1983). By the end of the
century the bishop was relatively independent, while the office itself had
fallen into the hands of men of higher social status. Although Catharism
existed in the region, Albi itself submitted to the crusaders early in the
conflict and was never a centre of resistance to Catholic authority.

The Bishop of Béziers, whose predecessors had been lords of the
town in the eleventh century, still had a feudal court in the mid-twelfth
century and received power over the whole of the town in 1204 when
Raimon-Roger Trencavel pledged it to him (Vidal 1951). The Bishop of
Agde controlled the town and became Viscount of Agde as well as hav-

ing rights in the rest of the diocese ceded by the Viscount of Nîmes in 1187.

The Third Council of Montpellier excommunicated the inhabitants of Capestang because they had captured, imprisoned and held to ransom the Bishop of Lodève, Raimon-Guilhelm (HGL 6: 171–2). He was the son of Guilhem IV, Viscount of Montpellier, and he had become the secular Viscount of Lodève in a series of acquisitions between 1167 and 1192. Purchases included the castle of Montbrun. He thus united bishopric and secular rule and laid himself open to attacks of the kind a secular ruler might expect (HGL 6: 118). At Uzès the bishops doubled the size of their domains in the second half of the century and were the rulers of the town as well as holding many castles (Dossat 1944). The bishops of Languedoc, often members of the ruling houses of the region, advanced their secular power as the century advanced. By uniting lay authority – and often ruling powers – to their spiritual offices they were taking advantage of the relative political weakness of their area to extend the authority of their families as much as the authority of the Church.

Not all bishoprics offered the same opportunities. The Bishop of Toulouse was in a difficult position; he was poor, but his diocese was vast. Fulcrand was bishop from 1179 to 1201. According to Guilhem de Puylaurens he had very little in the way of income, receiving nothing in tithes which all belonged to monasteries or to laymen. His income from property only allowed him to live like a townsman and when he wanted to visit his diocese he had to beg a bodyguard from the nobles whose districts he wished to enter. His successor, Raimon de Rabastens, was accused of simony and spent three years fighting a war against his vassal, Raimon Fort de Belpech, bankrupting the bishopric in the process (Duvernoy 1976: 43–5). Possibly because of this poverty the organisation of the diocese had not kept pace with demographic changes. In the mid-century there were only four archdeaconries for the whole diocese, which was too big to be controlled easily from Toulouse. For financial support the bishop might have looked to the Count. But the counts themselves were not wealthy and preferred to give patronage to prestigious regular orders such as the Cistercians and the Templars. Without large numbers of churches under his direct control, from which the bishop might draw revenue, he was left only with the proceeds of a small customary tax paid annually by each church. Collection of the tax was difficult and payments were often years in arrears (Ourliac and Magnou 1984). We should not imagine that the bishopric had only become weak and ineffective in the last years of the century. It is likely that the poverty and lack of power had been evident sixty years earlier, when Henry the Petrobrusian had been active.

At Carcassonne the bishop had a smaller diocese to administer which covered only the old Carolingian *pagus* of Carcassonne (Griffe 1936). But the see was poor and this may explain why the bishops had such a dismal reputation in the later years of the century. In 1198 Othon resigned because his great age made it impossible for him to carry out his duties and he was succeeded by his nephew, Berengar, archdeacon at the Cathedral, whose preaching against heresy led to his expulsion from the city by the inhabitants, not long before the Crusade. According to Pierre des Vaux-de-Cernay, he told them that they would be destroyed by people from other parts of the world. He forecast a crusade (Guébin et Maisonneuve 1951: 44). His successor, Bernard-Raimon, was deposed in 1211, probably because his background made him unacceptable to the conquerors. He came from the Black Mountains and from a family which contained many Cathars. His mother was supposed to have been a *perfecta* and his brother, Guilhem de Rochefort, was a member of the garrison of the castle of Termes (Roquebert 1970: 148).

It would be anachronistic to see the archbishops as normally exercising a high degree of supervision over their bishops. Such co-ordinated policy as did exist was exercised through such functions as synods. Implementation of policy and the dissemination of canons were normally carried on at the level of the archdiocese, under the control of the archbishop and so co-ordination throughout the Languedoc, divided between different archbishops, was difficult. The organisation of the Church in the Languedoc had not kept pace with the demographic and settlement changes of the eleventh and twelfth centuries. Those bishops with relatively small territories and considerable revenues and political powers generally controlled dioceses in which heresy was a relatively minor problem; those who lacked income or had extended dioceses did less well. The bishops of the Languedoc were badly organised and hindered by the political geography of the Languedoc, but it is difficult to argue that they were uniquely decadent, corrupt or idle. Their problems and their defects were far from unique and could be found in many other parts of Europe. What they lacked was consistent political support.

## The parish church

One fact seems certain about the Church in the countryside: there were a great many churches. Recent research in the area around Rieux suggests that by the thirteenth century there was about one church with parochial rights for every 800 hectares of land. As a result there were some 300 churches in the district. The same area today has 120 functioning churches in 110 communes. This large number of churches

reflects the density of population in an area which had been heavily
colonised in the eleventh and twelfth centuries. Tithings within parishes
were about 400 hectares in extent on arable plain-land and seem to have
had about 150–200 inhabitants. Typically, there was one church for
every 300–400 people (Menard 1990).

Elsewhere, in countryside which had been well settled since Roman
times, churches seem to have existed since the fifth or sixth centuries,
usually at villa sites. These were the churches with burial rights and all
the other functions associated with the later parish church. During the
eleventh and twelfth centuries the growth of *castra* and the consequent
movement of population led to the construction of new churches at
these new centres of population. The old villa churches were then often
left as cemetery churches in the countryside, while the tithes were collected by the incumbents of the new churches (Ramière de Fortanier
1990). The typical village incumbent probably did not actually enjoy
the tithes of his church. By the end of the century the monastery of St-
Lezat had rights over about 140 rural churches (Ourliac and Magnou
1984). The monastery of Lagrasse controlled about one hundred
churches. St-Benoit of Castres had 22 churches in 1122 and that number increased slightly during the century. Other monasteries also held
churches, so that by the end of the century the majority of village
churches must have belonged to outside organisations which received
most of the tithes. Where the tithes were not owned by an ecclesiastical
body they normally belonged to a major landowner. Most incumbents
therefore, probably lived on the glebe of their churches. When the
church of Maurressac was founded in 859, Ermentrude, the benefactor,
granted land for the church and cemetery plus twenty arpents of arable,
five vines and two arpents of woodland – a Carolingian *mansus* (Ourliac
and Magnou 1984). As elsewhere, the priest was expected to support
himself – and, until the banning of clerical families, his wife and children – from the *mansus* in return for performance of the rituals of the
church.

There are some signs that the older pre-parochial organisation of
rural churches could exist in more distant parts of the countryside. The
priory of St-Beat in Commignes was a dependency of St-Lezat, but had
once been independent. Eighteen surrounding churches were directly
dependent upon St-Beat. All their tithes went to the priory and children
could only be christened at the mother church at the great festival times
(Ourliac and Magnou 1984). St-Beat had probably been the first church
in the region and had built the churches on land round about which it
may have owned at the time. The churches had not become fully fledged
parish churches because of the inherent conservatism of the monastery

and its desire to retain the income from the tithes during a period of rising population and rising output.

Monastic influence upon the rural population was increased by the practice of maintaining priories as dependencies of larger monasteries. It is clear that some of the priories were ancient monastic institutions which had fallen under the control of large neighbours, often in the tenth or eleventh centuries, perhaps because of financial difficulties, perhaps to escape the clutches of a lay protector. Although these institutions normally had a secular priest who held the cure of souls for the lay community, the priory church was usually the parish church also and the monks controlled the village cemetery. Separation of the monks from the parish work had been one of the policies of the Gregorian reformers and was generally adhered to in the monastic world. Nevertheless, policy was clearly in their hands (Avril 1984). The number of monks in such institutions was often very small. Strictly a monk needed one *socius* (companion), but even this rule was not always observed.

In other places monastic control of rural parishes led to the emergence of a system of curates. Both the monasteries of Moissac and Montolieu granted the care of parishes to clerks who farmed the tithes and other income, paying the monastery a fixed rent and serving the cure themselves or paying someone else to do so. Such men were probably of superior status, since they were also offered the chance to become monks of the abbey, perhaps when death approached (Avril 1984).

## The Church in the towns

In the towns the picture was a little different. Although the towns grew very fast, it was only slowly that the Church organisation adapted. At Toulouse it was only in the mid-twelfth century that the three major churches of the town fixed their respective parish boundaries. Within the old *cité* the cathedral of St-Etienne was also the parish church and in the new *bourg* St-Sernin, the monastic and pilgrim church, became a parish church. The other church to take over this role was the church of St-Pierre-des-Cuisines which stood on an ancient extramural graveyard and had been in existence since the fifth century. The extramural suburb within which St-Pierre stood was eventually swallowed by the *bourg* of St-Sernin. St-Pierre kept its independence and became a parish church because the land around and the church itself had been granted to the Abbey of Moissac between 1055 and 1061 (Gérard 1990). Considering the size of the town population the number of churches available to the citizens seems meagre compared with the supply in the countryside. However the relatively small number of churches inside the city was not unusual. In other parts of western Europe some towns had many churches but in southern parts one (or a few) seems to have been more normal (Brooke 1970).

### Parish priests

It is difficult to say much about the parish clergy who served the rural churches, or those in the smaller towns. In theory at least the spread of the reform movement had helped bishops to control the quality of their clergy more effectively. The bishop's right to approve all candidates to cures, established by the Lateran Councils of the twelfth century, should have presented a powerful weapon with which to ensure the quality of the parish priest. Many of the monasteries which had effective control over parish churches were able to present candidates to office without the approval of the bishop – they simply went ahead and ignored his rights. Other monasteries negotiated with their local bishop, giving up rights claimed over some churches in order to gain immunity for others (Avril 1984).

Since so many of the offices granted to ordinary parish priests were poor, simony was probably not much of a problem. Much more important was the problem of clerical marriage and concubinage. The introduction of strict measures against clerical marriage had taken place in the 1070s and by the mid-twelfth century it is likely that there were few priests who could be described as married. At Padern in 1060 laymen gave the church and its tithes to an association of six priests who were to serve the church, choosing a successor, normally a son, to succeed when a priest died (Ourliac and Magnou 1984). The Second Lateran Council of 1139 had declared that a marriage entered into by a subdeacon, deacon or priest was not a marriage; and where a marriage had taken place before ordination, the new priest was increasingly required to leave his wife (Morris 1989: 104–5). This new emphasis on the other-worldliness of the priest was a development which ran parallel to the growing elaboration of the ritual of the Mass and its increasing distance from the laity. For the reformers abstinence from sexual relationships was a matter of ritual purity, driven by a belief that intercourse was dirty, and ultimately degrading and sinful and therefore a fatal impediment to the pure administration of the sacrament of the Mass. In the eleventh century the reformers had urged lay parishioners to boycott 'incontinent' priests and tied the chastity of the secular clergy to the example provided by the monastics.

The practical effect of such a movement was that it placed the priest in the close community of the parish, in a position of neutrality in which he could stand outside the everyday concerns of his flock, especially if he had not bought his office but been appointed on some basis of merit. It would certainly have broken the family control of the church of Padern. If the priest was not married, then he could not pass on his office to a son. Unlike almost every other position in medieval society, it could not be passed down through a family and it could not therefore become a species of property, as had threatened in the tenth and eleventh centuries. The outlawing of marriage struck a blow against the hereditary principle which was so powerful in lay life. The village priest was on his way to being professionalised just at the point that professional administrators were beginning to appear in secular governments and in the courts. It seems unlikely that this ideal was easily achieved in the Languedoc. The decrees of the Lateran Council of 1179 show the common problems with which the reformers still wrestled. The decrees forbade the sale of the sacraments and the taking of money for marriages and burials. No one might have the cure of souls before his twenty-fifth year and persons chosen should be of exemplary character. Bishops should be at least thirty years old and must be legitimate. Plurality was condemned and bishops were to maintain clerks they ordained who had no benefice. Clerks were not to accept secular posts and they were not to maintain women (Mansi 1961, vol. 22: cols 218–33). The restatement of all these provisions suggests that the old problems continued.

If the priests of the Languedoc were little different from those elsewhere in western Europe it is probable that they rarely if ever were capable of preaching. At this time preaching was still officially the prerogative of the bishop and his assistants, and one of the distinguishing characteristics of many of the great reformers of the eleventh and twelfth centuries was their skill and success as preachers. Most preachers spoke to the educated inside the hierarchy of the church, to monks or to scholars. However, in the twelfth century there was a great outburst of preaching which affected the lives of ordinary people. Great reformers such as Norbert of Xanten, Bernard of Tiron and Robert of Arbrissel, in the early part of the century, began a tradition of preaching to ordinary people (Morris 1989: 306). Other great figures, such as Bernard of Clairvaux, continued the practice and Bernard preached successfully in Toulouse and other cities of the Languedoc in an attempt to counter Henry the Petrobrusian.

That was the problem, since a preaching tour was a spectacular and relatively rare event. Most laymen in the countryside would perhaps have heard such a man once only in a lifetime. Perhaps even that is too high an estimate. Almost certainly there was a demand for teaching in this style, a demand which was not met. There is no evidence that sufficient training was available to most parish clergy, or that they would have been

expected to preach. The breach was to some extent filled by the Cathar
and Waldensian preachers. The local priest, where he fulfilled his function properly, provided the ritual framework through his celebration of
the Mass and the administration of the other sacraments, but he did not
meet the new needs of his flock. That need for teaching was another
aspect of the expansion of self-consciousness which was taking place all
over the western European world, but which could not be met by the
parish priest.

## The monasteries

It is clear that clerical reformers of the twelfth century saw a godly
clergy as the key to success in their relationships with the laity and were
anxious to see the secular clergy reformed and well ordered; but spiritual prestige still lay chiefly with the monastic orders. We have already
seen the extent to which reforms affected the monasteries of the
Languedoc in the eleventh century. The financial health of the older
Cluniac and Benedictine monasteries is difficult to gauge, but the experience of Lagrasse suggests that it was often bad. Although the
monastery had nine dependent houses, lands in seven dioceses and over
one hundred dependent churches it got into severe financial difficulties
in the second half of the century. Much land had been enfeoffed. Effectively this meant that the abbey had permanently alienated the territory,
getting only homage and no service. Its other estates were nearly all
farmed out for fixed rents, so that as prices rose the abbey suffered a
progressive loss. Recovery did not come until the mid-thirteenth century and by then the enfeoffed lands had gone for good (Pailhes 1984).
However, the older monasteries still continued to control vast territories, and as major landowners and lords were deeply involved in local
issues.

In the twelfth century, as elsewhere in Europe, the new and more
austere orders captured the imagination of southern laymen. These new
orders, usually eremitical in their inspiration, were often founded by
laymen or were enthusiastically adopted by men and women who had
not been brought up in the cloister in the old way. The ardour of men
like Robert of Arbrissel or Stephen of Muret was channelled into foundations which grew large and developed rules. The hierarchy which
gave such pre-eminence to the role of the priest captured and tamed
these orders, so that among the Cistercians or the Premonstratensians it
came to be the clergy who took the leading roles as choir monks and also
rulers of the communities, while the laymen and women were relegated
to subsidiary roles as *conversi*. But before that happened in the Languedoc

the eremitical movement seems to have been as successful as elsewhere in attracting converts.

The most important and successful of these orders, at least in sheer numbers, was the Cistercians. During the course of the century Cistercian monasteries were founded at Ardorel and Candeil in the diocese of Albi; at Belleperche, Bonnefont, Boulbonne, Calers, Eaunes, Escladieu, Feuillant, Grandselve, Nizors and St-Marcel in the diocese of Toulouse; Fontfroide in the diocese of Narbonne; Franquevaux in the diocese of Nîmes; Jau in the diocese of Elne; Valmagne in the diocese of Agde and Villelongue in the diocese of Carcassonne (Berman 1986). Also in the twelfth century, houses for Cistercian women were founded at St-Felix-de-Montseau and St-Marie-de-Bonlieu in the diocese of Maguelonne; Les Olieux in the diocese of Narbonne and St-Marie-de-Rieunette in the diocese of Carcassonne (Moreau 1988). Many of these houses started as Benedictine foundations, or in the case of some of the men's houses as groups of unattached hermits who subsequently petitioned to join the order.

In this way Grandselve was founded in 1114 by Gerald of Sales, a follower of Robert of Arbrissel, as a house for an eremitical group (Leyser 1983). Its connection with the lands of the dukes of Aquitaine, patrons of Robert, cannot have helped the house after Aquitainian rule was overthrown. In 1145 it sought to enter the Cistercian order, taking its tutelage from Clairvaux (Cottineau 1939). Silvanes, in the Rodez area, began as an independent group of hermits which joined the Cistercians (Leyser 1983: 35 & 40). Fontfroide had been founded as a Benedictine house in 1093, under the protection of the viscounts of Narbonne. In 1145 it asked for help from Grandselve, itself just going through reform, and joined the Cistercian movement (Cottineau 1939). It is surely no coincidence that Saint Bernard was preaching against heresy in the region just at this time.

Several of the tiny communities of women in the Languedoc seem to have begun as informal groups of men and women, devoting themselves to the religious life without a formal foundation and often in mixed communities. This seems to have been the case for St-Leon-de-Montmel and at Vignogoul, and it has been suggested that this was true also for La Rieunette and perhaps other houses (Moreau 1988: 70–1). The formal foundation of these monasteries seems to have been the work of the local bishops, probably anxious to avoid a cause for scandal. Such establishments demonstrate the strength of local religious feelings and show that, even in the later twelfth century, orthodox popular sentiment could often step outside the bounds of what the Church regarded as proper.

It is quite clear that the Cistercians enjoyed considerable success in the Languedoc. As elsewhere they attracted extensive gifts of land from laymen and most of the property they were given was on settled lands, providing rents. Constance Berman makes the point that out of thousands of gifts recorded in chartularies for these houses, less than twenty refer to uncultivated and waste lands (Berman 1986). This means that the gifts were not easy to make. The donors gave up actual revenues in order to make them, not abstract rights over virgin and uninhabited lands. The impact of the Cistercians was therefore sufficient to cause landowners to alienate real income. With the aid of these gifts the monks built up formidable territories, transforming the landscape and agricultural practice of the region in which their granges stood. The quantity of land they came to possess could be very large. By the end of the century Grandmont, the house which stood to the north-west of Toulouse, owned at least 16,000 hectares of land of differing types, scattered among eighteen estate centres organised as granges (Mousnier 1983).

The transactions by which these estates were built, some gifts, others purchases, were very numerous. This was not a case of monasteries benefiting from a few huge gifts by well disposed grandees. Between 1130 and 1169 the abbey of Silvanes benefited from no less than 203 grants. The best years were between 1146 and 1165 when 138 of the grants were made. Thereafter grants declined very sharply and virtually ceased after 1170. Grants came from many members of the landed classes. Multiplied by the number of houses in the region it is clear that the Cistercians attracted numerous gifts from a wide cross-section of the landed population. Their spiritual prestige was high in the Languedoc, at least in the early and middle years of the century (Verlaguet 1910).

Other reformed orders also settled in the Languedoc. The Premonstratensians at first had no houses closer than Gascony. The first settlement, at Casedieu, was founded in 1135 by Count Pierre of Bigorre and the Archbishop of Auch in order to combat Peter de Bruis's preaching. This house was the mother for a series of foundations along both sides of the Pyrenees (Bond 1993: 169). The monastery of Fontcaude in the diocese of Béziers, starting as an Augustinian canonry in 1154, became a Premonstratensian foundation in 1164. That it was not followed by other houses suggests that the order was too late in the Languedoc. It is likely that other orders, particularly the Cistercians, had received the major grants and that the perception among the laity was that they could no longer afford to make such gifts.

These orders all catered for men and women who were attracted to an austere spiritual life. As we have seen, many of the initial foundations were the result of individual initiative and enthusiasm, usually with local support. The increasing systematisation of Church structure, and the anxiety of Church authorities to control and channel all expressions of religious fervour, swept up these disparate beginnings into larger organisations. The result was that the informal route into the ideal life was no longer easily available. Even *conversi* needed to bring property with them when they entered a monastery, so that the decision, taken by a peasant farmer, often entailed the destruction of the family.

The Templars and the Knights Hospitaller had about forty different houses in the Toulousain alone (Mundy 1981). The chivalric new orders, which for the first time allowed the knight to combine his aristocratic military training with religious service and thus the salvation of the soul, were popular in the Languedoc from the beginning. At Douzens, near Carcassonne, the Templars had a commandery and the first grant seems to have been made as early as 1128. Much property was accumulated between 1133 and 1181. Houses, mills, lands, vineyards, orchards, pastures as well as the service of peasants were granted all over the north-western Corbières by local laymen. It was from among these people that recruits for the order were drawn, some to become knights, others seeking to be associated with the order to receive its spiritual benefits (Gerard and Magnou 1965). By the mid-twelfth century the order had preceptories at Montsaunès, La Selve, Rodez, Pézenas, St-Gilles as well as Douzens. These houses were part of a swathe of property which ran from Richerenches in Provence to Ambel, south of Zaragoza (Barber 1994: 20–3).

The Hospitallers were also very influential in the region. The Preceptory of the Hospitallers at St-Gilles had certainly been founded by 1112. In February of the following year a Bull of Pope Pascal II confirmed Gerard as the Prior of the Hospital in Jerusalem and listed seven other houses, of which the first was the establishment in St-Gilles. It was probably the first foundation outside Jerusalem itself. Count Bertrand of St-Gilles was almost certainly the patron who encouraged its establishment. As the first foundation the house at St-Gilles went on to become the administrative centre in the Languedoc for the Order and came to control fifty preceptories in Languedoc, Gascony and Provence. The Hospitallers also had a large establishment in Toulouse, founded in 1120 with the aid of Amelius, the Bishop of Toulouse (HGL 3: 601–4).

## Church and laity

It is difficult to know much of how ordinary people in town and countryside viewed either the Church as an institution, or religious belief as an expression of their own place in the world, except when they expressed a negative position and embraced Catharism. Even then it is not easy to be sure that many ordinary people regarded the differences between the Church and the heretics as either clear cut or significant, especially when viewed doctrinally. It is likely that it was the outward expression of belief, particularly as expressed in preaching and ritual activities, and in monastic observance, which most affected laypeople and that acceptance of doctrine followed the emotional approval of the lives of the *perfecti*.

There is plenty of evidence that, at least in the big towns, practical expression of the Gospel in such activities as the provision of charity to the sick and the poor affected ordinary laymen and women and that the teaching of the Church had a practical outcome. At Toulouse in the twelfth century there is clear evidence of the practice of charitable giving which was organised through Church institutions but largely paid for by laypeople. Traditionally the indigent were cared for by charity dispensed at cathedral and monastery doors. From the middle of the twelfth century this system was increasingly supplemented by a network of hospitals and hospices, offering care for the sick on a specialised and increasingly professional basis. Thus, in Toulouse, the hospital of St-Raimon in the Bourg was founded between 1075 and 1078 as a dependency of St-Sernin. Before 1114 the old hospital of St-Rézémy was given to the Hospitallers, who reorganised it. Between 1119 and 1130 the hospital of the Blessed Virgin of the Daurade was founded. In 1147 Bernardo and Petrona de Naso gave their property to Grandselve and committed themselves to the monastery's service also. They seem to have founded a hospital at their home which they ran and which after their deaths was organised and administered by the monastery. In all, by 1200 the city had at least eleven such institutions, all run by religious organisations (Mundy 1966).

Narbonne had five hospitals founded during the century and in 1177 a committee of laypeople was set up to administer relief measures for the poor (Mollat 1986: 100). When Peter Valdes started his movement of preachers his first act was to give away his considerable wealth to the poor of Lyon. By doing so he expiated the sin he felt he had accumulated from a lifetime of merchant activity. The desire to perform a good work for the salvation of the soul was what drove the citizens of Toulouse also in their giving. At the same time the gift placed the giver in a powerful position in a community which valued charitable giving. In some ways their foundations or gifts to hospitals imitated the gifts given by great nobles to monasteries.

Popular religious sentiment could be expressed by giving to found charitable institutions but the most common activity for the laity, and

one which they shared with the clergy, was the enthusiasm for pilgrimages. The deeply felt acceptance of the Crusade as an expression of religious belief, which engulfed the aristocracy of the south, was only one
part of a much greater outpouring. The rebuilt pilgrimage churches of
the Santiago de Compostela route, with their local saints, St-Gilles, St-
Tiberius, St-Modestus, St-Florence and St-Saturninus, provided a focus
for popular sentiment.

Most ordinary folk were hardly affected by the preoccupations of
the nobility, tithes and the like, but it is likely that they still shared some
concerns with the great. The area of everyday life where the Church
intruded and which most affected peasants and artisans had to do with
marriage and with sexual relationships. By the mid-twelfth century the
Church had gained effective control of the institution of marriage. Central to this control, which gave the Church increasing power over the
actual behaviour of individuals and deeply influenced the course of their
lives, was the extension and enforcement of the prohibited degrees. In
1059 Pope Nicholas II had defined the prohibition on marriage as running as far as the seventh degree. In 1063 Peter Damien, in his *De par-
entelae gradibus*, set out the Germanic system of calculation and this was
accepted by Alexander II in 1076. By this system marriage was forbidden as far as sixth cousins. The same system also applied to marriage
within spiritual relations as created by the godparent relationship
(Goody 1983: 134–6).

The degrees were so wide that strict enforcement would have made
it impossible to find a partner within a village community, or indeed
within a small town, and it actually had to be relaxed, to the fourth
degree, at the Fourth Lateran Council. Much later, in the eighteenth century, there is evidence from rural France that marriage to first cousins
was very common and that the Church granted regular dispensations.
This enabled property to remain within the peasant family (Goody
1983: 187). It seems entirely likely that this same problem affected the
peasants of the Languedoc in the twelfth century, where they held or
owned property. There are no registers of formal dispensations, but at
the very least there must have been tensions between laypeople and
clergy. Writing about Cathar practice in the thirteenth century, Nelli suggests that in the light of their beliefs the *perfecti* regarded marriage and
concubinage as very similar and of relatively little importance, but by the
mid-century they were urging the credentes to marry within the community of believers and actually conducting marriage services (Nelli
1969: 58–9).

The Cathars seem to have ignored the Church's new rules on the
prohibited degrees and preserved an older and more traditionally based

view of marriage. The evidence of Beatrice de Plannisoles is unequivo-
cal. She quoted her former lover, the priest of Montaillou, Peter de Cler-
gues, speaking towards the end of the thirteenth century:

> Look, there are four of us brothers – I'm a priest and I don't want to marry.
> If William and Bernard my brothers had married our sisters Esclarmonde
> and Wilhelma our family wouldn't have been ruined, because the property
> which my sisters had as dowry would have remained inside the family.
> With the woman brought into the house by our brother Bernard we would
> have had enough women and the family would be richer than it is now. So
> it would be better that brother should marry sister than take a wife from
> outside and also that sister should marry brother rather than that, when she
> is sent out from the family home with a great deal of wealth and given in
> marriage to a man from outside, the paternal family should thereby be
> destroyed. (Duvernoy 1965: vol. 1, 225–6)

The twelfth century was also a time when the Church first began to
elaborate the Canon Law on sexual matters. Concern about sexual behaviour, both inside and outside marriage, was increasing among theologians, and although the practice of regular confession for the laity had
not yet been instituted, canon lawyers clearly knew enough about sexual practices to comment upon them (Brundage 1993: 361–85).
Although the canon lawyers liberalised their attitudes towards sex inside
marriage during the period it is clear that the Church was increasingly
anxious to regulate sexual activity, simply because it had taken a more
positive attitude towards marriage by sacramentalising it (Brundage
1993b: 1–16). If sexual relations inside marriage were to be accepted,
even grudgingly, then sexual relations outside marriage would need to
be condemned with more vigour as wicked. But it is clear that practice
in sexual matters was almost impossible to control in the twelfth century, if the evidence of the later thirteenth and early fourteenth centuries
is any guide. Beatrice de Plannisoles and her lover practised a form of
contraception, another sin to compound the others they were commit-
ting, which was under the man's control. He refused to allow Beatrice
access to it lest, freed from the fear of pregnancy, she find another lover
(Duvernoy 1965: vol. 1, 244). If such attitudes were at all widespread
in the late thirteenth century, it seems probable that they presented a
near insuperable problem for conscientious priests in the twelfth, dealing with their parishioners.

The sin which became the over-riding preoccupation of the moral-
ists and preachers of the twelfth century was *cupiditas*, avarice. Usury was
seen as the form of the sin which was the most depraved and which presented the greatest danger to the soul. During the century the old injunc-
tions against usury were sharpened and defined as the need for credit

spread through the merchant world and into the countryside. The Second Lateran Council of 1139 condemned usury as ignominious and the Third in 1179 condemned the 'open usurer', that is the common moneylender, to excommunication and exclusion from Christian burial (Le Goff 1979: 28). The lending of money for commercial purposes, including mortgages, in several different forms came to be recognised as a necessity and allowed as an exception to the general rule (Gilchrist 1969: 62–5).

We have already seen that banking was an everyday activity and that in the second half of the century loans as well as mortgages were a normal feature of commercial life, recorded in the commercial records of the city. Many major towns developed a class of bankers. The merchants of Cahors were so famous that the term 'Cahorsini' was used to mean 'moneylenders'. While banking for merchants became respectable, lending to the poor never was. An annual rate of about 43 per cent seems to have been common (Gilchrist 1969: 64). Whatever distinctions were commonly made the result was a tension between the economic activity of some laymen, often powerful and successful, and the clergy as guardians and shapers of the official conscience of society. One productive outcome was the foundation of hospitals and hospices by conscience stricken merchants in the towns. On the other hand, tensions between different interest groups, lenders and borrowers could easily be exacerbated. In this atmosphere there were a growing number of successful merchants in the many towns whose relations with the clergy were potentially bad (figure 18).

## The Church and the nobility

Although so many members of the minor aristocracy were sympathisers with the Cathars by the end of the century, and some had become believers, this did not mean that as a group they were uniformly hostile to the Catholic Church or that Cathar sympathisers broke off relationships with orthodox believers. Even late in the century important noblemen could still have relationships with monastic communities. Aimery de Montréal, whose mother Blanche was the leader of a house of *perfectae*, nevertheless gave land to the monastery of Boulbonne in 1200 and Roger Trencavel gave property in Carcassonne to the same monastery in 1203 (Duvernoy 1994).

[At the highest level the rulers of the Languedoc often had very bad relations with individual monasteries or prelates, but they never rejected the Church as an institution.] Alfons-Jordan was excommunicated as a result of violence towards the monks of St-Gilles in a dispute over property (Gordon 1992). Raimon V had a long dispute with the Bishop of

Vaison. In 1160 he had seized the episcopal palace and demesne, seeking recognition that the bishop held his temporalities from the count. The next bishop, Bertrand, once elected in 1178, regained the episcopal property by force of arms and held it until his death. His successor in 1185 was asked to do homage for the property and refused. He was driven out by Raimon V and, withdrawing to his castle of Entrechaut, excommunicated Raimon. This quarrel rumbled on throughout the time of Raimon VI and was not settled until 1211 (HGL 6: 147).

Raimon VI was regarded as worse than his father in his quarrels with the Church. Certainly, he was supposed to have burnt a church in the diocese of Carpentras with sixty worshippers inside it and he had lasting quarrels with the abbots of Moissac and Montauban (Dossat 1944). In 1195 the Pope wrote to the archbishops of Narbonne, Arles, Aix and Bourges ordering them to excommunicate Raimon VI because of his treatment of the Abbey of St-Gilles. On their lands he had constructed the castle of Mirapetra and, far from pulling it down, had continued to strengthen it despite promises to the contrary (HGL 6: 171–87).

Pierre des Vaux-de-Cernay told even worse stories about Raimon-Roger, Count of Foix, talking of his 'cruel malignity and malign cruelty'. He was accused of supporting his wife and two sisters out of the revenues of the town of Pamiers, the property of the canons there; of building a house – a house of *perfectae* – on the abbey's lands and of being a party to the wounding of a canon in a church and the blinding of others. Finally he locked the canons in their church for three days and sacked their property before having them turned out of the town. (Guébin et Maisonneuve 1951: 82–3). Roger Trencavel was accused of imprisoning the Bishop of Albi in 1178 and of extorting 30,000 sous from the monastery of St-Pons-de-Thomières in 1179 (Dossat 1965).

Financial relationships between laypeople and the Church changed during the century. At the beginning, many well to do laypeople were giving tithes which they owned to the Church. Many rights to tithes went with churches and came into the hands of monasteries as churches were granted. We have already seen how large the monastic holdings of churches could be. But this movement soon stopped and tithes began to find their way into the hands of the laity again. At Lezat the monastery began to farm many of its churches and the farmers were often laypeople, so that there was always a possibility that the arrangement would become semi-permanent. However, the newer orders were able to become very successful financially. Fontfroide built substantial reserves of cash by the end of the century from profits from its wool trade (Grezes-Rueff 1977), as did other Cistercian houses, and their wealth was widely noted and widely resented.

Concepts of religious poverty, as understood by the laity, and the wealth of the new orders contrasted sharply. When the Cathar *perfecti* preached, they pointed to the wealth of the monasteries and contrasted it with the call of the Gospel and their own adherence to that ideal. There can have been few more telling or effective propaganda points. Raimon VI was deeply suspicious or perhaps jealous of the Cistercians, not only because he saw their campaigning against the Cathars as dangerous to himself, but also because of their wealth. He was reported to have told Fulk of Marseille that the Cistercians could not be saved because they kept sheep which led them into lives of luxury (Guébin et Maisonneuve 1951: 17). Raimon VI's view was one which was quite widely shared at the end of the century.

If the violent behaviour of men like Raimon VI contrasted strangely with the pious donation of property by members of the same group, we need to consider three factors. The first is that such violent action most commonly came from the most powerful rulers, who formed only a small proportion of the class, although their actions were all the more shocking because of their high status. Similar action by men of humbler origin, as at Capestang, was rare. Secondly, the older communities of canons and Benedictines were most likely to be the object of attack. At Moissac, the town – which was at loggerheads with the monastery – received support from Raimon VI. Such political quarrels were always likely where a church or monastery was also a powerful landlord and even more likely to occur where an ecclesiastic exercised real power, as was the case with several of the bishops in Septimania. The various Benedictines had always assumed that they would be a part of the aristocratic landowning community, and in some cases the monasteries had become powerful secular rulers, carried along like their lay neighbours by the tide of population growth and rising wealth.

When churchmen behaved like laymen they were easily drawn into quarrels which resulted in private war. Similar problems occurred in many other parts of Europe, often leading to violent action against Church property. Elsewhere, increasingly powerful rulers allied themselves with the Church to control such attacks, or, where the interests of ruler and Church diverged, set out to find an accommodation which would avoid the use of powers of excommunication in non-religious quarrels. In the Languedoc the slow development of authority made such an accommodation difficult. Lastly, the quarrels and violence became worse towards the end of the century. Partly this was because both monasteries and nobility were in increasing financial difficulties, partly that the continuing denunciation of heretics – and of rulers for not suppressing them – made relationships worse as the two sides, clerics and lay rulers became increasingly suspicious of one another.

There is evidence to show that members of the nobility patronised both the Church and the Cathars. Thus the Abbot of Lezat in 1188, Raimon-Gautier, was a close friend of Raimon de Justiniac who died at the monastery but had been received into the house of heretics at Durfort; while several other families with strong heretical links, the Durforts, the Roudeilles and the Tersacs, also retained links with the abbey (Ourliac and Magnou 1984). Many noblemen and women were anxious to support upright behaviour, wherever they found it. Since heresy was still an ill defined concept for the laity in the twelfth century, the Cathars were not easily seen as unorthodox. After all, many of the ill-organised eremitical groups must have seemed unorthodox compared with the staid Benedictines. Just like the Cathars they often offered preaching to the laity and attracted many followers to their austere way of life. These groups attracted donations of land and money, long before they had the support and approval of ecclesiastical authorities. The Cathars must often have seemed much the same. This was not so much a belief in 'tolerance', as a desire to support the righteous as defined by the views espoused by the Gregorian reformers (Gordon 1992).

At the highest levels relations between the nobility and the Church presented a patchwork of attitudes. Serious men and women had supported the expansion of monasticism, but by the end of the century that support was faltering. Many people supported both Cathars and clergy, seeking exemplars for the holy life. Where physical quarrels arose they were often caused by a clash of economic interests in a world where opportunities for expanded exploitation were becoming smaller. Resentment about Church wealth grew and relations between rulers and Church became increasingly strained as the Church applied pressure over heresy.

The twelfth century was a time of religious turmoil in which the laity were trying to find their place in the great renewal of religious life. They were exhorted to live more Christian lives and offered new ideals, although these were often presented as if they were a return to old ways. Some of the consequences of the changes were extremely uncomfortable for clergy and laity alike and in those circumstances Catharism could be seen as a way of reaffirming traditional stability. Because it regarded the world as evil, and society as a transient and unimportant ordering of things, which was in its origin evil, most of the social regulation which the Church was attempting could be seen as worthless. Catharism did not object to the taking of interest, was not in favour of the new way of looking at marriage, regarded the prohibited degrees as unimportant,

did not struggle with concepts of sin or crime in sexuality and regarded
the whole physical organisation of the Church as hopelessly corrupt. It
did not seek to build churches or accumulate estates. It disapproved of
tithes. In its individualistic appeal Catharism was revolutionary. To
regard the world as intrinsically valueless, a vale of tears and a place of
tribulation, called into question the whole structure of society. It seems
unlikely that many of the believers who listened to the sermons of the
*perfecti* realised the implications of the new doctrines. Instead, much of
Catharism must have seemed conservative and comforting, endorsing
the familiar world and resisting change and interference and regulation
from outside. For people threatened by change it offered safety.

It would be wrong to imagine that the clergy of the Languedoc set
out, almost like sleepwalkers, to antagonise the laity. Most of the imper-
fections of organisation, the frictions over landowning, tithes and role
of monastic communities in local society, were common to many other
parts of western Europe. Problems about marriage and sex or about
money were to be found everywhere, and lawless and violent acts against
churchmen were common. The difference in the Languedoc lay in the
relationships between rulers and bishops and in the contrast between the
rapid expansion of the economy at all levels and the failure of the lay
rulers to establish effective methods of governing the region. There was
no alliance of interest between the Church and the nascent states; and in
such conditions the fear of churchmen, that heresy was spreading like a
plague against which they were powerless, seemed self-evidently true.

# 5

## The response to heresy

### Early policy

It is impossible to know to what extent the policies of the papacy towards the Cathars were coherent. At first it seems unlikely that any of the popes formulated a consistent policy, other than the general objective that the heretics must, somehow, be repressed. Successive popes likened the heresy to a pestilence or a plague. Canon IV of the Council of Tours in 1163 described the heresy as like a cancer (Mansi 21: cols 1177–8) and Lucius III in the decretal of 1184 called it a pestilence (Mansi 22: cols 476–8). Innocent III used similar language when he wrote to the Archbishop of Auch that the heresy *velut cancer irrepit* (PL 214: col. 71). In a century when men were becoming preoccupied with sickness and when concerted measures against leprosy isolated sufferers and assumed that their illness was an outward sign of sin, the use of such terms allowed the hierarchy to think of heroic or even violent measures. Almost anything would be permissible if this epidemic of 'disease' was to be stemmed.

As the twelfth century wore on a number of strands of policy became apparent. There could of course be no compromise with the heretics. However, they could be called to repentance and reconverted to the fold. To this end the Pope and other members of the Curia were prepared for their agents to meet heretics and attempt to convert them. This was mostly seen as an exercise in debate at which the heretics would naturally be shown to be in error, either because they were too ignorant to understand the Scriptures or theological methods or because they were too blinded by their error to wish to understand. As a result there could be only one outcome to a debate, however or wherever it was staged. This stratagem was aimed at the leaders of the sect. However, not everyone could be accommodated by a debate. The numbers of heretics, especially in some of the towns, was too great for that. Here the church

sought to regain control of the masses by preaching, confident as conservative institutions almost always are, that the 'simple' can be controlled once they hear the true voice of authority.

Direct action to persuade was important, but the Church was under
no illusions about the value of coercion. It was always effective.
Throughout the twelfth century it was clear that the Church could only
coerce with the aid of secular authorities. Writing to his legate Raoul in
1206, the Pope could say *dificiente materiale gladio, spiritualis contemptu habeatur*
(with the physical sword lacking, the spiritual [sword] is held in con-
tempt) (PL 215: letter 175). For that reason the hierarchy was prepared
to expend much effort on trying to persuade the rulers of the Languedoc to co-operate in the programme of persecution. The failure of the
nobility, and particularly the ruling nobility, to respond caused deep dis-
may in clerical circles, reflected in displays of anger and in escalating
demands for violent action. In the end it was this reluctance on the part
of the secular rulers to aid the religious that led to the calling of the Crusade.

Allied to the policy of persuading the princes and magnates to act
was the use of the concept of the 'Peace'. This movement had been a
powerful influence in the tenth and the eleventh centuries. In essence an
alliance between the Church and the peasantry, aided by the princes, it
sought to control the lesser aristocracy and their soldiery. The greatest
beneficiaries of the movement were probably the churches, especially
the monasteries, as the scheme helped to protect their lands. The Peace
was revived in 1139 with a proclamation at Auch. During the second
half of the twelfth century the bishops of the region took the lead in
declaring the Peace and persuading the local magnates to join in sharing
with them. Similar 'Institutes of the Peace' were instituted at Elne in
1156, at Toulouse *c.* 1163, in the diocese of Commignes in 1170, at
Rodez 1169–70, at Béziers in 1170 and at Albi in 1171. Clement III in
1190 confirmed the Peace in the Narbonne archdiocese. The Peace consisted of mutual assurances, through oaths administered and guaranteed
by the Church, that each person would keep the Peace and would aid in
the repression of those who broke it by acts of violence of any kind. It
thus expressed a strong desire in society at large to see a secure world
and placed enormous social pressure upon everyone who subscribed to
conform and left those who would not join in an extremely exposed
position. The Peace explicitly linked fighting to subdue peace-breakers
with fighting on behalf of the Church and offered indulgences to those
who undertook the work (HGL I: Instrumenta, 162). By inference those
who would not join in the work, or worse, were breakers of the Peace,
were clearly the enemies of God.

The agency which was supposed to oversee the enforcement of the Peace in the Languedoc was the Order of the Temple and to that end they were able to collect a small tax on each ox used by the peasantry. There is little evidence that the Templars ever did anything effective to enforce the Peace. In some parts of the Languedoc peasants contributed through this payment to the support of a militia, used to attack peace-breakers (Bisson 1977). The Council of Montpellier, meeting in 1195, began its proceedings with a declaration of the Peace, reiterating the canons issued by Second and Third Lateran Councils:

> In primis, ut pax in tota Narbonensi provincia, sicut jurata fuerat antea de voluntate domini comitis Tolosan. Et postmodum in praesentia ejusdem legati, apud sanctum Aegidium, a vener-abilibus Uticensi et Nemausensi episcopis, et abbate sancti Aegidii pro se et omnibus terris jura-mento firmata, sine omni malo ingenio et cum bona fide servetur, nec aliquis eam violare presumat.

> (Firstly that the Peace throughout the whole Province of Narbonne, as it was previously sworn by the will of the Lord Count of Toulouse and sub-sequently in the presence of the same legate at St-Gilles was confirmed by oath to cover all their lands, to the venerable bishops of Uzés and Nîmes and the abbot of St-Gilles, should be preserved without any bad intention and with good faith. And neither should anyone dare to break it). (Mansi 22: col. 667)

Clearly the Church gained an enormous political advantage by its control of the Peace mechanism. It could always use the system as part of its own strategy for control of the region. For Church leaders the heretics could easily be seen as disturbers of the Peace. As a group, the *perfecti* were in any case quite outside the system, since they refused to take oaths and we can assume that their followers were also reluctant to take part in a process which ran so counter to their beliefs. The need to maintain the Peace provided part at least of the rationale behind the use of organised military force against heretical groups, such as those at Lavaur. Just as importantly, the Peace provided an important mechanism with which magnates who failed to provide the necessary support or who actively damaged the interests of the Church could be disciplined. Since it was mostly the magnates who maintained and employed the *routiers* – mercenary soldiers, often from the Spanish kingdoms, who were by definition outside the Peace – princes, who usually could not avoid subscribing to the Peace were most vulnerable to charges of break-ing it. Failure to control the Peace was politically very damaging.

The final area of activity was within the Church itself. Throughout the struggle with the Cathars the Church was immeasurably aided by the enormous progress made in the century by the academic study of theology. The subject was recognised as a discipline and the doctrines of the Church were defined and refined in such a way that the differences between the orthodox faithful and the heretics were clear to the hierarchy. Although it was possible for theologians to differ about doctrine, as Saint Bernard and Abelard did, nevertheless by the end of the century bishops and other officers had been provided with a coherent list of the sacraments and a clear doctrine about their natures (Morris 1989: 360–86). This made possible the debates which were such a common feature of attempts to convert the *perfecti* and made it easy for presiding officers to get their opponents to subscribe to professions of faith. As a result the Papacy could act by refining the rules which governed the way in which heretics and their supporters were defined and treated.

The other area of internal church activity consisted of a policy of reforming the hierarchy of the Church in the Languedoc to make it responsive to the demands placed upon it from outside. The great General Councils of the Church, particularly the third Lateran Council of 1179, provided the Pope with the opportunity to seek a consensus from the bishops and abbots and provided a way of spreading the reforms throughout the whole of western Christendom. During the twelfth century a view of the nature of the Pope's office developed, which gave to the Pope supreme authority over the hierarchy of the Church. He claimed to be acting as the representative of Jesus Christ himself rather than that of Saint Peter. As a result he could claim to exercise an unchallengable authority over other members of the hierarchy, allowing him to claim control over the appointment of bishops during the struggles with the emperor. Such powers were actually used very sparingly (Morris 1989: 225), but were of the greatest importance in the struggle of Innocent III to make the bishops of the Languedoc do what was necessary.

## Alexander III and Lucius III

In 1162 reverses suffered by Alexander III in his quarrels with the emperor led to his strategic withdrawal to the safety of the lands of the kings of France and of England (Baldwin 1968: 58–61). He landed from Italy at Maguelonne and moved from there to Montpellier, where he met Count Raimon V of Toulouse, as well as Guilhem of Montpellier. The next year, at the Council of Tours, the 'damnable heresy' which had appeared recently in the Toulouse region was condemned and its adherents anathematised (Mansi 21: cols 1177–8). Clearly the time spent in Gaul enabled the Pope to learn of the rise of Catharism in the Toulouse region, though there is nothing in the canon to suggest that the detail of Cathar doctrine was yet clear. Characterised as being 'like a cancer' it was described as spreading into Gascony. The faithful were forbidden to have anything to do with the heretics. Their goods were to be seized and sold by the local rulers and their heretical conventicles were to be sought out and dealt with.

It was only after this Council at Tours that the local bishops were stirred to call the Council at Lombers in 1165. It was held on the initiative of the Bishop of Albi, perhaps after pressure from the Archbishop of Bourges (HGL 6: 3). The bishops took the precaution of trying to spread support for their actions as widely as possible. Six bishops, including Pons d'Arsac, Archbishop of Narbonne, were present, together with eight abbots, the provosts of Toulouse and Albi and the archdeacons of Narbonne and Agde. Probably more important was the presence of Constance of Toulouse and the Trencavel Viscount of Albi and Béziers. The condemnation of the heretics, issued at Lombers, was repeated at another council held at Capestang in 1166. These councils were essentially attempts to persuade the secular rulers to put their weight behind the Church by showing them how dangerous and wrong the heresy was. They also sought to persuade the local hierarchy to act and by providing them with authoritative backing hoped to give them more credibility in their dioceses.

Little seems to have happened in the next few years to affect the Cathars. From the Council at St-Felix in 1167, until the letter of Raimon V in 1177, there was no effective check on their activities. Local bishops were unable to take any coercive measures. In 1172 Pons d'Arsac, the then archbishop of Narbonne, had written to the King of France complaining of the danger and urging him to take action, but nothing came of this plea. Raimon's letter, however had a deep impact outside the Languedoc. It seems likely that the appeal from so well connected a prince suggested to both Henry de Marsiac and the Pope that some effective secular support might be forthcoming. Apparently Henry II and Louis VII both responded. The result was an expedition to the Languedoc, which was both royal and ecclesiastical, led by four great princes of the Church, Henry de Marsiac, Abbot of Clairvaux and thus leader of the Cistercian Order, the cardinal, Peter of Pavia, the Pope's legate, Reginald, bishop of Bath, and John, the bishop of Poitiers.

The commission was able to use force as well as to preach and the visit was a major undertaking with the commissioners working in Toulouse for three months (HGL 6: 77–86 and 7: 11–14). With Raimon of Toulouse, the viscount of Turenne and Raimon of Châteauneuf to support them, the churchmen were able to overawe the city population. For Raimon V his support for the Commission may have been a weapon in his struggle with the consuls for control of the city and the attacks upon

the heretics were part of the political struggle which was taking place in
the town (Mundy 1954: 60). The bishop of Toulouse and the senior
clergy together with the consuls were made to take an oath to denounce
the heretics and their supporters. In this way the commissioners were
able to arrest Pierre Maurand, the most prominent heretic in the city, and
to force him to renounce his beliefs publicly. Many lesser folk were then
frightened into retraction. (Stubbs 1867–8: 152).

Peter of Pavia also publicly examined two heretics, Raimon Baimiac
and Bernard Raimon. These two did not live in Toulouse, but in Albi.
They had been expelled from Toulouse by the count and only returned
there under safe conduct (HGL 6: 82). Bernard Raimon was the Cathar
bishop of Toulouse, consecrated at the Council of St-Felix, and Raimon
de Baimiac was his *filius maior*. Although they denied heretical beliefs,
they refused to take the oath. Peter betrayed his attitude when he
described the two as fools, who did not understand scripture. He made
it plain that the two had to be examined on matters of doctrine in the
vernacular since they 'could scarcely put two words of Latin together'. It
was, he said, absurd to discuss such matters as the sacraments of the
Church in such a way (Stubbs 1867–8: 157).

The Third Lateran Council met in March 1179. Although the council was called to deal with issues raised by the ending of the schism, it
also dealt with many of the matters which concerned the Church in the
Languedoc. Most of the canons were concerned with the regulation of
the clergy, including the election of the Pope himself. Canon IV attacked
the luxurious life-style of the bishops and senior clergy; canons VII, VIII
and XV tried to stop commercial trafficking in clerical offices and canon
XVIII required the appointment of a master to teach clerks and poor
scholars at each cathedral. Canon XXVII repeated the provisions of the
Council of Tours against the heretics in the Languedoc and linked them
with the *routiers*, the mercenary soldiers of the region, thus associating
them with the breach of the Peace,

> since in Gascony, in the area of Albi, the territory of Toulouse, and in other
> places, the damned perversity of the heretics, whom some call Cathars, oth-
> ers Paterenes, others again Publicans, and others by other names, has grown
> so strong that, no longer in secret as some do, they attract the simple and
> the weak; we resolve that they, their defenders and supporters are subject to
> anathema, and we forbid under anathema anyone to presume to keep them
> in his residence, or on his land, or to aid or transact business with them. ...
> concerning the Brabantians, Aragonese, Navarese, Basques, Coterelles and
> Triaverdans who practise such enormity upon Christians that they would
> defer neither to churches nor to monasteries, nor to widows or children ...
> similarly we decree that those who would have employed them or shall
> have kept them in the regions in which they rave so madly, shall be publicly

denounced on Sundays and on other days throughout the churches and shall be subject to exactly the same punishments as the aforesaid heretics. (Mansi 22: cols 230–2)

The canon then went on to release subjects of supporters of heretics from obligations of fealty and homage and more radically, offered two years' indulgence for those who took up arms against the heretics. Connected with the condemnation of the *routiers* went a reaffirmation of the Church's regard for the Truce of God. Canon XXI laid down the times of the Truce, both for daily use and for the long truces of Christmas and Easter (Mansi 22: col. 229).

After the council, Archbishop Pons of Narbonne sent letters to all his bishops and abbots ordering them to excommunicate heretics and their supporters (HGL 6: 86). The practical result of the council was the first attempt at a crusade in the Languedoc. In 1181, Henry de Marsiac, now cardinal–bishop of Albano, arrived in the Midi and in June led a small army of local knights against the town of Lavaur, the seat of the Cathar bishop of Toulouse. The two heretics, Bernard Raimon and Raimon de Baimiac, who had been examined at Toulouse in 1172 and who had taken refuge in the town were captured after the Viscountess Adela surrendered the town. They were taken off to Le Puy, well outside their home territory and too far away for a rescue. Here they both abjured their beliefs (Roquebert 1970: vol. 1, 91). They were then offered positions inside the Church. Bernard Raimon became a canon of the Cathedral of St-Etienne in Toulouse and his companion a canon of St-Sernin. Guilhem de Puylaurens, one of the chroniclers of the Crusade, commented that he had been told about these two canons and their origins when he was a boy (Duvernoy 1976: 29).

This was an extraordinary move and one which was to be repeated many years later. By admitting the two men to positions of such prestige within the local community the Church marked their social positions in the Languedoc and also served notice that these men had been serious heretics, leaders of a community, and not the 'simple' men heretics were supposed to be. In view of their assimilation into the local hierarchy of the Church we may question whether these two were as ignorant of Latin as the cardinal's letter suggested. Strong evidence has been adduced recently to suggest that the Cathars of the Languedoc were a literate community whose normal ritual language was Latin and whose theological and administrative writings were normally in Latin also (Biller 1994: 69). The Cathar bishop of Toulouse might be expected to be a man of some learning and worth capturing for the Church.

The initiative of Cardinal Henry went further. Unable to destroy the heretics himself, he could at least do something about the Catholic Church and he deposed Pons of Narbonne. But nothing systematic was done to pursue the heretics. Perhaps that was not surprising. In the same year Stephen of Tournai wrote to John of Poitiers, recently elected as archbishop of Lyon, congratulating him that his election to Narbonne had been abrogated by his election to Lyon. He was thus

> exempt from the barbarousness of the Goths, the fickleness of the Gascons, the savage habits of the people of Septimania, where reigns unfaithfulness, deceit and distress. I have seen in the last place, passing through the country when the king sent me to Toulouse, an image of death, the more terrible for being always before my eyes. I have seen churches burnt and practically destroyed and the habitation of men serving as shelter for animals. (HGL 6: 96–7)

Henry of Albano continued with councils in Le Puy, Bazas in Gascony and Bourges and Bordeaux. Such councils served to spread word of the growing opposition of the hierarchy to the heretics, even though it did nothing to hinder their progress in the Languedoc.

Alexander III had died in 1181 and in 1184 Pope Lucius III, in the course of seeking an agreement with Frederick Barbarossa, issued a new Decretal at Verona (Mansi 22: cols 476–8). This Bull, *Ad abolendam*, condemned all the known heretical and dissident groups, including the Waldensians and the Cathars. The Cathars of the Languedoc were simply one of many groups attacked in the measure. At Verona the Pope was in the part of the Italian peninsula most deeply affected by Catharism, which had become widespread, affecting even the papal lands (Thouzellier 1969: 45). As in previous canons, those who harboured or supported the heretics were to share in their condemnation. For the first time the decretal laid down the procedures the bishop should use to counter heresy in his diocese. He should visit the parishes of his diocese on a regular basis (in practice deputing this task to his archdeacons) and get persons in each community of known integrity to state on oath their knowledge of the activities of heretics, particularly secret meetings. They were also to indicate those whose lifestyle did not fit in with their neighbours. Refusal to take the oath was itself regarded as evidence which would lead to condemnation. People exposed in this way were to be brought before the bishop's court and those condemned would then be handed over to the secular authority for punishment. Members of the clergy found guilty of heresy were to lose their status, and once stripped of their privileges were also to be handed over to the secular authorities for punishment.

The procedure of the hearings laid down in the decretal made it clear that those accused had to prove their innocence, presumably by taking an oath. The Church always gave the heretic a chance to repent and be readmitted to the body of the faithful but those who repented and then relapsed were to be handed over for punishment without delay and their property seized for the use of the Church. In this way the hierarchy was feeling its way towards a codification of the investigative process which all bishops could undertake in their task of safeguarding the orthodoxy of their flocks. Eventually this codification provided the basis for the Inquisition. The decretal demonstrated the growing view inside the Church hierarchy, that the secular world was obliged to help in the control of the religious beliefs of its members. The decretal demanded that 'counts, barons, rectors, consuls of cities', on the summons of the local archbishop or bishop should promise to carry out the orders of the Church. They were threatened with loss of office, excommunication and – for their towns and lands – interdiction, for failure to co-operate.

None of this had much immediate impact in the Languedoc. Between 1181 and 1191 Archbishop Bernard Gaucelin of Narbonne called a council of clergy and laity which condemned the heretics without being able to carry through any of the measures laid down by the Verona decretal (HGL 6: 218–19). In December 1195 the papal legate Michael summoned another council to meet at Montpellier (HGL 6: 171). Once more the local bishops of the province of Narbonne were enjoined to enforce the terms of the canons of the Third Lateran Council. Canon XX ordered archbishops and bishops to consult on how they should publish an interdiction on the heretics in their area, taking care not to enforce a long interdiction which would play into the heretics' hands, by removing all sources of spiritual comfort and withdrawing the orthodox clergy. What was more significant was that the new council first demanded that the Peace should be promulgated and enforced, and then excommunicated not only heretics but also the Aragonese *routiers*.

This council, presided over by a papal legate, carried enough prestige to cause the attendance of Raimon VI of Toulouse, who was already a signatory to a Peace made at St-Gilles. It continued a trend which was noticeable in the work of earlier assemblies in linking the disturbances and lawlessness of the Languedoc with heresy. The bands of mercenaries, often unpaid, seized what they pleased but were supported by rulers, including Raimon VI, who would not have had an effective army without them. *Routiers* and heresy became linked in the eyes of the Church. Both were a sign that the local princes were neglecting their duty to rule properly, that is in accordance with standards laid down by the Church. Effective control of the *routiers* would open the way to an assault on the Cathars because it would show that rulers were prepared to follow a policy of which the Church approved.

The response of the papacy to the situation in the Languedoc had been a part only of its general response to the problems posed by heretical movements. On every occasion the Church had set out to condemn heresy, at first seeking to engage in a dialogue with the leaders of the dissidents and then, as the nature of the beliefs became clearer and the Cathars' organisation became stronger, routinely condemning both the heretics and those perceived as their protectors. By appointing legates, the popes of the second half of the twelfth century were able to see through a personal source of information what was happening in the Languedoc and also to influence the great political powers, the kings of the French and the English, so that they too took an interest in ecclesiastical matters in the Languedoc. Probably both saw it as a way of registering their political interests. Where papal legates were involved in councils of the Church in the Languedoc some physical action did take place, as at Toulouse and then Lavaur; but what is most striking about the years between the visit of Bernard of Clairvaux and 1198 was the ineffective nature of the action. There is nothing to suggest that the conduct or spread of Catharism was seriously hampered.

## Innocent III

Lothar of Segni became pope as Innocent III in January 1198, at the age of 37 or 38. He was a product of the University of Paris, had passed his career in papal service and owed his first promotion to his uncle Pope Clement III (Sayers 1994). The new pope was known as both a theologian[1] and a canon lawyer and he brought to his office a very consistent view of its nature. He remarked of himself that 'we are the successor of the Prince of the Apostles, but we are not his vicar, nor the vicar of any man or apostle, but the Vicar of Jesus Christ himself' (PL 214: col. 292). He thus encapsulated the claim to universal authority which he had inherited from his predecessors of the twelfth century – an authority which extended not only to the whole Church but also to lay rulers as part of the Christian world. As the universal monarch he was to be the

---

[1] Innocent was well known in the Middle Ages as the author of *De miseria condicionis humanae*, a work which summed up the medieval convention about the nature of man's life. It is notable for its disgust with procreation and its pessimistic views about human nature, and the physical and mental trials of life. The work was immensely popular, striking a chord with a great many medieval scholars and writers. The disgust expressed would have seemed quite natural to the Cathars, even if founded on a different cosmology (Lewis 1978).

final judge on 'matters of sin' such as legitimisation, the validity of oaths and the observance of treaties (Sayers 1994: 44–5). His inaugural sermon had been based upon a text from Jeremiah, chapter 1, verse 10: 'See, I have this day set thee over the nations and over the kingdoms, to root out and to pull down, and to destroy and to throw down, to build and to plant'. Such a view might be inconvenient and embarrassing to a monarch such as Philippe-Auguste or Richard I, but to a lesser man such as Raimon VI it could be dangerous.

The new Pope also brought to his office a consuming passion for the idea of the Crusade. He was dedicated to the ideal of the return of the Holy Places of Palestine to Christian hands and he pursued that ideal from 1198 onwards. His desire to rid Christendom of division and heresy was sharpened by the perception that it would be impossible to launch a successful Crusade against the Saracens while heresy was spreading in Europe (Foreville 1969). For Innocent III at first, the Cathars of the Languedoc were only a part of the more general problem of dissident and heretical groups. He was by no means automatically prejudiced against novel activities and his reactions to the reformed Waldensians and later to the newly emerging Franciscans showed that he was far from rigid in his views about the nature of the religious life. But his tolerance extended to an accommodation with groups with unusual new ideas about the nature of the Christian life, not to radical expressions of unorthodox opinion. In 1200 he issued the decree *Vergentis in senium* which laid down that loss of property was to be a major penalty for heresy, just as it was for treason against a secular rule. Like his predecessor's decree *Ad abolendam*, this ruling owed more to relationships with the emperor than to a special or over-riding interest in the problems of the Midi, but it was a statement of intent which was to prove useful against the Cathars of the Toulousain.

However, in the first year of his papacy he had sent two legates on a general mission to preach against heresy throughout the whole of the Languedoc and into Barcelona. They were to excommunicate heretics and their supporters and to urge rulers to co-operate. Once more he laid down that those who armed themselves against the heretics would receive an indulgence, this time the equivalent of the pilgrimage to Rome or Santiago de Compostela. The goods of heretics were to be confiscated. Over the next few years the continuing problems of the region increasingly attracted his attention. As early as the first year of his papacy he had commanded the bishops of the region to support the efforts of his legates. In 1203 he appointed a new legate, Peyre of Castelnau. He was a native of the Languedoc, from Castelnau-le-Lez, near Montpellier, who was first a canon and then archdeacon of the cathedral of

Maguelonne (1182–1198). Probably in 1200, he entered the Cistercian abbey of Fontfroide and by 1203 he appeared as papal legate in Toulouse (Martin-Chabot 1973–89: vol. 1, 14). In the following year the Pope appointed another legate, Arnald-Amalric, the abbot of Clairvaux and the head of the Cistercian Order. He, too, was a native of the South, having been abbot of Poblet, in the diocese of Tarragona, from 1196 to 1198 and then abbot of Grandselve, near Toulouse, until his election as head of the Order in 1200 (HGL 8: cols 1849–51). He had first-hand knowledge of the conditions in the Toulousain.

Before Arnald-Amalric was appointed, Peyre of Castelnau, together with his fellow legate, Raoul, another monk of Fontfroide, had been active in the campaign against the heretics. Recognising the importance of Toulouse as a major centre of activity, they started work there in December 1203. They pressured the consuls of the town and the senior inhabitants to swear to uphold the Catholic Faith (HGL 6: 229). Using the expectations about the Peace which had become commonplace, they pressed Raimon VI to act against the Cathars and to get rid of the *routiers*. The request was hardly realistic. Without them Raimon would have been left without soldiers and he was neither temperamentally inclined to persecute the Cathars, nor able to do anything effective.

During the next few years Innocent began a campaign aimed at reform of the bishops in the archdiocese of Narbonne. In 1204 he branded the bishops as 'those dumb dogs which aren't strong enough to bark; those shepherds who only care about themselves, who can't chase away with their voices or their sticks the wolves which ravage the Lord's sheepfold. So when the priest sins he drags the people down in his fall, the sheep wander away and are lost' (PL 215: col. 355). Innocent granted his legates the powers to command the bishops of the region to act against the heretics and to suspend those bishops who would not co-operate, a decision which deeply antagonised the archbishop and his diocesans (HGL 6: 231). The old bishop of Carcassonne had already resigned in 1198 in favour of his nephew Berenger, whose zeal caused his expulsion from Carcassonne (Guébin et Maisonneuve 1951: 44–5). The bishop of Béziers was the first to suffer. In 1203 he had failed to co-operate with the legates, Peyre and Raoul, and they had suspended him. In 1204 the Pope confirmed their actions (Roquebert 1970: vol. 1, 150). This bishop seems to have been killed in 1205 'through the treason of his own people' (HGL 6: 236).

The case of the bishop of Toulouse was much more notorious. As we have seen above, Raimon Rabastens, who became bishop in 1201, had wasted what was left of the bishop's revenues in a private war. An enquiry revealed that he had purchased his office by bribing the canons and that he had stifled the inquiry of the bishop of Limoges about these activities in the same way. He was deposed by the legates and, after a long interregnum, replaced by Fulk of Marseille who finally took up the office in 1206 (HGL 6: 226–8, 243). Although Raimon VI remained on friendly terms with Raimon de Rabastens, he certainly recognised Fulk as the bishop. This man had been well known as a merchant prince in Marseille and as a troubadour. In 1195 he had abandoned the world and, together with his wife and children, entered the Cistercian Order, he to the abbey of Thoronet, of which he became the abbot. Fulk was to show himself to be unswervingly loyal to the papacy and an implacable enemy of the Cathars, but for the moment he was dogged by poverty.

The archbishop of Narbonne was a much harder man to move. Innocent was well aware of the man's connections and of his outrageous behaviour. In 1203 he demanded that Raimon-Berenger should give up either the archiepiscopal see or the abbey of Mont-Aragon, and in the following year ordered legates to depose him. Raimon-Berenger was the uncle of a king and not so easily overawed by the legates or the Pope. He violently disputed the authority of the legates and went himself to see the Pope. The stratagem worked and he was allowed to retain the office. In 1204 the legates accused the archbishop of a number of serious abuses. Firstly, he had been grossly negligent in conducting the business of his diocese and province. He had harboured a notorious Aragonese routier called Nicol in one of his castles and allowed the man to ravage the countryside. What was more, this brigand had been excommunicated by the archbishop's predecessor, a fact which caused the archbishop no problem. He had allowed vacant churches in his own hands to stay vacant for long periods, in order to collect their revenues. He had extorted 400 sols from the bishop of Maguelonne before consenting to consecrate him and he had allowed the archdeacon of his cathedral to hold benefices in plurality. They also accused him of allowing the canonries of his cathedral to fall in number and of allowing monks and canons to leave the religious life.

This mixture of complaints, both on matters to do with the Peace and on matters of ecclesiastical discipline, was very serious and damaging (HGL 6: 232). Fresh trouble arose and the Pope again ordered his deposition in 1207. At this time Bertrand de Saissac, the guardian and tutor of Raimon-Roger, Viscount of Béziers and Carcassonne, disapproving of the election of Bernard de St-Ferréol, the abbot of St-Polycarpe, to the abbacy of Alet, had imprisoned the new abbot, placed the corpse of his dead predecessor at the head of the chapter and forced the election of his own candidate. The bishop of Carcassonne did not dare to interfere and the archbishop was paid off (HGL 6: 158). Again the

wily prelate managed to survive and was still in office in 1211, only suc-
cumbing to pressure in the following year (HGL 6: 234–8; Roquebert
1970: vol. 1, 153–4).

### The Preachers

Preaching, as a method of countering the heretics, along with public debates and disputations, had always been recognised as potentially
effective and Saint Bernard himself had been the first and the greatest of
the preachers to work in the Toulousain. The visit of Cardinal Peter of
Pavia and his three fellow legates to Toulouse in 1178 had also begun
with an effort at preaching to reconvert the people, not only in the city
but in the countryside round about. Preaching had again been a part of
the duties of the legates Peyre and Raoul when they visited Toulouse in
1203, and in February of the following year they conducted a conference with the heretics, presided over by the King of Aragon, at which
the heretics were inevitably condemned (HGL 6: 231).

In the same year, 1203, Bishop Diego of Osma and his sub-prior
Dominic arrived in Toulouse, en route for Denmark on an embassy for
Alfonso VIII, King of Castile and according to a biographer met heretics
there (Vicaire 1964: 50). The bishop and Dominic made a second visit
to Denmark in 1205. They returned from their diplomatic mission in
the summer of 1206, having first visited Rome and, now on their way
back to Spain, stopped at Montpellier. Here they met Peyre of Castelnau,
Arnald-Amalric and Raoul, who had tried preaching to the Cathars and
their followers and were so discouraged that they were considering
abandoning their work (HGL 6: 245). They had been consistently
reproached by their opponents with the scandalous lives of clerics. The
grand state in which the legates moved around the countryside caused
deep offence, while the poverty of life displayed by the perfecti fitted perfectly the view of the authentic apostolic life demanded by orthodox
reformers as well as by the Cathars and well understood by the laity.

What seems to have shocked the legates was that they were not only
rejected intellectually, but subject to ridicule and abuse. Cathar preachers appealed to their audiences from a position of near equality of status. Their mission sprang from within the community to which they
spoke and this gave their testimony a potential for consideration and
acceptance. The legates approached the task as outsiders who spoke from
a position of social and intellectual superiority, despite their cultural
roots in the south. They carried with them a baggage of clerical and corporate assumptions not easily put aside, and fatal in an anti-clerical
milieu. People in the Languedoc were increasingly conditioned by their
experience of preaching by the perfecti to expect an 'apostolic' approach.

Diego of Osma saw that if the policy of preaching was to continue –
and it was impossible to imagine the Church abandoning its founder's
injunction – then they must do as the *perfecti* did and as the Bible enjoined,
and go out barefoot and without money to preach the Gospel. Diego and
Dominic were willing to back their words with deeds and set out with
Peyre and Raoul on a bold journey which took them deep into the heart
of Cathar country (HGL 6: 245–6). The decision had the Pope's backing
for he wrote to Raoul that they should go out and preach in imitation of
the poverty of Christ (PL 215: letter 175). Visiting Servian they met two
leaders of the Cathars, one of whom was said to be a canon from Nevers
who had fled his own country after being condemned for heresy at Paris
(Guébin et Maisonneuve 1951: 12–13). They then made a lengthy visit
to Béziers, during which Peyre of Castelnau withdrew in fear of his life,
because he had become so unpopular. The remaining preachers then
moved on to Carcassonne and Montréal. Guilhem de Puylaurens claimed
that the preachers also visited Verfeil (Duvernoy 1976: 48–9).

During the next year Dominic and his companions again entered
into a long public disputation with the heretics at Montréal, one of several held at this time according to Guilhem de Puylaurens (Duvernoy
1976: 51). Unlike so many other conferences of this kind, this one was
held in circumstances which were hostile to the Catholic preachers and
they seem to have argued from a position of equality. As far as can be
gathered from the contemporary commentators, the preachers made little impression on the Cathars. The whole confrontation lasted several
days and was conducted by an exchange of written arguments, during
which the Cathars accused the preachers of representing the Church of
the Devil, of preaching the doctrines of demons. Their Church was 'the
mother of fornication and abomination, drunk with the blood of the
Saints and the Martyrs of Christ-Jesus'. The Church was neither good
nor holy; it was not instituted by Our Lord Jesus Christ, and Christ and
the Apostles had never instituted the rite of the Mass as it was then cel-
ebrated. The preachers responded with proofs of their position drawn
from the New Testament. To the horror of Guilhem de Puylaurens, the
statements were submitted to the judgement of laymen:

> What pain to see among Christians the position of the Church and the
> Catholic Faith had fallen into such a state of vilification that it was neces-
> sary to submit such outrageous matters to the judgement of laymen!
> (Duvernoy 1976: 52–3)

In the summer of the same year 1207, Arnald-Amalric returned to
the Languedoc after presiding over the Cistercian Chapter-General,
bringing with him twelve other abbots. This group then divided into

smaller parties and set off on foot and begging their food to continue the preaching offensive (HGL 6: 250). Diego and Dominic set off for Osma and at Pamiers met Raimon-Roger of Foix. At his palace they conducted another disputation at which Raimon-Roger's sister, Esclarmonde, was present. She was rudely rebuffed by one of the missionaries when she tried to join the debate, being told to attend to her spinning. The missionaries were said to have reconverted the town, getting their message across particularly to the poor (HGL 6: 252).

The bishop died soon after his return home and most of the abbots gave up and returned home, but Dominic remained, working mostly in the region between Foix and Carcassonne, where Catharism was strong. He began using the semi-derelict church at Prouille, close to Fanjeaux, as a centre for devotion at the end of 1206, and by March of 1207 he had founded a convent for the daughters of poor gentlemen (HGL 6: 252). Some of these girls, without the means to marry, had entered houses of perfectae. They were now provided with an orthodox conventual house. Dominic was to remain in the area, expanding his convent and working tirelessly as a missionary throughout the whole of the war. His immunity from attack by the Cathars was a sign that his sanctity of life and his sincerity was recognised and were his most important attributes for ordinary people.

### Innocent III and the Count of Toulouse

When Innocent III came to power, Raimon VI was living in a state of excommunication, imposed by Celestine III in 1195, because of his quarrel with the monastery of St-Gilles. Raimon VI was easily the most prominent prince in the region and the person to whom the Pope would normally and naturally turn to find an ally. Rainier, the Pope's legate, released the count from his excommunication, while the Pope wrote to tell him that his sin was so great that he should go on a crusade or a pilgrimage in the East to atone (HGL 6: 187). Almost immediately the abbot of St-Gilles complained again to the Pope that Raimon had failed to comply with the conditions laid upon him and that in particular he had not knocked down the castle of Mirapetra but had strengthened it (HGL 6: 188). The Pope once more wrote to Raimon urging him to comply with the agreement.

In the spring of 1204 Innocent III wrote to King Philippe-Auguste of France and his son Louis, urging them to act against the heretics and offering the indulgence normally offered to those who served in the Holy Land. The idea of a crusade against the Cathars was already firmly established in the Pope's mind. It would have seemed only right that the king of France should have an opportunity to lead such a cause because of the active part his predecessors had taken in earlier crusades to the Holy Land and because of the power and prestige of the king, whose authority now embraced the Auvergne. In the spring of the following year Innocent again wrote to Philippe-Auguste urging him to intervene against the heretics. He was thinking of the heretics in the south. He wrote urging the king to

> constrain the counts and barons to confiscate the goods of heretics, by the power you have received from on high, and use the same punishment against those lords who refuse to drive them from their lands. (HGL 6: 234)

Later in the same year pressure on Raimon VI succeeded in persuading him to agree to demands to pursue the heretics and *routiers*. It may well be that he knew of the appeals to Philippe-Auguste and felt that it was politic at least to pay lip-service to the demand.

In 1205 Raimon had made a promise to establish peace, dismiss the *routiers* and persecute the heretics. During the next two years Peyre of Castelnau spent some time in Provence persuading the nobility of the region (where heresy was much less prevalent than further west) to join a Peace, the aim of which was to attack heretics. By early 1207 the normally turbulent relations between Raimon and his vassals in the Marquisate of Provence, exacerbated by Peyre's activities, had deteriorated into war. Peyre reacted by asking Raimon once more to head the new Peace and to drive the heretics out; when Raimon refused, he was excommunicated. The excommunication was accompanied by an interdict across the count's lands (HGL 6: 249). An angry letter from the Pope written in May made clear how seriously the Pope and his legates viewed what they now saw as Raimon's wilful and sinful refusal to aid the Church and his continuing actions which flouted the promises he had made: 'So think, stupid man, think. Cannot God who is Lord of death and of life suddenly cut off your days … then His wrath will deliver you to eternal torment' (PL 215: col. 1167). He was accused of not keeping the Peace he had sworn to, of having joined enemies of the Faith, of attacking religious establishments, of invading the lands of the monastery of St-Gilles and of converting churches into fortresses, of ravaging the countryside, of turning out the bishop of Carpentras, of raising tolls, of giving public office to Jews and of supporting heretics. Those who supported the heretics, he was told, were likely to be suspected of heresy themselves.

By August of that year Raimon of Toulouse was ready to promise what was required. He made peace and was absolved, but it seems unlikely that the Pope believed the count's promises (HGL 6: 258). In the November of the same year the Pope wrote to the King of France and to many of the great princes of the north, the Duke of Burgundy, the Count of Nevers, the Count of Dreux, the Count of Troyes, the counts of the Vermandois and of Blois. He urged them to make war on the heretics as enemies of God and the Church and to confiscate the lands and goods of the heretics and their supporters and offered them a crusading indulgence (HGL 6: 261). Philippe-Auguste replied that he could not maintain a war against the English and carry on a crusade in the south, although he did not reject the idea completely.

Despite his promises of the summer, Raimon of Toulouse had done nothing to comply with the terms which he had agreed to in order to re-enter communion with the Church, and Peyre of Castelnau again excommunicated him. At Christmas 1207 Peyre of Castelnau visited the Count of Toulouse at his court at St-Gilles at the count's invitation and took part in a long series of discussions which achieved nothing except to drive the parties further apart. On 15 January 1208 Peyre and his entourage left the court. Stopping beside the Rhone, prior to taking a ferry across the river, the party was waylaid by a follower of the count and Peyre was stabbed in the back with a lance and died very quickly. The murdered man was taken back to the monastery of St-Gilles where he was buried, on the Pope's orders, close to the shrine of St-Gilles himself (HGL 6: 261–2). For the Pope the murder was a reminder of the fate of Thomas Becket and a deadly insult to his own person and authority, for this was the Pope's own legate. His patience with Raimon VI was exhausted and in his wrath he launched a Crusade.

A crusade is a war which is fought on Christ's behalf to defend the Christian world against attack by infidels or which is fought to recover Christian lands or property. The Pope alone has the authority to declare a crusade. The crusader is a soldier who takes up arms to take part in such a war. He is distinguished from other soldiers by a number of features. He is not paid for his endeavours, which spring from religious devotion. He is offered an indulgence which grants a full remission of his sins committed to date, with his action as a soldier in the crusade, if legitimate, counting as his penance. Finally the crusader takes a vow to fulfil his commitment. The idea that a vow to God, made in public, was binding in conscience on a Christian was extremely ancient. The increasing numbers of monks and nuns were defined in their calling by just such a vow, which by the end of the twelfth century had a legally binding force (Brundage 1968: 78–9).

The century before the Albigensian Crusade had been marked by advances in the concept of just war which had made it legitimate for the Church itself to initiate conflict, rather than waiting always for a secular ruler to act for it. In Northern France and Flanders, bishops had acted to maintain the peace in the absence of powerful secular authority, raising militias to defend the Church and the faithful against the lawless and blessing those who fought. Canonists developed legal justifications for the use of force by the Church and its allies, even against other Christians, where the welfare and peace of the Church and society were threatened (Houseley 1985).

We have already seen that Alexander III, at the Third Lateran Council of 1179, had sanctioned attack upon the heretics of the Languedoc and that this led to a practical attempt to lead a war against the Cathars in 1181 by Henry de Marsiac. The *routiers* as well as the heretics were the enemy to be attacked. They were all enemies of God and the Christian World and disturbers of the peace and unity of Christendom. In these circumstances this would be a Christian war on behalf of Christ himself – a true crusade. In so far as the King of France was not involved the war was removed at first from any charge that it was a feudal war or a war of conquest for gain. With the pope as its leader, represented by his legates, the Crusade could claim purity of intent and it is likely that many of the men who answered the call saw it in those terms. They were motivated by the fear of heresy in their midst which had been growing during the twelfth century. The south could be seen as the seat of that contagion, which they might destroy at source.

Innocent III was more interested in crusading than most of his predecessors. He had authorised the crusade in Livonia in 1199 and called the Fourth Crusade to the Holy Land, which turned into the attack upon Constantinople, aiding it by the first tax on clerical incomes; and he was thinking about another crusade to the East in 1208 (Riley-Smith 1987: 119–33). He took the crusading ideal and used it wherever it might aid the Church in its fight against those he saw as its enemies.

The Crusade against the Albigensians has been seen as the first Crusade against Christians, a radical departure, but this was not how it was seen by contemporaries. The Albigensians were heretics: people who by the very definition of the term were not followers of Christ, but people who did the Devil's work. They were not true Christians but dangerous adversaries sent to ensnare the faithful and lead them to hell (Riley-Smith 1992: 19). To make war against them when all else had failed was a practical, sensible and urgent step. It was not to be seen as an aggressive war, but as a necessary defence against an expanding inner enemy. Furthermore, the whole problem of the Languedoc was complicated by the *routiers*. In so far as these mercenary soldiers were outside decent society they had become a major problem for the Church as it tried to grapple with the problems of ensuring peace inside the Christian community. *Routiers* were a means whereby war could be spread and maintained indefinitely, provided they were paid. They were a technical development of warfare, like the crossbow, which the Church would have liked to ban (Foreville 1969). The *routiers* were particularly prominent in those areas where heresy was prevalent, filling the gap left by the relative weakness of feudal institutions. So they were associated with Raimon VI and with heresy. As an 'unchristian' force they could be included in the enemies of the Church and thus of the Crusade.

The events of the years of Innocent's reign seem to have an inevitability about them which led inexorably towards the Crusade. The reality is that although the Church was able to refine its doctrinal position and its internal organisation as well as launching a considerable missionary effort, without secular support it could not enforce or maintain a monopoly of religious belief and observance. It had always been the tacit assumption of the Church that Christianity was the only organised religious observance, except Judaism, which could exist inside the successor states of the Western Roman world, since Christianity made the claim to be the only true and therefore legitimate access to supernatural authority. The reluctance to tolerate rivals had led to increasingly precise definitions of doctrine and increasingly clear tests of orthodoxy. These served as means of defining those who, once excluded from the body of the faithful, could be persecuted by secular as well as Church authorities. In the Languedoc, despite the special measures the Pope was willing to employ, nothing worked. The assumption that the secular prince would always do the bidding of the Church in matters of the Faith had failed. The way to salvage the position was to redefine the prince as no longer fit to exercise his office and to call upon other laymen to take over from the defaulter, using the crusading weapon, originally developed to provide a method of aggressive expansion of papal authority. It was the logical and practical outcome of the new definition of the Pope as the ultimate source of all legitimate authority.

For over a century popes had been using the language of crusade, of a war launched at the behest of the Church, for ends which the Church defined as just and in the service of God. Peter the Venerable had written:

> An essential aspect of your office as a knight, and the reason why you took up arms, is that you should protect the Church of God from its assailants. … But perhaps, you will say: we took up arms against the pagans, not against Christians. Well, who deserves to be attacked more by you or your people, the pagan who does not know God, or the Christian who acknowledges God with his words but who fights against him with his deeds? (Houseley 1985: 24)

Now, in the Languedoc, Innocent offered a crusading indulgence and sent out a call to Crusade, just as if the crusaders were to depart to fight the Saracens in the Holy Land or in Spain (Houseley 1985: 28).

# 6

# The war in the Languedoc

## Calling the Crusade

When the Pope heard the news of the death of Peyre of Castelnau, Arnald-Amalric was present in the Curia (Martin-Chabot 1973–89: vol. 1, 17). Innocent solemnly anathematised and excommunicated Raimon VI. The decision to declare a Crusade was apparently taken with the aid of Arnald-Amalric who was depicted by William of Tudela as urging the Pope to issue a crusading indulgence. He was given the duty of organising and leading the crusading army and set off first to Cîteaux, where in September 1208 he presided over the annual Chapter-General of the Cistercian Order, promulgating to his fellow abbots the Bull of 28 March which offered the crusading indulgence and calling upon them to preach the Crusade.

There were many Cistercian houses in France, particularly in Burgundy and other eastern parts of the kingdom, and it was here that the effort was concentrated by the preachers (Martin-Chabot 1973–89: vol. 1, 25). The Pope's Bull of 9 October 1208, addressed to the prelates and nobility of France, offered crusading status to all who would take up arms against the heretics (PL 215: col. 1469). They were to wear the sign of the Cross and thus receive the protection offered by the Church to crusaders. Their possessions were to be under the protection of the Church; their debts were suspended for the duration of their service – no one might sue for the return of capital or interest; clerks who went on the Crusade might pledge two years' revenues from their benefices to help with expenses. This was an appeal directly to the French, over the head of their reluctant king. The Duke of Burgundy and the Count of Nevers were both very quickly persuaded (Martin-Chabot 1973–89: vol. 1, 25). In May 1209 Philippe-Auguste summoned a *Parlement* at Villeneuve-sur-Yonne. The Pope had written to the king urging him once more to take up arms to drive the Count of Toulouse from his lands (PL

215: col. 1358). The legates were present and were able to recruit more crusaders but the king himself refused to take part in the war. This was in line with his consistent refusal to embroil himself in a matter which offered little strategic or economic advantage, compared with the increasingly successful struggle with King John and, at the moment of the Crusade, his intervention in the contest for control of the Imperial crown (Baldwin 1986: 204–5). He told the pope's legates that he had two great lions worrying at his flanks, the so-called Emperor Otto and the King of England. His great vassals might go if they wished (Belperron 1942: 148–9).

Fortified with the protections offered by crusading status, the army assembled at Lyon in late June. It included the Duke of Burgundy, the Count of Nevers, the Count of St-Pol, the Count of Monfort, the Count of Bar-sur-Seine and many other noblemen, as well as the Archbishop of Sens and the bishops of Autun, Clermont and Nevers (Guébin et Maisonneuve 1951: 39). There were also contingents from Germany, as well as from Gascony, Poitou and the Saintonge. Another army of Gascons advanced through the Agenais (Martin-Chabot 1973–89: vol. 1, 38–41). Between them the aristocratic crusaders and their followers made a great army, duly reported to the Pope as the biggest ever to assemble in the Christian world (PL 210: col. 138). The motives of the crusaders were doubtless as mixed as those of people who join any great undertaking. Many saw an opportunity for plunder and profit and were not to be entirely disappointed. On the whole, though, the crusaders were primarily motivated by religious zeal, which expressed itself in the desire to gain the indulgence. With customary exaggeration the *Chanson* reported 20,000 knights and 100,000 common soldiers, many of whom were peasants (Martin-Chabot 1973–89: vol. 1, 37–8). The whole expedition was led by Arnald-Amalric, and it set out down the Rhone Valley.

Raimon VI viewed the preparations for the Crusade with growing alarm. During the winter of 1209 he had sent a delegation to Rome to plead his cause. Among the ambassadors, all of whom were prelates, was Raimon de Rabastens, the deposed bishop of Toulouse, who could hardly have appeared to the Pope as a respectable witness for Raimon VI's cause. According to the *Chanson*, the Pope offered Raimon VI terms which included the surrender, as pledges of good conduct, of seven castles and fortified towns in the Rhone valley, as well as the County of Maguio (Martin-Chabot 1973–89: vol. 1, 33). As the army advanced down the Rhone valley the Count of Toulouse travelled to Valence where he met the Pope's legate Milo. He was offered a reconciliation with the Church and therefore protection against the Crusade, in return for a promise of reparation for the damage done to the Church and action against the heretics. Raimon felt obliged to accept the terms in view of the size of the expeditionary force which was approaching. On 18 June 1209 he appeared before Milo at his eastern capital, St-Gilles, and offered himself as a penitent.

The ceremony of reconciliation took place in front of the monastic church of St-Gilles in the centre of the town, in the presence of the archbishops of Arles, Auch and Aix and nineteen bishops of the south (PL 216: col. 94). Naked to the waist and barefoot, he took the oath at a specially constructed altar, laden with relics. He promised to obey the commands of the Church. He promised to make amends or obey the Church on each of fifteen points. He would no longer support *routiers*; he would not allow Jews to hold public office; churches used as castles would be re-instated; new tolls would be abolished; the Bishop of Carpentras would be allowed to occupy the diocese from which he had been expelled; the Bishop of Vaison would be compensated for his imprisonment and the destruction of his palace. He also denied the charges that he had refused to swear to the Peace, that he had favoured heretics; that his own beliefs were suspect; that he had violated the Truce of God and above all that he had been involved in the death of Peyre of Castelnau.

After the conclusion of the ceremony, during which he had been ritually beaten, it became apparent that the press of people outside was so great that the count could not leave the church by the west door. He was led out through the crypt passing the tomb of Peyre of Castelnau:

> He had to go down into the crypt and pass naked in front of the tomb of the blessed martyr, Brother Peyre of Castelnau, whom he had had assassinated. This was God's just judgment. He was forced to pay respect to the body of him he had scorned during life. (Guébin et Maisonneuve 1951: 37)

Pierre des Vaux-de-Cernay was of course an ardent partisan of the Church and the North in his writing about the Crusade, but his judgement is essentially accurate. It is hard to imagine a more complete public humiliation for a ruler. Other vassals of his, as well as the consuls of Avignon, were associated with the count's oath, making the humiliation something shared by other members of the southern community.

### Beginning the war

Four days after his reconciliation Raimon VI took the Cross and joined the Crusade. His action made his lands throughout the Languedoc safe from attack (Guébin et Maisonneuve 1951: 37). This was just as well, since the army had reached Orange by 25 June 1209 and by mid-July the crusaders had crossed the Rhone at Beaucaire and reached Montpellier. As they moved south from Montpellier the crusaders entered the lands of Raimon-Roger Trencavel, Viscount of Béziers and Carcassonne and nephew of Raimon VI. According to the *Chanson*, Raimon VI had tried to come to an accord with his nephew during the preceding winter, with a view to an alliance against the crusaders. Raimon-Roger had rejected the offer (Martin-Chabot 1973–89: vol. 1, 27). Seeing the manoeuvres of his uncle during the winter, Raimon-Roger had tried for an agreement with the Church but had been rebuffed by the legate Milo. If Raimon-Roger had indeed rejected his uncle's overtures, it was probably because he feared ensnarement and felt that he could rely upon his overlord, King Pere of Aragon for protection. If that was so, it was a miscalculation and the young count found himself completely exposed. The army moved swiftly south and reached Béziers on 21 July, camping outside its walls (figure 19).

The opening act of hostility in the Crusade signalled the brutality with which it was to be pursued. Raimon-Roger Trencavel had decided that the city was not defensible and had left for Carcassonne. With him went the Jewish community, mindful of what had happened to Jews in the north. The community of Béziers, with a long record of municipal independence behind them, decided to defy the army despite an appeal by the bishop for their immediate capitulation (Martin-Chabot 1973–89: vol. 1, 51). The attack on the city was started by the camp followers who attacked the gates and walls with picks. Seeing their enthusiasm the soldiers then joined in without formal orders and the army seems to have broken into the city in a very short time, only two to three hours according to Arnald-Amalric himself (PL 216: col. 139). The citizens rushed to the cathedral for protection. Both church and town were looted and the inhabitants massacred, with clerics, women and children being killed inside the churches. When the leaders of the army confiscated booty from the camp followers the town was fired and burnt down. It was on this occasion that Arnald-Amalric is said to have been asked how the attackers should distinguish between heretic and Catholic and to have replied *caedite eos. Novit enim Dominus qui sunt eis* – 'kill them all, God will know his own' (Caesarius of Heisterbach: vol. II, 296–8).

In the official report, sent by Arnald-Amalric to the Pope, the legates claimed that 20,000 people had been killed (PL 216: col. 139). The city probably had a total population of about 10,000, so this claim can be seen as in line with the normal inability of commentators at his period to deal with large numbers (Wolff 1969: 99–114). Although the official report is quite explicit about the attack and massacre, the *Chanson* is rather uneasy about what happened (Martin-Chabot 1973–89: vol. 1, 59).

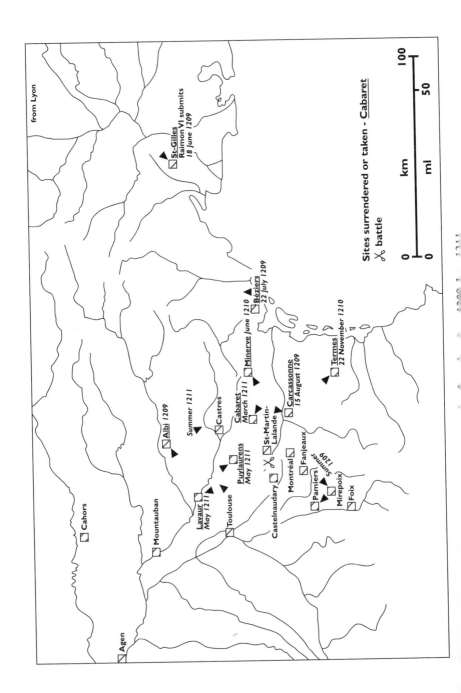

from Lyon

Cahors

Agen

Mountauban

Albi *1209*

*Summer 1211*

Castres

Lavaur
*May 1211*

Toulouse

Puylaurens
*May 1211*

Castelnaudary

Montréal

Fanjeaux

Pamiers

Mirepoix

Foix

*Summer 1209*

St-Martin-
Lalande

Cabaret
*March 1211*

Minerve *June 1210*

Béziers
*22 July 1209*

Carcassonne
*15 August 1209*

Termes
*22 November 1210*

St-Gilles
Raimon VI submits
*18 June 1209*

Sites surrendered or taken - <u>Cabaret</u>
✗ battle

0        km        100

0        ml        50

Pierre des Vaux-de-Cernay, on the other hand, justified the massacre as
punishment for the sins of the heretics in the town and for the politics
of previous years, when the townspeople had killed a previous viscount
in 1167 and for blasphemy against Mary Magdalen (Guébin et Maisonneuve 1951: 42). It seems unlikely that Arnald-Amalric actually uttered
the words attributed to him, since they are not quoted by the contemporary sources. Massacres of civilians, then as now, were not uncom-
mon. They were intended primarily to terrify the inhabitants of other
cities so that they would be more likely to submit without a siege and
the normal practice at this time allowed a conquered city to be sacked at
the will of the attackers, if it had not offered to surrender. Roquebert has
no doubt that the leaders of the crusaders had every intention of mas-
sacring the inhabitants and that only the way in which the attack started
surprised them (Roquebert 1970: 260-1). The immediate fruit of the
massacre was the unconditional submission of Narbonne through its
viscount and archbishop, who offered material support and promised to
deliver up their heretics to the army as well as the property the Béziers
Jews possessed there (Roquebert 1970: 265).

Wasting no time the crusaders marched on Carcassonne. According
to Arnald-Amalric more than a hundred of the fortified villages *en route*
were given up to them, such was the terror their passage inspired (PL
216: col. 139). They arrived before the city on the first of August and
found it already in a state of defence. Carcassonne was the military key
to the region and that was part of the reason why Raimon-Roger had
hurried to defend it. The city occupies the site of a Gallo-Roman fortress
at the north-western corner of the Corbières Mountains (figure 20). At
its foot the River Aude makes a sharp turn from its northerly course from
the Pyrenees and runs eastward through the valley between the Corbières to the south and the Black Mountains to the north. Through that
gap passed the old Roman road from Bordeaux and Toulouse to Narbonne, as do the modern railway, autoroute and the Canal du Midi. The
city looks westward across the plain towards Toulouse and south-west-
wards into Foix. It is not surprising therefore that there are indications
that the site was occupied as a hillfort at an early date with sixth century
BC Phoenician, Massilian, Etruscan and Attic wares as evidence of the
extent of its commerce (Gallia 1973: 477). The defences used in the
Crusade (figure 21) were the Roman walls of the late third or early
fourth century, which had been reconstructed and strengthened many
times over (Gallia 1981: 503; Rivet 1988: 136-9) (figure 6.4). Raimon-
Roger commanded the city from his comital castle, built round about
1130 at the western side of the town, overlooking the River Aude. He
had had time to erect timber hoardings around the tops of the walls and

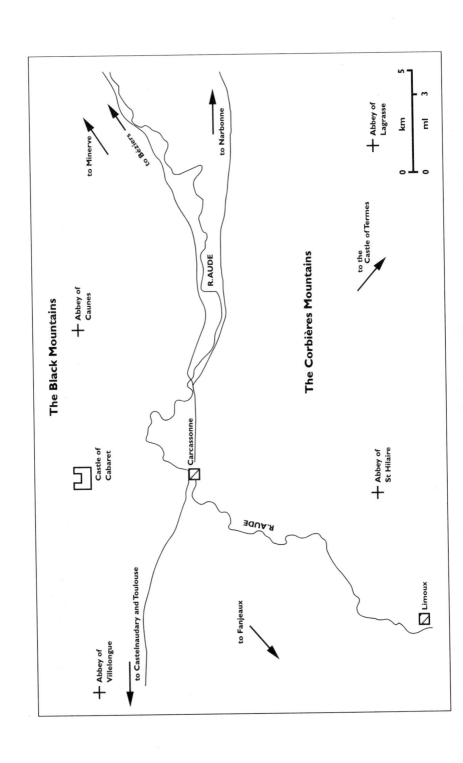

The Black Mountains

to Minerve

to Béziers

Abbey of Caunes

R. AUDE

to Narbonne

Castle of Cabaret

Carcassonne

The Corbières Mountains

to the Castle of Termes

Abbey of Lagrasse

km
ml
0          3          5

Abbey of St Hilaire

R. AUDE

Abbey of Villelongue

to Castelnaudary and Toulouse

to Fanjeaux

Limoux

Figure 21  Carcassonne city walls

he could reasonably hope to hold out against even a powerful army until help arrived or the enemy died of dysentery. But this was no ordinary army. It had something of the ferocity and self-belief which had made the First Crusade such a success.

The first targets were the two suburbs on the northern and southern flanks of the city, themselves defended with walls and ditches (Guébin et Maisonneuve 1951: 43). On 3 August 1209 the northern suburb was quickly assaulted and razed and the attack on the second suburb proceeded on 7–8 August. Within a week the crusaders had reached the walls of the city itself. At this point the King of Aragon, Pere II, arrived with a small retinue. Raimon-Roger might reasonably have expected some sort of help from his overlord, but according to William of Tudela the king was merely able to offer mediation, urging Raimon-Roger to seek a compromise with the French barons (Martin-Chabot 1973–89: vol. 1, 71–3). He was in a difficult position. He had himself issued decrees against the heretics in his own kingdom and he knew the dangers of publicly supporting a prince who was excommunicate and the subject of a crusade. He also knew about the sack of Béziers. On the other hand, this intrusion into Septimania threatened his family's sphere of influence. For the moment there was little Pere II could do. Using the king as an intermediary, the crusaders offered the viscount safe conduct for himself and eleven companions out of the city. The rest of the garrison and the inhabitants and the contents of the town were to be at the mercy of the besiegers. The viscount refused the offer, the attack was resumed and the king withdrew (Martin-Chabot 1973–89: vol. 1, 75).

A week later the viscount was offered a safe conduct to a conference to discuss surrender of the city, which was running short of water. The river was inaccessible because of the siege and the wells in the town had run dry (Martin-Chabot 1973–89: vol. 1, 77–9). The crusaders had decided that they needed Carcassonne as a base and that they needed the supplies which had been stockpiled within it (Guébin et Maisonneuve 1951: 44). At this point it seems that the viscount was seized and imprisoned, possibly as an agreed hostage for the performance of the terms of surrender, more likely as an act of treachery towards a man who was known to have been effectively abandoned by his overlord. With its leader gone, the city capitulated and the inhabitants were turned out of the town in their underwear and without any of their possessions. Some certainly had homes round about, others had relatives in the countryside. Others are known to have reached Toulouse and even Barcelona. Later many were allowed to return to the city, after all the goods had been seized. On 15 August the crusaders entered the empty and intact town, filled with supplies, and to many it must have seemed that they had fulfilled their crusading vows, as well, no doubt, as having filled their pockets from the sack of Béziers and the robbery of other people along the way.

## Simon de Montfort, Viscount of Béziers–Carcassonne

Up to this point the leadership of the Crusade rested with the papal legates, and particularly with Arnald-Amalric. The crusaders all felt the need for someone who could be regarded as the secular ruler of Carcassonne and they were prepared to accept a change of ruler as called for by the Pope. The nobility in the army, together with the great prelates, proceeded to an election. Their first choice was the Duke of Burgundy, the most senior layman on the expedition. When he refused they turned to the next most senior, the Count of Nevers, then the Count of St-Pol and when he refused they finally settled on Simon de Monfort. Diplomatically their choice could hardly have been bettered. He was the lord of Montfort l'Amaury, near Paris. He was also the titular Earl of Leicester, a claim which came from his mother Amicia, who had married Simon II of Monfort and who, with her sister, was daughter and co-heiress of Robert Earl of Leicester who had died in 1190. Because of the war between King John and the King of France the earldom itself was outside Simon's grasp. However, he maintained his claim which was eventually taken up by his youngest son Simon, who became Earl of Leicester in 1231 (Powicke 1953: 75, n.1). In a letter to Innocent III which announced his control of the Carcassonne and its viscounty, he called himself Earl of Leicester, Lord of Monfort and Viscount of Béziers and Carcassonne (PL 216: col. 141).

The impeccable social background of the new count meant he was the social equal of the men who had refused the title. He was, however, relatively poor, so that he posed less of a threat by his accession to the title than other great men and must have been reasonably acceptable to King Philippe. In theory the crusaders had precious little 'right' to offer the title and the lands to Simon. There was after all, still a viscount, albeit in prison. Furthermore, his overlord King Pere of Aragon had not been consulted about the change and had not given his consent. The offer came from the papal legate and was a practical example of the Pope's claim to be able to dispossess a heretical ruler. It showed how determined the Church was that there should be permanent changes in the secular leadership of the Languedoc and thus a guarantee that there would be permanent changes in the religious life of the region too. The whole issue was made much easier when Raimon-Roger died in prison in November.

Simon de Montfort was an experienced soldier with a long record as a crusader in the East. Born about 1153 he had fought for Philippe-Auguste against Richard I of England at Aumale, had taken part in the Fourth Crusade and had proved himself as a warrior and leader. Recognised as a devout Christian by churchmen, he was also able to command the loyalty of his soldiers among whom he had a reputation as an honest and honourable man.

Very quickly after the fall of Carcassonne the countryside to the west and south had capitulated. Both Montréal and Fanjeaux were garrisoned by the crusaders (Martin-Chabot 1973–89: vol. 1, 85). Castres submitted and Lombers offered to do the same. An assault on Cabaret was unsuccessful, but the new viscount was able to campaign southwards into the lands of the Count of Foix, seizing Mirepoix and Pamiers and then going north to Albi, where he accepted the submission of the town from its bishop (Guébin et Maisonneuve 1951: 50–3). A serious attack had been made on the lands where the concentration of Cathars was probably greatest.

The huge army now began to disintegrate. The crusaders felt that they had gained their indulgence, having served more than forty days, and having overthrown the Viscount of Béziers–Carcassonne. Most of them now returned to northern France, to their homes, their wives and their mortgages. Simon was left in possession of Carcassonne with a group of close followers and about 500 soldiers who served for double wages. The papal legates told the Pope that Simon was to rule all the lands of the viscounty (PL 216: col. 140), but the effective control soon shrank as the army disappeared.

An immediate effect of the coming of the crusaders was the beginning of serious persecution of the Cathars. Cathars began to be burnt at Castres when the town was surrendered (Guébin et Maisonneuve 1951: 51), while the crusaders also sent emissaries to Toulouse to place pressure upon the citizens to give up the heretics there (Martin-Chabot 1973–89: vol. 1, 97). However the shrinking authority of the new count meant that there was a respite during the winter. Simon was shut into a comparatively small area as the Count of Foix began to press to regain his land, while action by Pierre-Roger of Cabaret, the chief supporter of Viscount Raimon-Roger, and by other local lords to the north led to the capture of one of Simon's leading supporters and the loss of Saissac (Martin-Chabot 1973–89: vol. 1, 105). At the same time local lords who had done homage to Simon took the opportunity to throw off allegiance (Guébin et Maisonneuve 1951: 59). They also attempted to draw the King of Aragon into the conflict, with a general offer of homage. Pere refused this, but did negotiate protection for the Count of Foix (Guébin et Maisonneuve 1951: 63).

As the spring came new crusaders arrived from the north and an army was re-assembled. Simon began to campaign once more, reconquering the *pagus* of Carcassonne, so that by the summer only three great fortresses remained outside his control. To the south-east, in the Corbières was the chateau of Termes; to the north-east was the city and chateau of Minerve, chief place of the Minervois, and directly to the north of Carcassonne was the triple chateau of Cabaret. All three had to be captured. Termes and Cabaret were held by notorious supporters of the Cathars, believers themselves and still loyal to the memory of their dead viscount and committed to the maintenance of their own independence. Minerve was the home of the Cathar bishop of Carcassonne and a gathering place for *perfecti*, many of whom had fled there for safety after the fall of Carcassonne.

Minerve was the first place to be besieged, in June 1210 (Guébin et Maisonneuve 1951: 64). The village, as it now is, lies on a narrow projecting tongue of land between two deep river gorges which meet at the south-eastern end of the village. The leaf-shaped tongue of ground narrows at the north-western end of the village and at this point stood the castle protecting the entrance to the site. The clifftops were lined with walls and the houses filled the whole of the interior space. The village church contained then, as it still does, an altar dedicated there by Bishop Sergius of Narbonne in AD 456 (Wolff 1967). The weakness of the site was that the land surrounding the town, on either side of the gorges, was at the same height as the town and the distances across the gorges were not great, so that siege engines could be effective. Missiles were used to destroy access to the water supply, which was in a well at the foot of the cliff reached by a covered passage.

The surrender terms were dictated by Arnald-Amalric. Although the lives of the garrison and townspeople were spared, as were those of *credentes*, the *perfecti* were to be surrendered and would be spared if they converted. Pierre des Vaux-de-Cernay says that one of the senior crusaders was horrified at the thought that the *perfecti* might escape alive. He had come to see the heretics destroyed and was anxious that they should not be given an opportunity to escape. Arnald-Amalric reassured him that he thought very few would recant. When Pierre's master, the Abbot of Vaux-de-Cernay, entered he town he found a house filled with male *perfecti* who brusquely rejected his attempt to preach to them. A meeting of *perfectae* greeted him in the same way, saying 'neither death nor life can separate us from the faith to which we are joined'. The result was a great pyre on which the crusaders burnt some 140 *perfecti*, men and women (Guébin et Maisonneuve 1951: 64–7). This was the first of the mass executions which were to be a feature of the Crusade throughout the Languedoc.

The crusaders then moved on to Termes. This castle stood on a rock above a ravine, approachable from one side only. Raimon de Termes, the lord of the castle, was a well known heretic who ruled an area of mountainous territory in the Corbières. Unlike the attack upon Minerve the siege of Termes was a long drawn out affair. On the point of capitulation as a result of thirst, the garrison was saved by a cloudburst and the siege lasted into the autumn. Finally the garrison of the chateau abandoned the defence and left during the night of 22 November, fearing that Simon's sappers were about to break in. Raimon de Termes seems to have returned to the castle to get something and was captured and thrown into prison (Guébin et Maisonneuve 1951: 70–79; Martin-Chabot 1973–89: vol. 1, 13). It was not until the next spring (March 1211) that the chateau of Cabaret fell into Simon's hands, when he came to an agreement with Pierre-Roger, who received a fief near Béziers in exchange for its surrender.

The fall of these great fortresses much strengthened Simon's military position. Castles and fortified villages throughout the Corbières and the Albigeois were given up (Martin-Chabot 1973–89: vol. 1, 141) and he was in a position to consider an expansion of his sphere of activities. In the spring of 1211 Simon de Montfort and the crusaders turned their attention to Lavaur, a town about 32 km (20 ml) east-north-east of Toulouse, but a possession of the Viscount of Béziers–Carcassonne. The siege of the town lasted about a month (April–May 1211) and concluded when the besiegers cut a hole through the wall and burst into the town (Guébin et Maisonneuve 1951: 89–95). The town was defended by the lady of Lavaur, Geralda and her brother Aimery, who had been lord of Montréal until dispossessed by Simon. Since the town, the garrison and citizens were his to command, Simon ordered the execution of Aimery and eighty knights who had assisted him. They were, in his view, traitors who had resisted their rightful lord. He then had the lady of Lavaur killed by throwing her down a well which was then filled with stones. William of Tudela tells us that she screamed, wept and shouted (Martin-Chabot 1973–89: vol. 1, 173). He then recorded that at least 400 heretics were burnt in the town, a sight which – Pierre des Vaux-de-Cernay remarked – the crusaders greeted 'with great joy' (Martin-Chabot 1973–89: vol. 1, 173; Guébin et Maisonneuve 1951: 94).

## The Count of Toulouse

Raimon VI spent the winter of 1209 in feverish diplomatic activity. He visited Rome, with little success, and then paid a call on the Emperor Otto in Tuscany before visiting the King of France, who was not amused by his cousin's visit to the emperor. Requests for the king's support in the raising of tolls, which had been forbidden by the papal legates, met with refusal (Guébin et Maisonneuve 1951: 60). The legate Milo held a council at Avignon and excommunicated the consuls of Toulouse and laid the city under an interdict for its failure to give up the *perfecti* and their followers, as demanded by emissaries of the crusaders (Mansi 22: col. 795). During the spring Raimon continued to attempt a careful balancing act, fearful of the power of the crusading alliance between Arnald-Amalric and Simon de Montfort. The King of Aragon visited him and although, according to the chroniclers, this was of no material benefit to Raimon he must have hoped that it would send a signal to Simon. At the same time he hedged his bets with the crusaders by receiving a visit from Arnald-Amalric himself in Toulouse and allowing him and Bishop Fulk to preach in Toulouse and elsewhere in the Toulousain (Martin-Chabot 1973–89: vol. 1, 111). The advantage to the city was that the legate brought with him a papal Bull which released the city from the interdict, although only after the surrender of hostages and sureties to the legates.

The legates, with orders given by the Pope, were still anxious that Raimon VI should prove that his conversion to the cause of the Crusade was sincere and summoned him to a meeting at St-Gilles in July 1210. He was again condemned for his failure to meet the terms of the oath given at St-Gilles the year before. Raimon wept when told this (Mansi 22: cols 811–12). The next January (1211) another conference took place at Narbonne, attended by the King of Aragon, Simon de Montfort and Arnald-Amalric, which again pressed Raimon VI to expel the heretics from his lands. The plan was that he should expel the heretics from his own property and then expel them from places within his domains which were not held from him by feudal tenure (over five hundred sites), confiscating a quarter to third of the property for himself. Raimon was not prepared to adopt this plan (Mansi 22: cols 813–14). He doubtless realised that he was being invited to make war on his own county and that he could not carry through such a plan without outside help, provided no doubt by the crusaders. The King of Aragon was also anxious to protect the Count of Foix. In return for a promise not to attack the crusaders he would be left in peace, but Simon insisted on holding on to Pamiers. Simon de Montfort next persuaded the King of Aragon to accept his homage as Viscount of Béziers–Carcassonne. Pere recognised a *fait accompli* and Simon hoped to fend off any immediate attack by the King. The participants then moved on to Montpellier, where Simon agreed a betrothal between his daughter and the infant son of King Pere. A council also met which again pressed Raimon VI to meet the terms of his oath at St-Gilles but he left the town suddenly without making any formal promise. He was once more excommunicated (on 6 February 1211), a sentence which the Pope confirmed in April.

Raimon VI was vitally concerned by the siege of Lavaur, which was well within his own territory, although a possession of the Viscount of Béziers. He was accused by Pierre des Vaux-de-Cernay of secretly supplying soldiers to aid the town (Guébin et Maisonneuve 1951: 90–1). During the previous year, 1210, when Arnald-Amalric had visited Toulouse, he had encouraged the bishop to preach against usury. Many prominent merchants who were sympathisers of the Cathars lent money at interest, so that such preaching was socially divisive, setting the artisans, who were normally the borrowers, against the bourgeoisie. The bishop summoned moneylenders to appear before his courts and with the help of Arnald-Amalric organised a fraternity, a group of people, mostly inhabitants of the *cité* and therefore often attached to the church in some way. Their purpose was to attack moneylenders. Bound together by an oath and known as the 'white fraternity', these citizens began to attack moneylenders, pulling down their houses. The result was the formation of another fraternity, the 'black fraternity', in the *bourg*, devoted to opposing the 'white' (Duvernoy 1976: 67). There was fighting in the streets and the town became increasingly divided in its loyalties. According to William of Tudela this was encouraged by Fulk and Arnald-Amalric in order to weaken the town (Martin-Chabot 1973–89: vol. 1, 113). Between 15 March and 3 May 1211, some of the members of the white confraternity also took part in the siege of Lavaur, urged on by Bishop Fulk, in defiance of Raimon VI, weakening his position still further.

After his experiences at St-Gilles, Narbonne, Montpellier and finally in his own city of Toulouse, it was not surprising that Raimon, excommunicate again, should express hostility towards Fulk of Marseille. After nearly three weeks of pressure the bishop fled Toulouse just before Easter and went to join the siege of Lavaur (Guébin et Maisonneuve 1951: 91–2). A few weeks afterwards, early in May, the bishop ordered his clergy to follow him into exile, which they seem to have done (Guébin et Maisonneuve 1951: 97).

It is clear that opinion about the Crusade was far from united inside Toulouse. Raimon VI was not enormously popular. He rarely lived in the city and the influence of the orthodox was strong, particularly under Fulk of Marseille. Raimon had to forbid the townspeople to sell supplies to the besiegers at Lavaur. The decision by the bishop and the legate to foment dissension inside the town was a high-risk strategy, perhaps intended to lead to a general insurrection which would either lead to Raimon VI being expelled or give an opportunity for Simon de Monfort to intervene directly. In the ensuing power struggle Raimon VI was the victor and the political lines were drawn for the second phase of the war.

## The attack on the Toulousain

Raimon VI was no longer protected by his status as a crusader and the way was open for Simon and the crusaders to begin an attack on the Toulousain. Immediately after the fall of Lavaur Simon had seized the castle of Puylaurens, which lay within the Toulousain, and then moved on to besiege castles and towns belonging to the Count of Toulouse, burning the *perfecti* who had taken shelter in them. At Montferrand (figure 22) the crusaders were able to take the castle and receive the submission of Baldwin, the younger brother of Raimon VI, normally known as Count Baudouin. Simon then moved across the Tarn, back into the Albigeois and began to reduce the towns and castles there (Guébin et Maisonneuve 1951: 97–8)

By the middle of June 1211the crusaders were ready to assault Toulouse. The effect of withdrawing the clergy was to leave the town under an effective interdict. The crusaders advanced upon the city, killing Bertrand the bastard son of Raimon VI during a skirmish, and killing the peasants they found in the fields. Between 17 and 29 June 1211 the crusaders camped outside Toulouse. They were too few in number to surround the city completely, which had the advantage of lying beside a very wide river, which provided ready access. Despite the divisions among the citizens, the consuls were able to command the loyalty or acquiescence of most people in their decision to resist (Belperron 1942: 225–6). Raimon called upon his vassals, the counts of Foix and Commignes to help him and with them a number of *routiers*, led by the Navarrais Hugues d'Alfaro, who had married Raimon's illegitimate daughter, Guillaumette (Belperron 1942: 226). Since Toulouse was too large for the crusaders to capture and the attacks of the southerners were becoming more and more dangerous, Simon withdrew after twelve days, and sent an army south to devastate the county of Foix, while he moved north-west to receive the homage of the bishop of Cahors and the Quercy passed almost effortlessly into his hands. As most of his army now felt that they had completed their crusade the army began to break up again and by the late summer he had returned to Carcassonne.

By September 1211 Raimon had assembled a coalition of southern forces. These included the Count of Commignes, Gaston de Bearn and Savary de Mauleon, from Poitou, the seneschal of the King of England, who was present on the orders of King John, as well as militias sent by various towns. With these forces he was able to besiege Castelnaudary

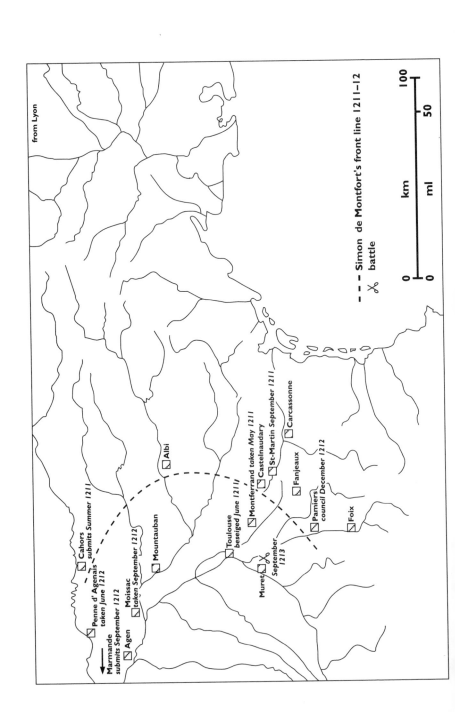

from Lyon

Cahors
submits Summer 1211

Penne d' Agenais
taken June 1212

Marmande
submits September 1212

Agen

Moissac
taken September 1212

Mountauban

Albi

Toulouse
beseiged June 1211

Montferrand taken May 1211

Castelnaudary

St-Martin September 1211

Carcassonne

Fanjeaux

Pamiers
council December 1212

Muret
September
1213

Foix

km

ml

— — Simon de Montfort's front line 1211–12

✂ battle

0        50        100

0

(Guébin et Maisonneuve 1951: 105). Simon found that he could not rely on support from his new subjects, as those who had done him homage from fear of the consequences began to desert him for Raimon and his allies. A battle at St-Martin-des-Landes, about 5 km (3 ml) from Castelnaudary ended in defeat for the Count of Foix. The fact that Simon de Monfort was able to take part in the battle showed that the 'siege' was far from complete, but despite Simon's comparative success the revolt among the southern towns and nobility continued to spread. However, throughout the winter of 1211–12 Simon still held Carcassonne, Albi and Pamiers and controlled all the territory behind that rather loose front line. The Bishop of Uzès, who was a papal legate, ordered the preaching of the Crusade in northern France during the winter (Guébin et Maisonneuve 1951: 115–16) and by Easter time Simon was relieved by the arrival of fresh troops.

During the spring of 1212 Simon was able to recapture the towns and castles lost during the winter, killing defenders and destroying ramparts. By early June the army had entered the Agenais and soon reached Penne d'Agenais which was besieged and captured before the end of the month (Martin-Chabot 1973–89: vol. 1, 259). The Crusade then swept south again, this time to the west of Toulouse. Moissac was besieged and taken between 14 August and 8 September and the garrison massacred. Marmande then capitulated, so that by the end of the campaigning season only Toulouse and Montauban remained outside his grasp. The south collapsed before him as he took control of Commignes and Foix.

## Southerners and the Crusade

As we have seen, the south was far from united in its views about Simon de Montfort and the Crusade, when it first began. There were after all many devout Catholics who saw the Crusade as the answer to their prayers. In Toulouse Fulk of Marseille was able to raise a substantial party of supporters, while Albi had submitted to Simon and remained firmly committed to him thereafter. At Cahors the rich merchants were the financial backers of the Crusade. In each case the support the Crusading side received sprang from the decision of someone in authority. At Cahors the bishop was the ruler of the town and the richer merchants made common cause with him. In Toulouse the bishop was the great leader of the cité. In Albi the bishop was the effective ruler of the town (figure 6.9).

Smaller towns were more of a problem. This was because so many of them had as lords local men who were committed to the cause of the Trencavels or the House of Toulouse. These were the men who were most closely associated with heresy. The war of sieges which Simon conducted usually led to the capitulation of these places, some of which were received back by their lords as vassals to Simon. In other cases their lords joined the *faidit*, members of the nobility dispossessed by the crusaders and living as wanderers and outlaws, and the town received a new lord imposed by Simon, sometimes a southerner, but often a northerner. In these circumstances Simon found he could not rely upon the good faith of the townsmen. In September 1211 the town of Puylaurens, which had been garrisoned for Simon was delivered by its inhabitants to its previous lord (Guébin et Maisonneuve 1951: 104). At about the same time the inhabitants of Lagrave in the diocese of Albi killed the knight who had been given the place and the few soldiers he had in the castle (Guébin et Maisonneuve 1951: 114–15). Pierre des Vaux-de-Cernay made much of the treachery and cruelty of the southerners, both lords and ordinary people. He expressed surprise and outrage when the southerners showed signs that their allegiance was forced or that the behaviour of the crusaders was resented.

The general revolt of the south from late 1211 to the autumn of 1212 was led by the nobility loyal to the House of Raimon and by the town consuls who were prepared to declare for him, as at Moissac (Martin-Chabot 1973–89: vol. 1, 263). It did not include areas to the east, near the Mediterranean, nor did it include Albi or Cahors. These areas were either anti-Raymondine or too firmly under Simon's military control to take part in the uprising. The revolt marked the point at which there was a general coming-together of most southerners against the crusaders. From this time onward the south began to regard the war as one of the Languedoc against the foreign, northern invaders. Toulouse itself was to be subject to a series of sieges and actually to be occupied by the crusaders, but it never rejected the House of Raimon, even when Raimon VI himself had failed the city most miserably at the battle of Muret, where the city lost many men from its militia.

### The Statute of Pamiers

Simon was able to winter at Pamiers where he summoned many of his followers and held a *Parlement* on 1 December 1212. He had been shaken by the revolt of the towns, and especially the nobility of the south. At the *Parlement* he began to lay down rules (now usually called the Statute of Pamiers) which would make it possible to control the Languedoc, by introducing political and social structures which were similar to those found in the north of France. He also began to arrange for his followers to receive permanent holdings and so avoid problems with local nobility.

The Church received all the privileges and property which it claimed had been taken by laymen. Clergy and their lands were exempt from taxation and from secular courts. The tax 'Peter's Pence' was imposed on everyone, marking Simon's recognition of the authority of the Pope in his new dominions. All laymen were ordered to attend church regularly on pain of payment of a fine and the property of heretics was to be handed over to the Church. The right of the Church to judge heretics was recognised and heretics who had been reconciled were forbidden to live in their own towns or to hold public office. Thus heresy, even when renounced, was defined as a secular crime with secular penalties attached. Those who permitted heretics to live on their property were also to forfeit it. Jews were forbidden to hold public office.

All the northern barons enfeoffed by Simon were to owe military service to him and all their knights were to be Frenchmen. Southerners might not be employed as knights for twenty years. All lands were to be held from the count on military terms and all castles were to be yielded to him on demand. Only Simon could authorise the building of a new castle. Failure to perform service on demand would lead to loss of property. Thus Simon hoped to provide permanent military forces without having to pay mercenaries and at the same time to guarantee loyalty amongst a sea of foreigners by inserting a northern military aristocracy. The nearest parallel might be William the Conqueror's parcelling out of England among his followers 150 years earlier.

Although the peasantry were assured of their personal freedom, since they might change their lords at will, they were to lose their property when they changed. This would have destroyed the allod and reduced the peasantry to a tenantry. They were also enjoined to seek redress for wrongs in the seigniorial courts. Thus the ideal pattern of a feudal hierarchy would extend from top to bottom of society, making control much easier at all levels. Finally, the new ruler introduced a new law of succession 'according to the law of France'. This meant descent of property normally to the eldest son and the exclusion of daughters from inheritance before brothers, as well as the loss of female property rights. Those women who inherited rights to fortresses were forbidden to marry southerners (HGL 8: cols 625–35).

## The death of King Pere

The practical effect of Simon's success was to drive Raimon VI to turn to King Pere for more support. In 1204 Raimon had married Pere's sister, while his infant son had been married to Sanchia, Pere's other sister. In the same year Pere had married Marie, the heir to the viscounty of Montpellier (Belperron 1942: 57). He had interests in Foix which were now threatened by Simon. The count was the vassal of King Pere for some of his lands, which if they fell into crusader hands, would leave Roussillon exposed. Already his vassals along the Languedoc coast were overwhelmed and his new possession at Montpellier was in the process of being surrounded. The Count of Commignes and Gaston de Bearn were also vassals and they too had been attacked by Simon. Pere II was at the height of his power and prestige, having taken part in the defeat of the Moors at the battle of Las Navas de Tolosa the previous year. He had the ear of the Pope who increasingly favoured him. When the bishops of the Languedoc met at Lavaur in January 1213, Pere set out to protect the Count of Toulouse who did him homage for his lands on 27 January.

During the summer Simon devoted himself to campaigning in the Toulousain, reducing and destroying castles, but without the strength to attack Toulouse directly (Guébin et Maisonneuve 1951: 171). The situation was resolved in the autumn. In September Pere II arrived in the Toulousain with an army, in aid of his brother-in-law. The combined armies of Raimon and Pere met the crusaders near Muret, which had been garrisoned by Simon. At the battle on 12 September the superior forces of the south were betrayed by poor leadership. Simon's smaller, but much more disciplined, army won a convincing victory. Pere II was killed on the battlefield and his infant son Jaime captured in the camp. Raimon VI fled leaving large numbers of his army, including the militia of Toulouse, dead or wounded. Simon de Montfort was able to ravage Foix once more and the whole of the Toulousain except for the Toulouse itself was under his control, although Simon did not feel confident enough of his power to take the city. Raimon VI and his son spent the Christmas of 1213 in London as the guests of his brother-in-law, King John.

The practical effect of the battle was to leave Simon free to campaign as he wished. By the spring of 1214 Raimon VI was back in the Toulousain, but in hardly better circumstances than many of his followers. Despoiled of their lands many had become wanderers, living as soldiers and known as faidits. Raimon's brother Baldwin, a supporter of Simon, was captured in February, and Raimon, the Count of Foix, and Bernard de Portella, a member of Pere II's household, hanged him at Montauban (Duvernoy 1976: 87–9; Guébin et Maisonneuve 1951: 191–2). Simon was able to continue to devastate lands outside the Toulousain, in Quercy and to pursue dynastic politics by marrying his eldest son Amaury to the daughter of the Dauphin of Vienne, the brother of the Duke of Burgundy (Guébin et Maisonneuve 1951: 197). By early 1215 only Toulouse itself was outside his grasp.

## Simon and the Church

The energetic support of the Crusade by senior churchmen was of the utmost importance to Simon. The reformed episcopacy of the south stood solidly behind him. Clerics continued to preach the Crusade in northern France, providing Simon with supplies of enthusiastic and free recruits for his army. During the summer of 1211 Simon de Monfort had visited Cahors and received the enthusiastic homage of the bishop, who claimed the title of count and was the effective ruler of the town (Belperron 1942: 228–9).

In mid-January 1213 a council of the Church had met at Lavaur (Belperron 1942: 258–9), with over twenty prelates present. Much of the time of the council was spent in negotiation with Pere II, trying to persuade him to abandon Raimon VI. Pere pleaded hard on behalf of Raimon and the Count of Foix, the Count of Commignes and Gaston of Bearn. The bishops judged Raimon to have absolutely failed to address any of the errors for which he had been condemned at earlier councils. A far as the bishops were concerned the Crusade against heresy meant a crusade against Raimon VI and their stand against him was uncompromising (PL 216: cols 834–51).

Innocent III was far removed from the everyday events of the war in the Toulousain. His knowledge came through letters and messengers, often long after the events reported. This had the disadvantage that he could not be involved in immediate decision making and had to leave most to his legates. The people he had put in charge, particularly Arnald-Amalric, were southerners themselves, but men with no time for the heretics and a strong desire to see the authority of the Church vindicated. Large councils, such as that which met at Lombers, were just as steely in their determination not to compromise as any single legate. Overall, the impression they leave from their records is of remarkable unanimity and consistency of purpose over long periods. On the other hand, Innocent had time to make his judgements and could see the campaign as it was, only a small part of the overall concerns of the Curia.

During the winter of 1212–13 ambassadors from Pere II had visited Innocent and the Pope wrote to Arnald-Amalric, now Archbishop of Narbonne, in January 1213 to halt the Crusade and to seek to divert the energy of the crusaders towards the Moslems of Spain and the Holy Land. Simon de Montfort was ordered to behave properly as the vassal of the King of Aragon. This was followed by letters accusing Simon and Arnald-Amalric of having despoiled the Count of Toulouse of lands which were not tainted by heresy. The Pope was also impressed by the ambassadors' argument that the punishment of the count by loss of his lands would be a punishment of his son and heir also, which would be unwarranted (See Belperron 1942: 252–8). By the spring however he had more news of the events from the legates. This time the Pope sent a message to Pere II warning him not to support heretics, which effectively allowed Simon de Monfort to continue with his attack upon the Toulousain.

However, the result of the battle of Muret was such that the Pope realised that the war he had unleashed had changed its nature. He had set out to use the secular arm to crush a heresy: now, a king he had not long since honoured was dead and many Catholics were caught up in the destruction. In January 1214 he issued instructions which protected Toulouse from further attack. Although neither side in the war ceased hostilities, the Pope had decided that he should be the arbiter of any final settlement. The Council of Montpellier met in January 1215. There were five archbishops and twenty-eight bishops present. They decided that Simon de Montfort should be recognised as the sole ruler of the Languedoc. The legates, however, pointed out that they could not put Simon in possession of the title without consulting the Pope himself. If Innocent was applying the novel doctrine that he could depose and make secular rulers as well as prelates he was careful not to allow the power to fall into the hands of others by careless delegation (Mansi 22: cols 935–7). Innocent's reaction was to call a council in Rome. This was to be the Fourth Lateran Council.

# 7

# The Pope and the king

## At the Fourth Lateran Council

Innocent III summoned the council to meet on 1 November 1215, in the Basilica of St-John Lateran in Rome. The purpose of the council was to call a Crusade to recover the Holy Land and to reform the Church. For the first time, lay representatives of great rulers attended. They were not there to deliberate, or to give their opinions, but to hear the decisions of the council. This was not to be about the Languedoc alone, but would cover the whole range of business with which the Pope and the bishops of the Church normally expected to be concerned, matters of the faith and of the order and good government of the Church (Sayers 1994: 95–7). Innocent was becoming increasingly preoccupied with the project for a Crusade and the opening words of his letter summoning the council were about the Holy Land (Mansi 22: col. 956). If the council condemned the heretics and settled matters relating to rulers who were at odds with the Church it would clear the way for a united and peaceful Christendom to assault the infidel.

However, any gathering to which secular rulers and their advisers and diplomats had been summoned was bound to be affected by lobbying. Raimon of Toulouse, his wife and his son were all present in person as was the Count of Foix (Duvernoy 1976: 93). Simon de Montfort was not in Rome, but he had sent his brother Guy (HGL 6: 470). Raimon can have had few advocates at the council. Simon, on the other hand, had many clerical supporters. Most of the hierarchy of the Languedoc were present.

The council began with pronouncements on heresy, first that of Joachim of Fiore on the Trinity (Mansi 22: cols 981–2) and then a more general condemnation of heretics, summing up the attacks made over previous years. All of the themes of previous councils were taken up and authoritative summations issued. The Pope was anxious to settle the specific problems raised by the war in the Languedoc, since they were a hindrance to his plans for a crusade and this gave an opening for Simon de Montfort and his clerical allies to present their case. According to the *Chanson* the deliberations of the Council and the debates before the Pope were exhaustive. Raimon-Roger of Foix and Raimon of Toulouse are depicted as arguing in person. On the other side the clerics urged the case of Simon de Montfort. The part of the council which most concerned Raimon of Toulouse was contained in a brief sentence which was issued separately from the canons of the Council (Mansi 22: cols 1069–70).

The outcome was a sweeping victory for the clerical party and for Simon. Although Raimon was not actually condemned as a heretic he was nevertheless stigmatised as at least negligent over his treatment of both heretics and *routiers* (Kuttner and Garcia y Garcia, 1964: 141). Raimon was to be permanently excluded from the County, although his wife, as a good Catholic, was to hold on to her dowry. For his support he was to receive an annual pension of 400 marks. All the land taken from the heretics by the crusaders was to remain under the control of Simon de Montfort, who was to hold it as a vassal of the King of France. The land which the crusaders had not taken, including the lands in Provence, was to be controlled by the Church on behalf of the young son of Raimon, the future Raimon VII, who would receive the land when he reached his majority, providing that he showed evidence of meriting it. The Pope is depicted as being concerned not to rob the young Raimon of his inheritance (Martin-Chabot 1973–89: vol. 2, 41–89).

Bearing in mind the general feelings among aristocratic circles in Europe about the sanctity of inheritance such concern may well have been genuine. Pierre des Vaux-de-Cernay stressed the decision of the Council as being that of the greatest number and the wisest of the council (Guébin et Maisonneuve 1951: 216). This certainly suggests that views among the clerics were not unanimous and it may well be that many of them shared the Pope's reluctance to see the young Raimon disinherited and perhaps felt reluctant to see a legitimate ruler deposed. The *Chanson* however, talks of the Pope being constrained by fear of the clergy who intimidated him (Martin-Chabot 1973–89: vol. 2, 43). Raimon VI was stunned by the treatment he received. 'I am completely overwhelmed', he told the Pope, 'that there should be a single person who could tell me that someone can legally strip me of my patrimony ... and as for my son, who is ignorant of blame or sin, you have ordered that his land should be taken from him and you have agreed to his dispossession' (Martin-Chabot 1973–89: vol. 2, 80–1).

A separate settlement was made for Raimon-Roger of Foix. Simon de Montfort was to give Foix itself to the guardianship of the Church while a commission investigated the claims and counterclaims of the local clergy and Raimon-Roger. In the end, of course, it was decisions about the government of the Church and the conduct of the faithful which had the most profound effect upon men's lives, but the political decisions about the Languedoc were those with the most immediate outcome.

## In the Languedoc

In the period between January 1214 and December 1215, when the final decisions were published, the position in the Languedoc had continued to change. The Church had gained control of Toulouse, the prize most desired by Simon. Earlier, during the Council of Montpellier, Fulk of Marseille had travelled to the town and taken possession of the Chateau Narbonnais, the Count of Toulouse's palace (Guébin et Maisonneuve 1951: 209). The count himself went to live with one of the merchants in the town (HGL 6: 453). During the spring of 1215 Louis, son of Philippe-Auguste, arrived in the Toulousain at the head of a crusading force. The King of France had decided to 'stake a claim' to the Languedoc by showing a material interest in the war there. Louis, together with Simon de Montfort, moved through the defeated Languedoc to Toulouse where the consuls submitted to him. There was no question of any resistance, and they were forced to demolish the walls of the town (Guébin et Maisonneuve 1951: 209–11, 213–14; HGL 6: 462). In May the consuls took an oath of allegiance to Simon while half the consuls were delivered up as hostages. Louis did not stay long, for his visit was a more formal pilgrimage than a campaign. By the beginning of June he had begun his journey back to Paris, taking with him part of the jaw of Saint Vincent which he gave to the monastery of St-Germain-des-Près (HGL 6: 463). The Chanson claimed that his father greeted news of the success and wealth of his vassal Simon with stony silence (Martin-Chabot 1973–89: vol. 2, 37).

When Raimon VI left Rome he travelled to Genoa, where he was joined by his son. The two then sailed to Marseille and from there travelled to Avignon where they were enthusiastically received. The majority, though by no means all, of the local nobility rallied to their cause, while the towns seem to have been particularly enthusiastic. The poets of the Languedoc reacted to the declarations of the Lateran Council by writing in support of Raimon and his son. They portrayed the settlement imposed as shameful and the decisions of the Church as false. They talked of 'the French'. After the battle of Muret, Guilhem Anelier had written: 'The Church was greatly lacking in wisdom when it wished to establish the French here where they have no right to be'. It looks as if the troubadours reflected the opinions of many members of the aristocratic classes throughout the Languedoc who found the French increasingly hard to accept, especially at their moment of victory (Siberry 1985: 162–3).

While Raimon VI went off to Spain to solicit help, the young Raimon set out to regain the castles, towns and lands of the Rhone valley (Martin-Chabot 1973–89: vol. 2, 91–105). The principal object was to regain control of the castle and town of Beaucaire. Overlooking the site of the famous fair, the castle controlled progress up and down the Rhone as well as guarding the much used crossing point of the ancient Via Domitia from the town of Tarascon on the east bank of the river. The long siege was complicated by the arrival of Simon de Montfort, early in June, from northern France where he had been recognised as Count of Toulouse by Philippe-Auguste and to whom he had done homage for the county (HGL 6: 483). He besieged the besiegers and a ferocious struggle ensued which included an indecisive pitched battle. Simon was unable to prevent the fall of the castle to the young Raimon and withdrew to Nîmes. He had lost control of the Rhone valley. News arrived that the citizens of Toulouse were in communication with Raimon VI and between 25 and 28 August Simon and a small band of followers rode the 240 km (150 ml) between Nîmes and Montgiscard near Toulouse (Martin-Chabot 1973–89: vol. 2, 199; Guébin et Maisonneuve 1951: 221–2).

His swift action forestalled an attempt by Raimon VI to regain the city and as a reprisal Simon set fire to part of the town and soon overcame an attempt to defend the bourg. He completed the work of destroying the walls, pillaged and destroyed houses in the town, and took hostages from among the citizens before going off to Gascony to marry his younger son Guy to Petronilla, Countess of Bigorre, widow of Gaston VI of Bearn (Guébin et Maisonneuve 1951: 222). From there, fortified by forced contributions of cash from Toulouse, he ravaged the county of Foix and passed the winter in a savage siege of the castle of Montgrenier, near Foix, while strengthening the garrison of Foix itself in order to stop the implementation of Innocent III's ruling which gave the county back to Raimon-Roger (Martin-Chabot 1973–89: vol. 2, 258 n.4). By the spring of 1217 he was campaigning in the Termenès, capturing castles, before moving into Provence, where he campaigned around Valence capturing Montelimar and Crest (HGL 6: 493–4).

Raimon VI had spent a long time in Spain and in the autumn of 1217, after secret dealings with envoys from Toulouse, he crossed the

Pyrenees and in September re-entered the city secretly, under cover of fog (Duvernoy 1976: 99–101). The invitation to return to his city was issued by its consuls, who seem to have expressed a popular desire and he was received with joy. The townspeople set to work to fortify the town and to besiege the Chateau Narbonnais which contained the wives and young children of the entire Montfort family in the Languedoc. Raimon VI was joined in the defence of the town by many southern noblemen who had been dispossessed by Simon (Martin-Chabot 1973–89: vol. 2, 297–9).

Simon de Montfort abandoned his activity in the Rhone Valley and made a truce with Raimon VII which enabled him to march to Toulouse (HGL 7: 508). He dispatched Fulk of Marseille to France to drum up support and began a siege of the city in late September. The Pope, Honorius III, wrote to young Raimon VII to warn him not to assist his father and he also wrote to bishops in the north to urge the faithful in France to go to Simon's aid.

The siege was bitterly contested. In Toulouse, the defence by the citizens was a communal effort. The men of the city laboured at the defences and women carried stones to be hurled by hand or by machines (Martin-Chabot 1973–89: vol. 3, 15). Early in the siege Guy, the younger son of Simon de Montfort, was gravely wounded and for once the two sides seem to have been more or less evenly matched. Certainly the men of Toulouse can have been under no illusions about their likely fate should Simon succeed in capturing the city.

By the spring Fulk of Marseille arrived from the north with reinforcements. They were especially valuable for Simon because they were crusaders and therefore did not need to be paid for the first forty days. Early in May Simon began the construction of a engine destined to help him break into the city. A great wheeled shelter, known as a 'chatte', was built. Under its cover workmen would advance to the edge of the ditch to fill it with rubble and then to the wall itself, so that it could be attacked directly. Meanwhile machines for hurling stones were also built to give support to the shelter (Martin-Chabot 1973–89: vol. 3, 105). The citizens of Toulouse were much helped by the sheer size of their town and its position on a great river. Simon could not surround it; provisions could be brought in and people could come and go. A direct assault on the town was therefore the only way of taking it and Simon intended to use his 'chatte' for this purpose.

On 25 June 1218, while supervising the deployment of the engine under fire, Simon was struck on the head by a stone fired from within the town. Despite wearing an iron helmet he was killed instantly. According the *Chanson* the engine which hurled the stone had been operated by women (Martin-Chabot 1973–89: vol. 3, 207). The *Chanson* allowed him no time to confess: 'the stone arrived just when it was needed'. Simon was no hero to the continuator of the *Chanson*, who later remarked:

> It says on his epitaph, for those who can read, that he is a saint and a martyr who will rise again and have his share and flourish in the marvellous joy, wearing a crown and enthroned in the Kingdom of Heaven. As for me, I have heard it said that that may be so if, by killing men and spilling blood, causing the loss of souls, approving of murders, following evil counsel, lighting fires, ruining barons and besmirching Paratge,[1] by seizing lands and maintaining Pride, by stoking up wickedness and stifling good, by massacring women and slaughtering children, a man can overcome Christ Jesus in this world and so he can have the right to wear the crown and to shine forth in Heaven. (Martin-Chabot 1973–89: vol. 3, 207 and 229).

Pierre des Vaux-de-Cernay gave him long enough to 'twice strike himself on the chest, commending himself to God and the Blessed Virgin' (Guébin et Maisonneuve 1951: 234). Simon was succeeded by his son Amaury, who took his father's body to Carcassonne for burial, but so great was the loss of morale on the crusading side that Amaury abandoned the siege at the end of July and withdrew to Carcassonne.

Simon's energy and ability as a soldier were manifest throughout the whole nine years of his campaigning in the Languedoc. He fought unceasingly and normally with great success. He was also a devoutly religious man. Pierre de Vaux-des-Cernay makes him the epitome of noble piety with a story which makes him stay at Mass just before his death, despite increasingly urgent calls for his presence at the front line (Guébin et Maisonneuve 1951: 233). He clearly felt an unwavering belief in the justice of his cause and he was probably encouraged in that belief by local and Frankish prelates for whom every advance he made strengthened the power of the Church throughout the Languedoc. Simon himself and many of his followers, encouraged by churchmen, were able to throw off the conventions of feudal warfare. As society had developed in the north it became normal for members of the aristocratic chivalrous class not to be killed when they were defeated in battle, unless from the accidents of the battle itself. The conventions of private warfare had developed to stop the wholesale slaughter of members of the ruling group (Strickland 1992).

Rebellion was rarely punished with death. It was also rare for a fam-

---

[1] *Parage* was the term used to describe the quality of courtly, aristocratic life in the Languedoc. The Crusade had ruined the small noble courts of the south and driven many of their lords into exile, damaging courtly cultivation and manners and breaking up the network which supported this culture.

ily to lose its lands permanently. Even if a disloyal nobleman was expropriated his family would often receive the land back again when the wrongdoer was dead. In the Languedoc the local inhabitants were treated as infidels and therefore the conventions were much weakened. Still at first Simon saw many local noblemen as part of the class to which he belonged and was willing to accept them as vassals. But it took only two years of campaigning and revolt for Simon to begin to replace them with Franks. The killing of the Lord of Montréal and the Lady of Lavaur at the fall of Lavaur probably marked a turning point for the crusaders. A woman of the ruling class had been put to death with extreme cruelty and with no pretence of a judicial process because she was a heretic. This view of the southerners, as heretics who had no rights, justified a war of expropriation, blessed by the pronouncements of successive popes and urged on by local churchmen.

The disadvantage faced by the South was that, initially, it was far from united in the face of the onslaught. Although Simon and his army often treated local Catholics almost as badly as Cathars, there were always some supporters among the local population. We have seen that Albi remained loyal to Simon throughout the war, as did Cahors. The town of Moissac, firmly in the hands of its lord the abbot after its reduction by Simon in September 1212, was always available to him. Simon certainly had some members of the southern nobility on his side during the final siege of Toulouse (HGL 7: 510). Even as late as 1224 Amaury still had staunch southern supporters, noblemen such as Raimon of Capendu, Berenger of Montlaur and Raimon-Arnaud of Saissac (Belperron 1942: 356). However, the longer the war lasted the more supporters Raimon VI gathered. By the time he was invited back to Toulouse in 1217, there was no suggestion of an opposition to him within the town and its successful defence was largely the result of the determination of its citizens to resist the assaults and exactions of Simon de Montfort.

Simon had also long since alienated the citizens of Narbonne. After the death of Pere II of Aragon and the installation of Arnald-Amalric of Cîteaux as Archbishop of Narbonne it seems likely that the Viscount of Narbonne felt increasingly hemmed in by the crusaders. By 1214 Simon was devastating the Narbonnais (Guébin et Maisonneuve 1951: 192). Even the citizens of Montpellier, a staunchly Catholic city under the Guilhems, showed their hostility, refusing to allow Simon into the town during the Council of Montpellier in 1214 (Guébin et Maisonneuve 1951: 207). In the Rhone Valley, after the Fourth Lateran Council, the support for the House of Raimon was overwhelming, coming from local nobility and from the municipalities. Much of this support probably sprang from opposition to Simon de Montfort's financial exactions.

Since he had so little land in the north he had few private sources of revenue and was heavily reliant upon crusaders, who came free for the first forty days, but he also needed to maintain large numbers of paid troops permanently at work. They could only be paid for by the forced contributions from the towns, by taxes and by loans. Guilhem de Puylaurens described Simon in 1216 as exhausted by the expense of the siege of Beaucaire and lacking funds (Duvernoy 1976: 99). Once Simon was established as Count of Toulouse it became increasingly difficult to recruit crusaders and by the time of his death in 1218 many of his soldiers were unpaid. Amaury found he had no money for their wages and this was a major reason for his withdrawal.

The continuing war, the expropriation of many members of the nobility, the financial pressure on towns, above all the political settlement of the Fourth Lateran Council all combined to turn sentiment against the northerners and against the Crusade. It was only at this point that some of the troubadour poets began to criticise the Crusade. They criticised it for no longer being a crusade and reminded their listeners that the crusade in the Holy Land should now be the priority (Siberry 1985: 162–5). The sense that this was a war of northerners against southerners was very strong, and probably represented a feeling widespread among their patrons.

## The King of France in the Languedoc

By September 1218 Amaury de Montfort had decided to try to hold on to his father's conquests and he moved to Albi. This town, led by the bishop, had been consistently loyal to his father. From there he moved to secure Moissac and then into the Agenais where he besieged Marmande during the winter of 1218–19 (Martin-Chabot 1973–89: vol. 3, 253–5). Meanwhile his friends Jean and Foucault de Berzy, aided by the Viscount of Lautrec, a southerner, pillaged the Lauragais, driving off flocks of sheep as booty (Duvernoy 1976: 105). They were not alone in this, since the district had become a disputed territory between Carcassonne and Toulouse. Roger-Bernard and Loup de Foix, the leaders of a band of faidits, also swept through the countryside seizing cattle and men (Martin-Chabot 1973–89: vol. 3, 261). They were soon joined by the young Count Raimon VII, to whom his father had relinquished government and campaigning. The Lauragais, a fertile district of rolling countryside and prosperous small towns, had always been an area where the Cathars were most active and well organised. The two sides met near Bazièges in a battle won by the southerners. The Berzy brothers were captured and taken to Toulouse, where they were executed.

Meanwhile the Crusade had been preached again in the north.

Philippe-Auguste was still reluctant to get bogged down in a southern war, but when the Pope suggested that Thibaut, the Count of Champagne, should lead the campaign the king reluctantly agreed that his son Prince Louis should lead an expedition (Baldwin 1986: 338). The army from the north marched into the south by the western route and came first to Marmande. They were joined in the June of 1219 by Prince Louis. Marmande was surrendered (Duvernoy 1976: 109) and its inhabitants massacred (Martin-Chabot 1973–89: vol. 3, 291). The crusading army then moved on to besiege Toulouse but Prince Louis decided that his pilgrimage was over – he had passed the necessary forty days on the Crusade – raised the siege and returned to France (Duvernoy 1976: 109). There is a suggestion from French chroniclers that Louis was hampered by dissension among his barons, who saw little prospect of profit from the expedition. He seems in any case always to have been half-hearted about the whole project (Petit-Dutaillis 1894: 200–1). One of the companions who went from the royal court on the expedition was Guérin, Bishop of Senlis, the most trusted advisor and administrator of the king. It is possible that the king was anxious not to be drawn too deeply into the south and had sent Guérin to make sure nothing happened.

During the next two years the southerners recovered one stronghold after another. The siege of Castelnaudary by Amaury from July 1220 to March 1221 led to the capture and then the death from wounds of Amaury's brother Guy. In August of 1221 Agen declared for Raimon VII, followed by Moissac and the Quercy. By the late summer of 1223 Amaury was besieged in Carcassonne by Raimon VII and Roger-Bernard of Foix. Here he was gradually deserted by his French knights because he was unable to pay their wages. On 24 January 1224 he came to an agreement with Raimon which allowed him a truce of two months. The next day he left Carcassonne never to return, taking with him his father's body. In his place the young Raimon Trencavel, the son of Raimon-Roger who had died in prison in 1209, resumed his place as Viscount of Carcassonne and Béziers.

Other people had also left the scene. In August 1222 Raimon VI had died suddenly in Toulouse at the age of sixty-six. Unable to speak at the last, he kissed the robe of the Hospitallers, hastily thrown over him as a sign of his admission to the order. He died excommunicate and despite his son's best efforts lay unburied in the garden of the Hospital of St-John, gradually rotting away. His skull was preserved by the Hospitallers but seems never to have received a burial (Duvernoy 1976: 113). In 1223 Raimon-Roger of Foix also died. On 14 July 1223 Philippe-Auguste died at Mantes.

The new King Louis VIII immediately showed his interest in the sit-

uation in the south. Simon de Montfort had sworn allegiance to
Philippe-Auguste for his conquered lands in the south in April 1216
(HGL 7: 483) and Louis maintained that interest. It was a sign of how
the political situation in France had changed during the reign of his
father, that the first reaction of the clergy of the Languedoc to Amaury's
withdrawal was to write to the king telling him of the situation and ask
him to undertake another Crusade (HGL 7: preuve 782). The bishop of
Cahors offered his homage to the king for his County of Cahors in February 1224 and the king was pleased to accept it, giving his backing to
the bishop's attempt to recover lands taken by the Count of Toulouse
(Petit-Dutaillis 1894: 459, no. 78). The expansion of the Kingdom of
France into the south, already begun by Philippe-Auguste, was to continue. The Midi was an area of political weakness which might be filled
by the kings of Aragon or even the kings of England if something positive was not done.

Immediately after his arrival in the north Amaury ceded his claims
in the Toulousain to the king who began to plan an expedition to the
south. He wrote immediately to the citizens of Narbonne to tell them
that he was planning to campaign against the heretics in the region and
bidding them to guard the city and its neighbourhood for him (HGL 8:
col. 790). However, Pope Honorius III, probably understanding very little of the extent to which the political situation in the French kingdom
had changed, proposed in a Bull of April 1224 that the king should ask
Raimon VII to make his peace with the Church and that Raimon VII
should be recognised in exchange for promises to eradicate the heretics
and compensate the Church. The result would be that there would be no
invasion by Louis VIII. Louis's response was to call a *Parlement* in which
he publicly declared that the religious question between the Church and
Raimon was nothing to do with him, but that his rights with regard to
fiefs were. However, he did not feel strong enough to defy the Pope and
carry through his intentions (Belperron 1942: 365).

Honorius called a Council at Montpellier in August 1224, led by
Arnald-Amalric, Archbishop of Narbonne. There Raimon VII swore to
support the Church and maintain its rights, to persecute the heretics, to
confiscate their property and that of their supporters, to get rid of the
*routiers* and to maintain the Peace; all the things his father had sometimes
promised to do and sometimes refused to do and had never been able to
deliver. He also offered the Church 20,000 silver marks and the Pope
three castles as a pledge of his good faith (Mansi 22: cols 1207–8). During the autumn a group of ambassadors representing the clergy of the
Languedoc and Raimon went to Rome. The negotiations were protracted
and there were envoys from Louis VIII also present. It seems likely that

they were anxious to persuade the Pope against a recognition of Raimon. They succeeded, in that the Pope made no definite pronouncement in Raimon's favour and in the spring of 1225 sent to the French court the legate, Cardinal Romain.

Romain, whose powers covered the whole of France and the Languedoc, was charged with telling Raimon that he would not obtain absolution unless he ceased troubling the Church. In effect Romain was given *carte blanche* to deal with the affair as he saw fit, and he persuaded the king that a new crusade was a necessity. In November 1225 Raimon VII appeared before a new council held at Bourges before 14 archbishops, 113 bishops and 150 abbots. Raimon expected absolution and confirmation of his position and again gave the promises he had made the year before, while Amaury de Montfort offered the letters of Innocent III and King Philippe-Auguste, made in favour of his father. The council condemned Raimon and in January 1226 the Cardinal–Legate excommunicated him, leaving the way clear for the king to begin a crusade.

Although this was a 'crusade' Louis summoned his feudal army. By June the army had reached Avignon, where a promise of submission was withdrawn when the size of the army became apparent. A siege followed which lasted until the early part of September before the king could bring the city and its inhabitants to heel (Petit-Dutaillis 1894: 309). The legate then took possession of all Count Raimon's lands in Provence on behalf of the Pope. The siege made a deep impression on the nobility of the Languedoc and even while it continued they hastened to make their peace with the king, offering their allegiance to him. The towns were also anxious to placate him. Nîmes submitted in June (Petit-Dutaillis 1894: no. 381), as did Castres. Carcassonne, of all places, submitted on the sixteenth of the same month, and its viscount was forced to withdraw south to Limoux. Montpellier and Narbonne also sought royal protection. All the great towns of the Rhone valley were in Louis's hands by the time his siege of Avignon had ended (Belperron 1942: 371).

Neither the towns of the Rhone valley and the seaboard of the Languedoc, nor the Count of Toulouse, could look for outside help. The Pope had forbidden Jaime I, King of Aragon, to intervene, ordering him to forbid his subjects to help heretics. Raimon had only Toulouse, the Count of Foix and the Viscount of Carcassonne, and the towns of Limoux and Agen behind him. The king was able to make a progress through the Languedoc without even bothering to move his siege engines from St-Gilles. Carcassonne and other eastern towns were garrisoned on his behalf and the walls of Montolieu demolished. He left his cousin, Humbert de Beaujeu, as his lieutenant in Albi. As on previous occasions Toulouse stood out against the king and prepared to defend itself but he did not bother to approach the city for it was October and far too late in the year to begin a siege (Duvernoy 1956: 123). Instead he made his way northward through the Auvergne and died at the village of Montpensier on 8 November 1226 (Petit-Dutaillis 1894: 326).

The new king, Louis IX, was a child and the regency was undertaken by his mother, Blanche of Castile. She determined to continue the policy of support for the Church and the extension of royal power in the south, taking an aid from the northern French clergy, which had been granted for five years to Louis VIII. This provided the cash with which Humbert de Beaujeu was able to campaign in the summer of 1227, without a check from Raimon VII. The following summer Humbert spent three months in the Toulousain, close to the city, systematically destroying the vineyards, the crops and the fortified houses of the countryside (Duvernoy 1976; 131). By the end of the year it was clear that the city of Toulouse and the countryside round about could no longer sustain the war. There was no evidence that Raimon VII could defend the country against the devastation. The abbot of Grandselve, the Cistercian monastery near Toulouse, acted as negotiator. A treaty was finally negotiated in the spring of 1229 at Meaux. The Archbishop of Narbonne and the bishops of his archdiocese as well as Raimon VII and some of the leading citizens from Toulouse attended the signing. The Peace accord was completed on 12 April 1229 and on the same day Raimon was reconciled to the Church. Barefoot and clad only in his underwear he was led to the altar in Notre Dame de Paris in a ceremony, more orderly, but no less humiliating than that suffered by his father at the beginning of the war (Duvernoy 1976: 133).

Raimon promised to support king and Church and to work to stamp out heresy. He would get rid of the *routiers* and would promise not to allow public employment of heretics or Jews. He would restore Church property; he would make people pay tithes; he would pay 20,000 marks in all to the monasteries of Citeaux, Clairvaux, Grandselve, Belleperche and Candeil, and to the king for maintenance of the Chateau Narbonnais which was pledged to him as security for the Peace. He would found a university at Toulouse; he would take the Cross and go to the Holy Land to serve there for five years. Neither side – Raimon on one side and the king and the Church on the other – would molest the count's subjects because they had fought on the other side in the war.

Then followed the political and territorial dispositions. Raimon's daughter Jeanne would marry one of the king's brothers. Raimon would do liege homage to the king and would hold his lands as a fief of the King of France. In return the king would grant him the whole of the diocese of Toulouse (except for a part of the Razès), the Agenais, the Rouerge, the Albigeois north of the Tarn, and Quercy (except for Cahors). The lands which lay outside Francia, on the east side of the Rhone, Raimon ceded to the Church. In return also, all the grants made by the crown and by the counts de Montfort within Raimon's domains were cancelled and all those who had left the lands because of persecution by the Church, unless they were proven heretics, might return. (Those grants made in the viscounty of Carcassonne continued to be observed. The king was the effective direct ruler there, through his seneschal.) Raimon also agreed to destroy the walls of Toulouse and of all the major towns in his domains as well as promising not to build more castles.

The most onerous part of the treaty concerned the inheritance of the County. Only the children of Jeanne and the king's brother, Alphonse, whom she was to marry, might succeed. Failing heirs, the King of France would inherit, not a relative chosen by Raimon. At the time the treaty probably seemed the best that could be got and potentially offered many advantages. The title, Count of Toulouse, and the sovereign powers which went with it were guaranteed. The days when a count might hope to play kings one against another were gone. In any case, the English king was a shadow of Henry II his grandfather, while the King of France was immeasurably stronger than before. If independence was reduced, security was enhanced. In any case, there was always a strong possibility that Raimon VII might have a son, who might reasonably be expected to inherit before his sister.

## The failure of hope

Of all the opponents of heresy and of the House of Raimon none had been more consistent than Fulk of Marseille. As a result of the peace settlement he resumed his seat in Toulouse, but he found it hard to collect the tithes upon which he depended for an income and the restitution of which had formed part of the peace treaty. He died in December 1231, bitterly holding Raimon VII responsible for his difficulties. His successor, Raimon de Fauga, was a local man, but a member of the Dominican Order and no friend of the heretics. The papacy continued to keep a very close watch on the region. The Church continued to press for the extermination of the heretics, and the new power in the hands of churchmen, as well as the growing desire by Raimon to see some of his independence restored, made for a very uneasy peace.

The establishment of a general inquisition (1233) made relations between the disaffected and the heretical and the Church even more difficult, while Raimon was forced to support the bishops. In 1232 he and the new Bishop of Toulouse captured nineteen heretics in the mountains but the count became 'lukewarm and negligent, and was seen to be lacking in enthusiasm in the pursuit of the Cause of the Peace and the Faith'. The legate in Paris used the royal power to force the count to come into line (Duvernoy 1976: 147–9). During the next few years, as the Inquisition set to work, with the acquiescence of the count and the ultimate sanction of the authority of the crown, real persecution of the Cathars developed and much popular and aristocratic opposition to it grew.

The first open revolt came from Raimon Trencavel, the deposed son of Raymond-Roger of Carcassonne. In 1224 he had returned to Carcassonne, only to be driven out again by Louis VIII. In 1227 he also lost control of Limoux and the Razès and went into exile at the court of the King of Aragon, for whom he fought. Around him rallied the dispossessed nobility of the region, permanently excluded from their lands by the men who had been enfeoffed by Simon de Montfort.

In the summer of 1242 Raimon Trencavel entered the Languedoc, seized the castles of the central Corbières Mountains and took Alet, Limoux and Montréal. By September the rebels were hammering on the gates of Carcassonne. The *bourg* was surrendered to them and thirty-three priests massacred. The rebels besieged the *cité*. After a month the siege was relieved by a royal army and Raimon Trencavel and his chief supporters fled to Montréal where they were themselves besieged. The counts of Foix and Toulouse then intervened to arrange a capitulation which allowed Raimon Trencavel and his supporters to withdraw to Barcelona. The rebel towns were severely punished by being devastated and paying heavy fines.

Although Raimon VII had taken no part in the revolt, neither had he supported the king and the Church. He was pressed to promise that he would capture Montségur when possible and hunt down the *faidits*. In the face of this pressure he found it politic to abandon his war in Provence against Raimon-Berenger and thus attempt a rapprochement with the King of Aragon. He next decided to divorce his wife, Sanchia, who had given him only the one child, Jeanne. She was put away on the grounds of consanguinity – his father Raimon VI, had been married to Sanchia's sister – and Raimon arranged to marry the third daughter of his erstwhile enemy, the Count of Provence. This man had nothing but daughters and had married the eldest to Louis IX and the second to Henry III. Rather confusingly, this prospective bride was also called Sanchia. Although the match had support from the girl's father and her uncle, King Jaime of Aragon, the long vacancy of eighteen months after the death of Pope Celestine IV (died October 1241) frustrated the plan and the girl married Richard of Cornwall, younger brother of Henry III of England.

Raimon had hoped that he might get a male heir through a new marriage. He also hoped to begin to move into a new relationship with

Jaime of Aragon and with the King of England. Henry III had returned to Gascony in 1242 and this seemed to promise a situation of the type which had existed in the previous century, where kings might be played off one against another. For Henry III the Languedoc might provide an arena where he might embarrass the King of France by stirring up trouble. The occasion was provided by Hugh de la Marche, head of the Lusignan family and the most powerful of the lords of western France who was increasingly alarmed by the growing influence of the King Louis, whose brother was now married to Jeanne of Toulouse and had also been invested with the county of Poitou. Hugh hatched a plot for a rebellion which would draw in Henry III and the Count of Toulouse, who would marry his daughter Marguerite. However, Henry III found that his barons were unwilling to commit themselves to a war on the continent. Nevertheless he sailed to Bordeaux. The promised concerted rebellion failed to materialise and in July 1242 Henry was defeated at Taillebourg whereupon Hugh de la Marche deserted him and joined the King of France (Powicke 1953: 99–103).

Raimon VII had taken steps to make sure that the whole of the Languedoc would join him in the revolt. Many of the leading nobility of the region between Toulouse and Narbonne joined with him.[2] A sign of the confidence felt by the rebels, though not by Raimon himself, was the massacre of the inquisitors at Avignonet on the night of 28–29 May 1242 (Duvernoy 1976: 167). The murders were carried out by a group led by Pierre-Roger of Mirepoix, who had come from the fortress of Montségur, to which they returned after the assassinations. Raimon VII did nothing effective to pursue them.

The rebellion foundered on the lack of co-ordination and above all on the failure of the English king. When it became apparent that the Count of Foix had deserted Raimon and was preparing to transfer his allegiance to King Louis there was nothing left for Raimon to do but seek the King's mercy (Duvernoy 1976: 169). In January 1243 he agreed to the Treaty of Lorris in which he promised to stand by the terms of the treaty of 1229 and was allowed to resume his position as count, although he had to seize and hang those of the inquisitors' murderers he could find.

---

[2] William of Puylaurens named The Viscount of Narbonne, the Count of Comminges, Jordan de l'Isle, the Count of Armagnac, the Viscount of Lomagne, the Count of Foix, the Viscount of Lautrec and even the citizens of Albi as involved (Duvernoy 1976: 169). The standing of the rebels shows how seriously the revolt was taken in the Languedoc, but it seems that the rebels were unaware of the wider events and lacked an appreciation of the way in which the political and military situation had changed over the years.

## The chateau of Montségur

Montségur was a terrible provocation to the Church, and to the king and his local officers. In 1241, at Montargis, Raimon VII had promised the king that he would do everything in his power to attack and subdue Montségur (HGL 8: cols 1053–4). It was from Montségur that the assassins of the inquisitors of Avignonet had come and to which they had returned for safety afterwards. It was a nest of heresy which needed to be destroyed.

The castle of Montségur stands on a rocky hilltop 1,200 m (3,900 ft) high, about 6.5 km (4 ml) south of Lavelanet. There seems to have been a castrum, a fortified village, on the hilltop in the twelfth century, but it had fallen into ruin by the beginning of the thirteenth century. The castrum was apparently rebuilt c. 1204 by the lord of the district, Raimon de Péreille: 'Because of the pressing demands and requests of Raimon de Mirepoix, of Raimon Blasco and other heretics, I rebuilt the castrum of Montségur which up to then was ruinous. ... It was some forty years ago' (quoted by Roquebert 1989: 27). It was hardly possible in 1204 to forecast the war which was to erupt. It is likely that the castrum was rebuilt in response to a general feeling of insecurity. The general attacks on the heretics by the Church and the well publicised attempts to persuade Raimon VI to persecute the Cathars probably made the believers in the Mirepoix area increasingly uneasy.

Montségur lay on the edge of the territories of the Count of Cerdagne, a vassal of the Count of Barcelona, the Viscount of Carcassonne and the Count of Foix. It stood in the foothills of the Pyrenees, countryside which was mountainous and lawless and likely to be disputed in any conflict. By the time of the Fourth Lateran Council it was clearly recognised as a Cathar refuge. Fulk of Toulouse, within whose diocese Montségur stood, accused the Count of Foix of allowing it to harbour the Cathars, claiming 'that the mountain-top of Montségur had been fortified precisely to serve as their defence and that he tolerated them'. The Count of Foix replied that he was not the overlord of the castrum (Martin-Chabot 1973–89: 1989, vol. 2: 49–53). It actually stood in the jurisdiction of the Viscount of Béziers and Carcassonne (HGL 6: 768).

In the years after the Treaty of Meaux, as persecution of the Cathars became more organised, Montségur became increasingly attractive as a refuge. Raimon de Péreille came from a family of Cathars. In middle age, his mother had abandoned her family to become a perfecta, first at Mirepoix and then Lavelanet, before moving to Montségur itself (Roquebert 1989: 31–2). In the 1230s, as life became more difficult for the Cathar perfecti, Montségur developed as a refuge, so that there were always some living there, although most spent some time at least working through-out the Languedoc. From 1232 onwards the *castrum* became the seat of the Cathar bishop of Carcassonne (Duvernoy 1968). Among the population were a number of *faidits* and their families, and a garrison of ordinary soldiers. The whole group was headed by the lord of the *castrum* and his family. It has been calculated that the total population at the beginning of the siege was 361 people, including children. Of this population 211 were religious (Roquebert 1989: 358–67). They formed a considerable Cathar community, effectively defying the will of the Church and living a life independent of civil community (Roquebert 1989: 162–213). They had withdrawn into what was really the old-fashioned world of the semi-independent nobleman in his castle, surrounded by his household and supporters.

In the spring of 1243, the Archbishop of Narbonne, the Bishop of Albi and Humbert de Beaujeu, the king's seneschal in Carcassonne, set out to besiege Montségur with an army which included royal soldiers as well as levies led by the bishops and from surrounding districts (Duvernoy 1979: 289–90). The difficulty of access to the site and the size of the hilltop upon which the castle sits, made it impossible to surround the castle completely, so that starving the defenders into submission was impossible. The alternative was to attack the castle. The fighting lasted ten months. For a long time the attack was ineffective. The hill is very high and very steep. Engines of any sort were useless and it was impossible to throw missiles from mangonels far enough to reach the castle. However, during the autumn, under cover of darkness, the attackers managed to climb the sheer cliffs on the south-east and reach a subsidiary summit on which stood a tower, which they captured. This was a very hazardous exploit and William de Puylaurens reported that the soldiers who had made the climb were horrified when they saw the climb they had made: 'they saw with astonishment the terrible route by which they had climbed in the night, which they would never have dared to try in the daylight' (Duvernoy 1976: 175).

At this vantage point, still well below the castle and its village, they built engines with which they bombarded the defenders. By the middle of February 1244 the attackers had pushed forward to the barbican. At the beginning of March, Pierre-Roger of Mirepoix began negotiations for a surrender. The terms he obtained were surprisingly generous in view of the ferocity of the siege and perhaps reflected the anxiety of the king's general to keep down casualties on his own side. The civilians and the soldiers were to be allowed to leave the hill. The *perfecti*, men and women as well as the believers who had been consoled and refused to abjure, were condemned to death.

A fourteen day truce was negotiated which was to expire on 16 March. The *perfecti* distributed their money and goods to those who were to leave. William of Puylaurens reported;

> As those who were inside had no rest day or night and those miscreants could not withstand the attacks of the faithful, they accepted terms to save their lives and gave up to the attackers the castle and the robed heretics, who, men and women together, were about two hundred in number. Among them was Bertrand Marty whom they had made their bishop. As they refused the invitation to convert, they were burnt in an enclosure made of palings and posts, within which was set the fire and they passed into the flames of Tartarus. (Duvernoy 1976: 175–7)

This great bonfire was sited at Montségur itself, probably close to the bottom of the hill, where the monument now stands. The executions took place on 16 March 1244, the day on which the truce ended (Roquebert 1989: 412). There is no suggestion that the Cathars of Montségur resisted the massacre. They died secure in the knowledge that they had run their course to perfection and that they were indeed saved.

### The last act

Despite the best efforts of Raimon VII he was not able to re-marry. His attempt to marry Béatrice, the youngest daughter of Raimon-Berenger and heir to the County of Provence, was foiled by her guardians who married her to Charles of Anjou, Louis IX's youngest brother. In August 1246 Raimon Trencavel submitted to Louis IX and relinquished his claim to the viscounty of Béziers and Carcassonne. He received a pension secured on revenues from Beaucaire and followed Louis to the Holy Land. He took with him to the Crusade five knights and five crossbowmen. His rent was finally exchanged for land worth 500 livres in the Béziers–Carcassonne area. He probably finished his days as a minor country landowner. In 1332 his granddaughter lived at Cesseras, near Minerve, where some of his rents had been based (Alauzier 1950: 181).

Raimon VII had also taken the cross in 1247, but in August 1249 he was taken ill at Millau after visiting his daughter and her husband at Aigues-Mortes, where they were preparing to follow Louis IX to the Holy Land. He died on 27 September 1249 at Pris, near Rodez, aged fifty-two (Duvernoy 1976: 185). His embalmed body was taken via Albi, Gaillac and Rabastens, first to Toulouse and then by boat down the Garonne to the nunnery of Paravis and in the following spring, as Raimon had requested in his will, he was carried to Fontevrault where he was buried with the Plantagenets, his mother's family.

# 8

## The Inquisition

### Before the Inquisition

Although the war brought many Cathar deaths it did little to control the heresy. The disruptions caused by the war gave little opportunity for the Church systematically to repress heretics, and the attacks by the crusaders and their supporters related mostly to their campaigns or to fairly short periods when they occupied towns or districts. After Simon de Montfort's death and the resurgence of the power of the Raimondines the way was clear for the Cathars to continue with their practices. In addition the return of noble families who were friendly to the faith, as well as a feeling that the heretics had been vindicated by the apparent success of the southern cause, probably all helped to reinforce Catharism.

The movements of prominent *perfecti* during the years after the death of Simon de Montfort are well documented and so it is possible to trace the places where Catharism flourished. The deacon, Bernard de Lamothe, has been traced at Castelsarrasin after 1218 and then over the years up to 1226 at Villemur, Montauban, Moissac, Toulouse, Montesquieu, Montgiscard, Gardouch, Saverdun, Foix, Lanta, Fourquevaux, Caraman, Laurac, Fanjeaux, Montréal, Saissac, Verdun-Lauragais, Limoux and Pieusse. During that time (1225) he became the *filius maior* for Toulouse, receiving his new rank before a large congregation of noble ladies (Duvernoy 1979: 261–2). Similarly Guilhabert de Castres, who became the Cathar bishop of Toulouse, was first mentioned at Fanjeaux around about 1195. In 1204 he received Esclarmonde of Foix as a *perfecta* and defended Catharism in debates at Montréal and Laurac in 1207 and 1208. In 1219 he was at Dun. In 1221 he was at Mirepoix where he conferred with the Viscount Arnald de Castellbo and the Count of Pallars. By 1225 he had established a house in Fanjeaux where he lived more or less openly, while one of his sisters, a *perfecta*, also lived there unmolested (Duvernoy 1979: 265–6). In 1224 in the new town of Cordes the *perfectus* Sicard of Figueiras opened a weaving workshop, which also served as a seminary for novices (Duvernoy 1979: 261).

Depositions made by witnesses, although often made long after the events, show that the audiences for preachers were often very large and that the local nobility were prominent as protectors and supporters of the sect. In another instructive case a group of *perfectae* were shown in 1224 to be living in a monastery as nuns:

> One day my sister Peironne and I and my mother who was ill, agreed with the *perfectus* Bernard de Lamothe and his companion that we would leave Montauban. We set out for Linas where some *perfectae* were living as nuns. Peironne, my mother Astorgue and I pretended to wish to take the habit. We got the prioress of Linas and her companion (they were *perfectae*) to come and with them we left Montauban and came to Linas. While we were living there the *perfectus* Giraud Abit arrived with his companion and heard the confessions of all the *perfectae* who were in the convent of Linas, which was some sixteen. (quoted Duvernoy 1979: 258)

There were a number of other monastic establishments where similar conditions prevailed.

In 1226 the Cathars were still powerful enough to hold a council at Pieusse, a village just north of Limoux. At least a hundred *perfecti* were present who had travelled from all over the Toulousain, the Carcassonnais and the Razès. The most important act of this council was to create a new diocese for the Razès. Clearly the number of adherents in the area made such a course spiritually worthwhile and financially feasible. Benoit of Termes was consecrated as bishop for the new diocese. The adherence of the nobility, given as a reason for the success of Catharism in the region, was still widespread. Even in 1229 Raimon de Niort could maintain heretics in his castle of Luisignan. The core area of Cathar heresy was so deeply penetrated that the prospect of eradicating the heresy must have seemed doubtful. Even in the mid-thirteenth century the origins of Cathars called before the inquisitors ranged from the Pyrenees in the south to the northern Albigeois, and from Carcassonne westwards into the Agenais, with the greatest concentration in the Toulousain and Foix (Duvernoy 1985: map 29).

The Cathar church had proved surprisingly resilient in the face of so much hostility. In the period up to 1226 it was able to develop a social organisation much like that of the Catholic Church. The constant attendance of the *perfecti* on the dying, as with their orthodox counterparts, made it possible for them to receive bequests, and the system of exchange of goods for deathbed benefits which was becoming so common among the orthodox provided a source of income for the Cathar church also. In addition the faithful had become used to supporting their *perfecti*, whose needs were fairly simple. The *perfecti* also customarily worked as craftsmen or doctors when settled. It is likely that this integration of the *perfecti* into peasant and bourgeois social and economic life, as well as their connections with the aristocracy and the robust local organisation, enabled the Church to last so long once persecution became common.

The Waldensians also continued to exist as an organised group. They were heretic also and as such just as much at risk from the Inquisition as the Cathars. However, there were fewer of them. Pierre Sellan's work as inquisitor in the diocese of Cahors in 1241–2 shows him issuing a total of 671 condemnations. Of these 116 were of Waldensians, over half of whom came from Montauban (Duvernoy 1994: 87). It would be dangerous to extrapolate such figures for the rest of the Languedoc, but it does suggest that the Waldensians made up a substantial minority of the dissenting population, even in the mid-thirteenth century. Another group of Waldensians was discovered at Pamiers in 1320, having emigrated from the Jura (Duvernoy 1965: vol. 1, 25, 40–127). They seem to have affected the aristocracy of the Languedoc less than the Cathars and it may be that the lesser dependence upon them enabled the Waldensians to survive longer than the Cathars.

When Louis VIII progressed through the Midi in 1226 one of his acts was to issue a decree against the heretics in April which said that 'All heretics condemned as such by the bishop's tribunal will without delay be punished as *animadversio debita* and supporters will be branded as infamous' (Fliche, Thouzellier and Azais 1950: 300). This and other ordinances issued before his death marked the determination of the Crown to pursue the heretics. Some fled to the mountains at his approach. However, it was not until 1229 that persecution began to threaten the life of the Cathar Church seriously. In the years 1229–33 the Church reorganised its method of enquiry into heresy – the inquisition. Instead of being an *ad hoc* tribunal organised by a bishop for a particular problem in his diocese, it became an arm of the Church, with its own rules of conduct and even its own specialist personnel.

## The Organisation of the Inquisition

All of the means which were needed to pursue the heretics were available to the bishops of the south. Canon Law over the previous century had followed a consistent line in its approach to heresy, making clear the duty of the bishop, to seek out heretics and of the laity to assist in the process. This sprang from the general duty of the bishop, which he had always had, to oversee the beliefs of his flock for whose spiritual welfare he was responsible. No particular rules were laid down for the way in which the bishop should conduct his inquisitio; it was simply an inquiry in which he would call before him the accused party and the accusers and question the suspect on his beliefs.

During the twelfth century the bishops' courts developed the methods which were to be taken up and refined in the Inquisition proper. They came to rely upon written evidence and upon careful witness statements, made on oath in court, copied by a notary and signed by the witness. The ordeal was abandoned. Instead of a jury of peers the Church court reached its decision through the judge (the bishop or his appointee), aided often by expert assistants, usually lawyers and theologians. Such courts were all-purpose bodies and could deal with all the business of the Church (Le Bras 1964: 242–3). The work of canon lawyers and the decrees of the popes deeply affected these courts by providing them with new bodies of law to administer, particularly where matters of belief were concerned, and new and more efficient ways of carrying out their work. During the century both laymen and clerics became used to viewing the Church as a body with powerful judicial functions which reached almost every part of the lives of laymen as well as churchmen (Duggan 1995: 192–9). The actions of the popes, both as the source of law and of judgment, provided a powerful impetus towards making the Inquisition an effective, standardised institution with procedures recognised everywhere.

As early as 1140 Gratian had condensed many other canonists to define heresy and lay down penalties such as loss of property, physical punishment and death (Thouzellier 1968). At the Council of Tours under Alexander III, it was decreed that a search be made for heretics and when found they were to be imprisoned and their goods seized by the lay power (Mansi 21: col. 1177). Lucius III had similarly ordered each bishop to proceed against the heretics in his diocese. He or his archdeacon was to go once or twice each year to parishes where heresy was suspected and enquire either through the testimony of two or three honest people or if necessary by compelling the whole neighbourhood to testify, whether or not there were people holding secret meetings or who were known to be heretics. The bishop was then to call those people before him for examination and judgment (Mansi 22: cols 476–8). This order was repeated at the Fourth Lateran Council of 1215, with further obligations laid upon secular rulers to aid the bishop in this work (Mansi 22: cols 986–90).

The Provincial Council of Narbonne, held in 1227, was a particularly vindictive affair, beginning its decrees with one on excommunication. Canon 24 ordered that there should be someone in each parish who would report to the bishop about heretics (Mansi 23: cols 21–4). However, it was the Council of Toulouse held in 1229, under the leadership of Cardinal Romain, which really set up the machinery to pursue the heretics. The first canon laid down that in each parish there should be a committee of a priest and two or three laymen, bound by oath to seek out heretics. Both they and local lords were enjoined to seek out the hiding places of the heretics, such as cellars and isolated houses, and destroy them. Those who allowed heretics to dwell on their property were to lose it. Houses where heretics were discovered were to be pulled down. Laymen were forbidden to own the Bible, whether Old or New Testament, although the Psalter, the Breviary and books of Hours in the Latin were allowed. Translations into Occitan were forbidden. All adults were to give evidence on oath to the bishop's court and heretics were forbidden to act as doctors. Those who converted back to Catholicism of their own free will were to wear crosses on their clothes. Those who recanted only from fear of death were to be imprisoned (Mansi 23: cols 191–205). Such repressive measures were aimed as much at Waldensians as at Cathars and demonstrated the determination of the clergy to take charge of the lives of the laity.

The Treaty of Meaux had placed heavy obligations on Raimon VII to help in the pursuit of heretics and so the Church authorities were free to do as they pleased. The legate gave the lead by beginning an inquiry into heresy in the Toulouse. A former perfectus, Guilhem de Soler, who had voluntarily given up his beliefs, proved very useful as a source of information. His conversion was worth a canon's prebend. The inquiry then proceeded to use evidence given by anonymous informants. The subjects of the inquiries were constrained to severe penance (Duvernoy 1976: 139). A council similar to that at Toulouse was held at Béziers in 1232 and promulgated the same rules. At Toulouse the Council had declared that all parishioners should attend church on feast days and again the Council of Béziers issued the same ruling, insisting that parish priests should report people who failed to attend as suspected heretics (Mansi 23: col. 271).

In April 1233 Pope Gregory sent instructions to the archbishops of the whole of the Languedoc: Embrun, Aix, Arles, Vienne, Narbonne, Bourges, Auch and Bordeaux. He ordered them to hand over to the Dominicans the work of seeking out and prosecuting the heretics. He instructed the Prior of the Dominicans in Provence to chose brothers to carry on the work and told the newly appointed inquisitors to get on with their work with the aid of the civil authorities and without allowing any right of appeal. This last instruction was in the spirit of the Bull

*Excommunicamus*, issued in 1231, which – as well as laying down that heretics should be excommunicated – laid down physical penalties for heretics who recanted, but who would receive life imprisonment as their penance.

From the start the Inquisition was conceived as an emergency measure against an overwhelming danger. The inquisitors, with the aid of the secular authorities, could arrest whom they pleased on suspicion of heresy. The suspect had no rights and could be held in the bishop's or inquisitor's prison indefinitely. But the most repressive and tyrannical measures were the denial of legal assistance and the denial of a right of appeal. Lawyers were threatened with loss of their legal status if they assisted the accused (Dossat 1959: 111–19). The old bishop's inquisition was a public affair, attended at least by a number of interested clergy. The new Inquisition was essentially a closed administrative procedure, by which the accused was questioned about beliefs and actions by the inquisitor and his assistants who did not reveal the evidence to the accused. Accusers were never brought before the accused and the proceedings could be adjourned at will for indefinite periods by the inquisitor. Only at the end of the process would a final statement of guilt and of punishment be made in public. Thus the Roman Law characteristics which had become the normal practice in Church courts were extended into an administrative procedure which had no element of public justice and which left the accused with no safeguards.

The opposition to this method of proceeding was so widespread that by 1243, at the Council of Narbonne, the rules were modified somewhat (Mansi 23: cols 353–66). Only those who were manifestly and clearly guilty were to be condemned, since 'it is better for the guilty to go unpunished than that the innocent should be condemned' (c. 23), while those who converted of their own free will were to be treated leniently. The council also laid down rules about how heretics were to be recognised: did they bow to heretics; had they asked for their prayers; had they adored the good men; had they been consoled; had they received heretics, and so on. The *Ordo processus Narbonnensis* of 1244 laid down the forms to be used: letters of citation; the form of the abjuration to be used before the interrogator; formulas for interrogation and reconciliation; model letters of penitence and models of sentences to be used to release the convicted to the secular arm were all laid out and subsequently adopted elsewhere (Fliche, Thouzellier and Azais 1950: vol. 10, 335–6). By 1248–9 the first of many handbooks for the conduct of the Inquisition had been produced (Dossat 1959: 167). The *processus inquisitiones* was written for the benefit of the new Inquisition which was set up in Catalonia and it showed in brief the procedures in use: the letter to summon the inhabitants of a parish; the oath of abjuration and promise to aid the inquiry which all those who appeared were required to take; a plan of interrogation; the form of individual citations to appear; formulae for reconcilations, condemnations, sentences of imprisonment and letters of penitence; the formula for abandonment to the secular arm and the sentence of posthumous condemnation (Dossat 1971).

So the General Inquisition was established in the Midi. The use of the Dominicans as inquisitors across a wide area had already been implemented in parts of Italy and the Holy Roman Empire in the preceding three years and the various measures which together formed the working practice of the Inquisition had been gradually assembled. In the Languedoc the whole machine was set to work. The twelfth century had been a period when everywhere the legal system had developed with astonishing speed. Inside the Church itself Canon Law had been organised into a coherent body of theory and practice, while in the secular world the Church had brought about the gradual abandonment of irrational methods of judgment such as the ordeal. Everywhere courts followed practices which allowed men to know their accusers and to seek legal representation, with judgment given by men's peers. Doubtless the new rules were often ignored, and judges and jurors were often corrupt, but an ideal of justice was widely spread. Now the Church in its rage and fear cast aside the safeguards which were being developed and employed instead an administrative procedure aimed at something wider than the individual swept up by it. An apparatus of repression aimed at controlling the behaviour, the beliefs and the freedom of expression of the population was set up, tempered only by the opposition of many members of society and above all by the inability of the medieval world to make any organisation run for long with any sort of efficiency. The new Inquisition was a professional organisation set up to deal with widespread and organised 'subversion'. It was the prototype of the numerous secret police forces which have plagued Europe throughout modern times.

## The Dominicans as inquisitors

As early as 1215 Bishop Fulk of Toulouse had seen the potential of the Dominicans as a weapon against the heretics, describing them as 'preachers instituted in the diocese to extirpate the corruption of heresy, hunt down vice, teach the signs of the faith and inculcate sound morals into men' and Saint Dominic himself had certainly been prepared to see violence used against the heretics, even if he did not foresee the way in which his new preachers would be used as inquisitors. In a sermon preached at Prouille in 1217 he said that for many years I have spoken to you with gentle words, preaching, begging, weeping. But, as the proverb says in my country, 'where fine words don't help, clubs prevail'. So we will call up against you the princes and the prelates. They will gather nations and kingdoms together against your country. Many will perish by the sword, towers will be thrown down, walls demolished and ruined, and – what misery – you will all be reduced to slavery. (Vicaire 1967)

In 1221 Honorius III described the Dominicans as ordained for the repression of heresy and the reform of the Church.

Once Toulouse had fallen into the hands of the Church in 1215 it was possible for Dominic to transfer his centre of operations from Prouille to Toulouse, under the protection of the papal legate. At the same time Dominic and his small group of followers were given some property in Toulouse which gave them a permanent base (Vicaire 1964: 179). The Lateran Council of 1215 had turned the somewhat informal body of canons led by Dominic into an order. It has also been suggested that Dominic's view of the nature of his group was changed by a meeting with Saint Francis at the council. From the first it was intended that the new order should concentrate upon preaching to the faithful as well as the heretics and that it should use the weapon of poverty, much as Dominic had first done when he began to work in the Languedoc (Brooke 1970: 60). New houses in other cities in the Languedoc soon followed, since – although they needed a benefactor to provide a house – their lives of poverty required little in the way of endowment. Montpellier had a house in 1220, Narbonne in 1231 with Béziers and Carcassonne close behind. By the end of century there were forty-nine (Vicaire 1973). From the first, Dominic and his companions were clear that their work would be concentrated in the towns. The urgent task of the Church was to regain religious control of urban communities, lest they become autonomous religious entities, much as they had earlier threatened to become independent politically.

Canon 21 of the Fourth Lateran Council had placed the obligation on the adult faithful to confess their sins at least once a year. If followed through, this meant that every adult man and woman could be questioned once a year about the orthodoxy of their beliefs. The council also recognised that many parish priests were not capable of carrying out their duties as confessors, either through absence or ignorance (Canon 32). Dominic looked for well trained men coming from the new universities in Northern France and Italy, and from the beginning the Dominicans were a well qualified and highly trained group (Brooke 1970: 60). The Dominicans quickly took on a specialised role as confessors as a result of their skills in theology, teaching, preaching and disputing with heretics, so it was natural that such skills should also be turned to examining putative heretics.

In January 1234 the first inquisitors were appointed in the dioceses of Toulouse and Albi. They were all Dominicans. Other tribunals were set up at Cahors and in Moissac. The inquiries began with a period of grace during which people could confess voluntarily and then receive a lighter penance than would later be required. During these early years much attention was paid to the dead and many known Cathars were exhumed from their graves and their bodies burnt. The Bishop of Toulouse marked the canonisation of Saint Dominic on his first Saint's Day, 4 August 1234, with the burning of a sick woman who confessed her heresy to him as she lay in a fever. She was carried on her bed to a meadow outside the city and consigned to the flames.[1] At Albi the inquisitor Arnald Catala burnt heretical corpses and sent the living on pilgrimages to the Holy Land (Wakefield 1974: 141), as well as burning two people.

At Narbonne in 1234 there was a revolt against the inquisitors, and in other large towns there was widespread opposition to their activities. Already the characteristics of inquisitorial practice were established: confiscation of property and disinheritance, secret depositions, anonymous accusations, lack of the right of appeal. Raimon VII was as outraged as the citizens of the towns by these procedures and appealed to the Pope. The reaction was to order the correction of abuses, but not to alter procedures or policies in any way. In Toulouse in the autumn of 1235 the inquisitors summoned twelve people, eight of whom came from prominent consular families. This action marked the beginning of a consistent policy. It was from among the wealthy and often aristocratic Cathars that the leaders of the sect tended to be drawn, so successful pursuit of the powerful and prominent among the heretics would make it much easier to destroy the heresy among the poor.

The citizens, led by the consuls, expelled the inquisitors and then the Dominicans from the city, whereupon they and Count Raimon were promptly excommunicated by the chief inquisitor, Guilhem Arnald, who had fled to the safety of the royal stronghold of Carcassonne. The restoration of the Dominicans and the Inquisition was inevitable, given the position of Raimon VII, and the next two years saw large numbers of convictions, both of the living and the dead, partly as the result of the

---

[1] This information comes from the *Chronicle of Guilhelm Pélhissou*, a Dominican friar and inquisitor who left an eyewitness account of some of the more dramatic events at Toulouse and elsewhere in the Languedoc. His chronicle is printed in an English translation in W. L. Wakefield 1974, 207–36, as *The Chronicle of William Pelhisson*.

voluntary conversion of the *perfectus* Raimon Gros (Wakefield 1974: 145–9). The search for heretics was gradually widened to cover smaller towns and their surrounding countryside. The Inquisition, led by Guilhem-Arnald in 1241–2, visited St-Paul-Cap-de-Jour, Lavaur, Labrugière, Auriac, St-Felix, Labècéde, Castelnaudry, Laurac and Fanjeaux, the heartland of the heresy in the diocese of Toulouse (Dossat 1959: 220). It is in the context of the spreading circles of persecution and hate that we must view the murder of the inquisitors Guilhem Arnald and Stephen of St Thibéry, together with their support staff, eleven persons in all, at Avignonet in May 1242. They had been working their way through the central Toulousain in 1241 and 1242, the heart of rural Catharism and they had become the objects of extreme hatred among the Cathars of the region.

## The Inquisition at work

The failure of Raimon VII's rebellion in 1242 signalled the end of effective resistance to the Inquisition. From then on there was nothing he could or would do to impede its activities and under Jeanne and Alphonse of Poitiers and later direct rule by the King, a policy of complete co-operation with the Church was consistently pursued. In 1254 Alphonse issued an Ordinance which placed the power of the government behind the Church, while Innocent IV's Bull *Ad Extirpanda* of 15 May 1252 allowed the use of torture to extract confessions.

The volume of work undertaken by the inquisitors was enormous. Pierre Cella was at work at Moissac and Montauban between 1241 and 1243. He pronounced about 730 sentences. Bernard de Caux worked as inquisitor at Agen and at Cahors between 1243 and 1245, where his sentences included at least twenty-five condemnations leading to confiscation of goods or sentences of perpetual imprisonment. In 1245–6 he worked in Toulouse. It seems that large groups of suspects were summoned from all over the diocese to a centre set up in the cloisters of the church of St-Sernin, near which the Inquisition had acquired a house to use as a prison. Only a fragmentary register of proceedings survives but it is clear that about fifty per cent of those who were condemned came from the Lauragais, forty per cent from Toulouse itself and ten per cent from the rest of the diocese, reflecting the spread of heresy. Two hundred and three condemnations were recorded, so it seems likely that lost records would reveal many more (Dossat 1971). To achieve that many condemnations the surviving records show that at least 5,599 people were interrogated (Dossat 1959: 232) and the inquisitors may have interviewed as many as eight to ten thousand (Hamilton 1981: 42). Investigation and interrogation on this scale was unprecedented and must have struck fear into many people, perhaps helping to disrupt the networks of believers even when the heretics themselves escaped punishment by flight. The continued progresses of the inquisitors through the region added to the pressure placed upon.

The characteristics of the Inquisition as a thought police is well illustrated by the case of Pere Garcias of Toulouse. During Lent 1247 this citizen of Toulouse had a series of conversations with his close relative Guilhem Garcias, who was a brother in the Order of Friars Minor in the city. In these conversations in the convent of the order, Pere revealed himself as a Cathar believer. Naively he thought he was speaking in private to a close and therefore trusted relative. In fact each conversation was monitored by a group of friars concealed in the room above. The subsequent depositions recorded the beliefs of Pere and were used to condemn him. He seems to have fled the city and his property was confiscated (Wakefield 1974: 242–7). It has been estimated that between 1237 and 1279, when the King issued an amnesty to heretics, at least 507 condemnations were issued for Toulouse alone and in most cases this resulted in loss of property. Many others, who were condemned to wear crosses as a sign of public penance but did not suffer confiscation, probably went unrecorded (Mundy 1985: 38–46). In Limoux, a town belonging to the Count of Foix and notorious for its heresy, the inquisitors condemned no less than 156 inhabitants to wear crosses as a public penance (Dossat 1971).

At Albi, despite its support for Simon de Montfort during the war, it seems that there were many heretics. The inquisitors sent there in 1234, Arnaud Catala and Guilhem Pélissou, started by digging up and burning several dead heretics in the face of determined and violent opposition from the citizens. In 1236 they condemned and burnt Arnald Giffre who had been captured in the Toulousain, but whose execution was easier in Albi because of the support of the bishop, Durand de Beaucaire and of the king's seneschal at Carcassonne who was the real secular authority in the area. Between 1240 and 1252 some sixty citizens were condemned, though it is not clear how many were actually punished. In 1247 the bishop received authority from the Pope to remit severe punishments and a relatively mild line was pursued from then until 1271. A long vacancy then ensued before the election of a new bishop in 1276. He was Bernard de Castenet, papal diplomat from the Montpellier region who was appointed by Innocent V, himself a Dominican, using his *plenitudo potestate*.

The new bishop attacked the problem of heresy which had grown in the absence of a bishop and inquiries in 1285 began with the interrogation of Bernard Lagarrigue, who had been *filius maior* in Albi.

Inquiries extended throughout the Albigeois and involved 137 people in the Gaillac-Lautrec area, 206 from Albi and another 63 from Castres. A further inquiry lasting only a few months – December 1299 to 30 March 1300 – named 35 suspects, 25 of them from Albi. In the end 211 people were implicated, all believers, from 23 places in the diocese (Biget 1971).

The vagaries of the Inquisition in Albi, with long periods of relatively mild treatment, interspersed with bouts of real persecution, have been ascribed to the shifting political relations between the town and the bishop, who was anxious to maintain his influence against the intervention of outside powers, particularly the king's officers. Even in 1234 the rioters were members of the leading families. Most of the people prosecuted were from well to do families and were mostly lawyers or merchants, the people who made up the town government and their allies, and it was the same group who were attacked in 1300.

The inquisitorial tribunal proceeded by taking evidence from witnesses to the heterodoxy of a suspect and then confronting the individual with the deposition, not the witnesses. A deposition was then taken from the suspect, who was not allowed to call a defence, only to deny or accept the evidence quoted. It was for the inquisitors to then judge the suspect's orthodoxy. They might remand the suspect in prison or on bail for further questioning and there was no time limit on this process. Some prisoners languished for years in prison without being condemned. Some of those arrested in Albi in 1300 were still in prison, unconvicted, in 1306 (Davis 1974: 44). After 1252 torture could be used against those suspected of withholding evidence, and although it was not often used the inquisitors were not squeamish. Some of those arrested at Albi in 1300 were certainly tortured and made confessions afterwards (Biget 1971).

The inquisitors were concerned to pursue two allied objectives. The most important was to destroy Catharism as a part of the social structure and as a belief system. The second objective was to regain control of those who no longer acknowledged the Church's spiritual authority. In some way they needed to be 'converted'. The first aim was met by the widespread net which enabled the inquisitors to question so many people. The methods used encouraged early confession and denunciation of other heretics and this spread fear and disruption through the Cathar community, although it must be said that the eradication of the heresy was a very long business. The second aim was achieved through the punishments or penances offered to the repentant. It is in this light that one must judge the paradox of an institution devoted to forgiveness and reconciliation which handed people to the 'secular arm' to be burnt to death and burnt the bones of the dead. The Inquisition was the most effective weapon in an ideological war. In such a war success is not to be measured in the numbers executed. The deaths are a mark of failure and so must be kept to a minimum. Rather, the acquiescence of previous opponents, even if gained by threats and force, was to be seen as a victory since it showed the faithful and the waverers alike the power of the Church as an institution and made further opposition less likely.

The *perfecti* normally refused to lie about their faith or to equivocate and they rarely converted. Such people were nearly always burnt. Guilhelm Pélissou frequently mentions *perfecti* who escaped burning by flight, often to Montségur, and many of those burnt after its fall were *perfecti* who had already been condemned. Those believers who were slow to confess and only did so under duress and after witnesses were brought against them were condemned to perpetual imprisonment and normally to the loss of their property. Prisons at Toulouse, Albi and Carcassonne held these people, each in their own small cell. They became known as the *immurati* and were held in very harsh conditions – no light, chained and fed a diet of bread and water. Only the habitual corruption of the middle ages made it possible for prisoners to receive extra food and clothing (Hamilton 1981: 53).

Many other reconciled heretics were sent on pilgrimages. This had long been a penitential practice, but the Inquisition turned it into a punishment. Some penitents were sent to the Holy Land, but many others were sent to Compostela, Rome, Cologne or Canterbury, as well as to other, closer shrines. A pilgrimage was often a dangerous and burdensome undertaking and always expensive. One man was sent as a pilgrim to fight for seven years against the Moslems in Valencia. Many pilgrims never returned. Those who did were obliged to visit their local churches once a month, naked and barefoot to be publicly scourged (Mundy 1985: 47). The most common punishment was to be made to wear yellow crosses on the shoulders of one's garments. This made the repentant sinner highly visible and no doubt open to derision and even abuse from the faithful. It made possible the sort of discrimination already practised against Jews. The provision was so unpopular that Raimon VII was forced to issue an order to his officers in Toulouse in April 1233 requiring them to see that the orders of the Inquisition were enforced (Maisonneuve 1960: 272).

The consequences of condemnation for heresy flowed beyond the humiliations and indignities visited upon the sinner. The children of the dead were disinherited and were disqualified from holding secular office for two generations (Hamilton 1981: 55). Those imprisoned, even if they did not have their goods confiscated, sometimes saw their great mansions pulled down where they were men of substance. These were secular punishments which humiliated whole families. The statistics which survive for the activities of Bernard de Caux in the Toulousain suggest that about ten per cent of those sentenced received perpetual imprisonment and the rest other penances (Dossat 1959: 257). Later in the century it seems as if about eight or nine per cent of those sentenced were condemned to death.

It was the intervention of the papacy which tempered the zeal of the local inquisitors. Between 1245 and 1249 Innocent IV received many appeals for clemency from the Languedoc and intervened to reduce sentences. When the inquisitors sentenced the 146 inhabitants of Limoux to wear crosses they appealed to the Pope and when he suggested that the penalty be reduced the inquisitors reacted by remitting the penances entirely and withdrawing from inquisitorial activity. The duties were taken over by local bishops and it was not until the accession of Alphonse that the Dominicans were recalled (Griffe 1980: 88–9).

## The Cathar response

Despite the growing persecution the Cathars remained a substantial and resilient minority in their heartland between Foix and Toulouse for some years after the fall of Montségur (figure 23). Seven deacons were still at work there in the late 1240s (Duvernoy 1979: 300) and it has been suggested that during the period 1241–54 there were perhaps 1,500 *perfecti* at work in the Languedoc. But during the next fifty years the position changed dramatically so that by 1300 there were probably only fifteen or sixteen active (Duvernoy 1985: 31–2).

We have already seen that part of the Cathar response to persecution was to riot and take up arms against the inquisitors. The believers were not forbidden to fight and the experience of the Crusade had made people very ready to turn to violence. At Roquefort the women of the community rescued two *perfectae* who had been seized by the agent of the abbot of Sorèze, beating him with sticks and stones and defying him when he tried to get the local lord to help.

Some *perfecti* were reconverted to Catholicism. Pierre Doat of Caraman had returned to Catholicism by 1256. The deacon of Laurac, Arnald Pradier, did the same in mid-century as did Sicard de Lunel. Such conversions were often devastating for the Cathars, since conversion nearly always led to the denunciations. Sicard de Lunel denounced several noble families in this way. He worked as an agent of the Inquisition until 1284. He and other apostates only survived in the Languedoc with the protection of the Church and civil authorities. Stephanie de Chateauverdun and

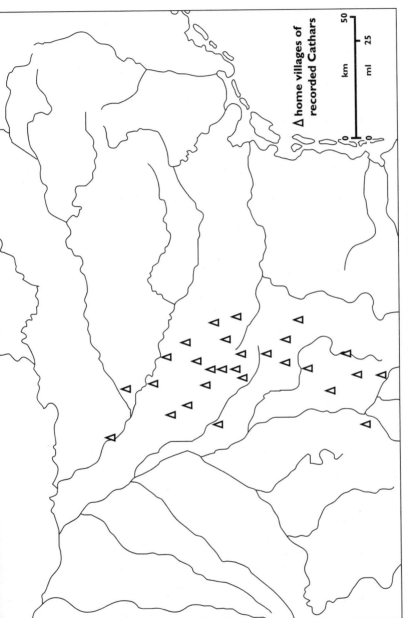

Figure 23  Catharism in the mid-thirteenth century. *Original map based on Duvernoy 1979: 230–2*

△ home villages of
recorded Cathars

km
ml

0    25    50
0

her husband Arnald Pradier were living in the Chateau Narbonnais when they visited there a prisoner held in chains, who had attempted suicide by running his head against the walls of his cell (Duvernoy 1979: 300–1).

Another response was to flee. Writing in 1250, Rainerius Sacconi, the Italian Cathar turned Dominican reckoned that the Cathar Church in the Languedoc numbered about 200 people and that the total number of Cathars in Europe, including the Byzantine Empire was less than 4,000. He presumably meant *perfecti* (Rainerius: 337). If so he was probably over-optimistic.

Some believers, including *perfecti*, began to leave for Lombardy after the Treaty of Paris and as persecution intensified it became a common way of avoiding capture. Cremona, Piacenza, Pavia, Alexandria and Verona all had colonies of Occitanian refugees (Griffe 1980: 121–35). Here small groups of believers gathered around *perfecti*, providing mutual support and a welcome for newcomers, as well as a group from which people might return to Languedoc. The tradition of refuge in Lombardy remained strong and continued into the early fourteenth century. Typical of the way in which Cathar sympathisers left the Languedoc was the case of Ponce de Gameville who left Toulouse in 1273, with his wife and children, to go on pilgrimage to Our Lady of Vauvert, near Nîmes. From there they fled to Italy (Dossat 1980). At that same date the depositions before the Inquisition in Toulouse revealed that many others from the city had also gone to Italy. Some had gone in organised groups. Most had sold up and taken their capital with them to live in modest circumstances in exile. Some Cathars fled to Aragon, but that was a less sure refuge than Lombardy, since the Inquisition was established in Barcelona in 1233, and in 1238 its authority spread to Castille, Leon and Navarre (Maisonneuve 1960: 275).

Those *perfecti* who remained lived as fugitives, hiding in woods and caves or in the houses of sympathisers, supported by their gifts and moving with guides only at night. During the Crusade artificially constructed cellars or caves hidden in the woods existed. The testimony of Philippa d'Albiac given at Toulouse in 1223 showed that her husband had rented some land in a wood to two *perfecti* who had worked the land and had built a cave or cellar to hide, which she, her husband and children had used as a refuge for three weeks, during an invasion by the crusaders (Duvernoy 1994: 226). Guilhem Fortis of Montaillou, testifying about events at the end of the thirteenth century, recalled visiting a house where someone had just died. He was asked, 'Would you like to see Pradas Tavernier, who is one of the good men?' When he said he would, the lady of the house opened the door to a room and out came two men.

They were two *perfecti* who had come secretly to administer the *consola-mentum* to the man who had just died (Duvernoy 1965: vol. 1, 443). At about the same time Alzais of Le Pech in Ariège recalled giving food to a *perfectus* who was hiding in a nearby house (Duvernoy 1965: vol. 1, 482). Bernard Marti from Junac, the brother of a *perfectus*, speaking of the early years of the fourteenth century, described meeting *perfecti* in a stable. He also described night-time journeys through the mountains with the *perfecti* as they were passed from one safe house to another.

Other *perfecti* made the journey to Lombardy only to return. In the last quarter of the century many made tours to preach and to console, sometimes returning again to Lombardy, sometimes being captured. Guilhem Pagès of La Tourette returned from Lombardy in 1262 and consoled a long list of nobility and clergy. Frère Isarn de Canois, a former Catholic priest, consoled the Prior of Mas-Cabardès and later a canon of Carcassonne, Guilhem-Arnald de Morlane. The brother of the prior, Arnald Morlane, rector of Pennautier, was consoled round about 1284 by two anonymous *perfecti*. Pierre Authié , a former lawyer and confidant of the Count of Foix, returned from Lombardy in 1300, stopping at Ax to speak to the believers in the town and then moving on to Toulouse. Along with a small group of other *perfecti*, including his son, he spent the next few years working throughout the region. His influence was considerable. New converts were made everywhere, but the point has been made that the new Cathars were from a different social group from the earlier generation. There seem to have been few from among the merchant classes in the towns or from among the nobility in the countryside. Instead the new believers were peasants and small rural and urban craftsmen. In 1308 the inquisitors used an informer to penetrate the group and arrested the entire population of the village of Montaillou. Many of the *perfecti* who were companions of Pierre Authié, his son included, were rounded up and executed. Captured in 1309, Pierre was condemned by the Inquisition in Toulouse and burnt to death on 9 April 1310 (Duvernoy 1979: 325–31).

Between 1308 and 1321, 25 believers were burnt to death, almost all in Toulouse. Three more were burnt to death at Carcassonne in 1329. The last *perfectus* to be burnt was Guilhem Belibaste, who was captured in 1321 and was executed at Villerouge-Termenès, at the castle of the Archbishop of Narbonne (Duvernoy 1979: 332–3) (figure 24). Sentences were passed on the heretics of Limoux by Bernard Gui in 1308 and 1313 and the bones of heretics were burnt at Carcassonne in 1318 and 1324 (Biget 1985: 315–16).

Many other believers were sent to prison, mostly in Carcassonne as the Bishop of Pamiers, Jacques Fournier, went about the work of

destroying the Cathar community at Montaillou and in the country round about. The Cathars he examined were mostly farmers and their relatives, shepherds who worked in the Pyrenees and Spain. The registers of Jacques Fournier show the faith deeply embedded in the family structure of the peasant communities of the mountains. But although their beliefs were often quite coherent they lacked the educated elite which alone could preserve their faith. Without the perfecti they were bound to disappear.

The destruction of Catharism was a long, slow process. Undoubtedly, the resistance of Raimon VII to the Inquisition and the opposition of the counts of Foix helped to protect the heretics. The advent of royal power, first in the diocese of Carcassonne, then in the county of Toulouse and finally after 1308 in the county of Foix, allowed the Church a free hand to pursue its enemies, despite the resistance of the countryside. In the last quarter of the thirteenth century the nobility finally fell away from Catharism. It seems likely that the lack of noble support damaged the faith by cutting off access to funds and material support for the perfecti and by removing the social influence which gave protection to individuals. In the towns, particularly Toulouse, the movement was all but extinct by the end of the century. The heresy had been strong in the city at a time when Toulouse was at its most independent. The rule of Alphonse of Poitiers and then of the king curbed that independence and allowed the Church into the fabric of town society.

In Albi, Toulouse and Narbonne the townsfolk started by revolting against the Inquisition, which used methods of procedure so unlike those normally used in the towns. An alternative and powerful jurisdiction had been introduced, which rivalled and soon overtopped the native power of the consuls. Once the political independence was removed, the town became a dangerous place for dissidents in which concealment was difficult (Biget 1985). Without the town's rulers to protect them, the artisan heretics were bound for extinction. The base in exile had also become less sure. After 1270 the rising power of Charles of Anjou and the Guelf party gave the Church and the Inquisition more influence and made Lombardy less secure (Manselli 1985). By the early fourteenth century the Cathars of the Languedoc were becoming isolated and poor. That was the mark of their decline. Their destruction was caused by the methodical pursuit of the Church with its new weapon, the Inquisition, supported by the secular government, now firmly behind the Church.

# 9

# The Languedoc as part of France

## The King's government

The death of Raimon VII brought about the integration of his county into the kingdom of France, but the king's control of the Languedoc had been advancing steadily ever since the siege of Avignon in 1226. Nîmes, Toulouse, Castres, Narbonne, Albi and Montpellier submitted to him almost immediately, as did many local noblemen (Petit-Dutaillis 1894: 501–3). These acknowledgements were of enormous importance to the royal government, since they provided precedents which would make it very difficult for citizens of the towns or for noblemen to resist in the future.

Carcassonne was placed directly under royal control by the appointment of a seneschal, who acted as the military governor of the viscounty and who worked in conjunction with his colleague the seneschal at Beaucaire, who controlled the Rhone Valley. The abortive attempt to recapture Carcassonne by the last Trencavel led to his submission to the king in 1240 and the final acknowledgement that the viscounty was lost. The king assumed his title and powers (Alauzier 1950). During the period prior to Louis IX's assumption of power there is evidence that the government officers in the Béziers–Carcassonne viscounty used their authority to enrich themselves and allowed their junior officials to do likewise. Since they had all paid for their offices the cost, and a good profit, had to be obtained by extortion. Taxes were arbitrarily raised and the courts used to extort money. The complaints of injustice which reached Paris paint a very black picture, suggesting that the seneschals and their officials behaved as conquerors (HGL 7: 467–70). It was not until after 1254, when Louis IX issued an Ordinance and appointed *inquisitores*, sent from the north that the problem was controlled and the complaints died down (HGL 7: 464).

French control over the town of Toulouse was not established until the death of Raimon VII, but by the end of 1249 royal commissioners were receiving oaths of loyalty to the new Count Alphonse from citizens and nobility in Toulouse and other major towns and during the next twenty years the county continued to be administered on his behalf. Alphonse and his wife, died childless, within three days of one another, in 1271 and the county reverted to the King of France, as provided in the Treaty of Meaux. His officers proceeded to take oaths of fealty and homage from towns and villages and from noblemen throughout the whole of his new territory (Bisson 1964: 171–85). These oaths undoubtedly had a strong political as well as psychological effect upon those who took them, since they were a public recognition of the legality and legitimacy of the new government. Neither were they a mere formality, since many of the towns insisted on recognition of their rights and privileges before they took the oath, or reserved matters of contention for negotiation.

The work of governing the new territories was deputed mostly to northerners, though in the Toulousain many of the Raimondine officials continued to serve. The king used the existing system of vicars and bailiffs, led by seneschals in Toulouse, Carcassonne and Beaucaire, appointed for a term of three years each, but filled the offices with Frenchmen (Armengaud et Lafont 1979: 336). This meant that local nobility were generally excluded from the government of the Languedoc. What the nobility lost was autonomy, since the new northern government now pressed in upon noblemen who had previously acted almost like independent rulers. Most affected by the loss of status were men like the viscounts of Narbonne, who had been sovereign within their territories. Narbonne, having submitted to the king, continued as a self-governing entity under its viscount, but he had lost the power to behave as a sovereign prince.

In the twelfth century his predecessors had chosen suzerains who protected but did not dominate them, playing off the counts of Barcelona against the counts of Toulouse. By the mid-century the viscount was treated as merely one of the nobles of the region, summoned to consult with the seneschal on the king's business at Narbonne, Carcassonne or Béziers as the seneschal thought fit (Bisson 1964: 187). In 1258 the kings of France and Aragon came to an agreement in the Treaty of Corbeil, concerning territorial disputes in the region (HGL 6: 858–61). The viscounts could never again think seriously of changing allegiance. In 1271 Aimeric of Narbonne refused to do homage to anyone but the King of France in person. It was an empty gesture. The viscount was required to summon the consuls, *consilium* and *universitas* of the citizens of Narbonne to take the oath to the king, promising to aid him, even against their lord. They swore (Bisson 1964: 166). The viscount's appeal to the King of Castile in 1275 was futile.

## The southerners

The Peace of 1229 had annulled the grants made by Simon de Montfort in the Toulousain. In the king's new territories of Béziers–Carcassonne such gifts needed his confirmation. Many members of the southern nobility who had been most fervently opposed to the Crusade and who had become *faidits*, were still dispossessed in 1258. The settlement of that date allowed those who had played only a minor part in the revolt of 1240 to recover their lands and granted them an amnesty, but after so many years the recovery of all their lands was impossible. Most found their properties much reduced and few were able to regain all they had lost. In addition most had heavy debts (HGL 7: 543–6).

The best known example is that of Olivier de Termes. Born in 1197, he was the son of the Cathar lord of Termes, so notorious as a heretic, who was dispossessed by Simon de Montfort in 1210. The young Olivier grew up as a Raimondine and became a *faidit*. In 1228 he was reconciled to the Church and remained a Catholic thereafter. Politically he remained a southerner and he took part in the attack upon Carcassonne in 1240. Excommunicated in 1242, he was not reconciled until 1247. Thereafter he fought in the Crusades with King Louis and he received back his father's lordships and territories of the Termenès and Aguilar, although not the castle of Termes. It was Olivier who conducted the siege of Queribus in 1254 and received its surrender in 1256. In 1264 and again in 1267 he went crusading. In 1270 he was present at Tunis and he set out for the Middle East for the last time in 1273 with a force of twenty-five knights and one hundred crossbowmen. He died there in 1275 (Peal 1986). He sold almost all his recovered lands to the Cistercian monastery of Fontfroide in order to pay his debts and meet his needs as a crusader.

His ally and vassal Guilhem de Minerve also lost his lands after the fall of Minerve but was compensated with land near Béziers. Although reconciled to the Church he too fought for the southern cause. His son Guilhem also later came to an accommodation with the king and went off to the Crusades. In 1254 he accepted a rent of 50 livres assigned from lands confiscated from his father. He had married Olivier's sister Blanche (Barber 1990: 18).

The Lord of Anduze, a close ally of Raimon VII, lost his chief lordships of Anduze and Sommières for his part in the revolt of 1242 and was forbidden to set foot in them (Armengaud et Lafont 1979: 337). William de Peyrepertuse ceded his castle and lands in the Corbières and received a pension in exchange. In all four cases the power and wealth of the families, although they survived, was severely reduced. By 1270 most of the greater vassal families of the twelfth century had disappeared, either from failure of male heirs or through poverty.

The nobility, in losing their autonomy, also lost their culture. It was difficult for the life of the roving troubadour to go on when the castles which had sheltered him were in the French king's hands or the families who had patronised him were in reduced circumstances. The noble culture of the Languedoc had rested on the brilliance and independence of the individual noble courts, led by the court of the counts of Toulouse. Alphonse and his wife lived mostly around Paris and did not visit the Toulousain. Alphonse was in any case a foreigner. Patronage at the highest level was gone and the connections with the equally brilliant court in Barcelona were made more difficult by the severing of connections between the Languedoc and Aragon.

## The northern landholders

Some of the northern soldiers and their descendants, who had come to the Languedoc with Simon de Montfort, continued to hold land in the Razès and the Carcassonnais in the thirteenth century. Guy de Levis, one of the closest supporters of Simon and Amaury, kept Mirepoix and extensive lands in the area. Philippe de Montfort, son of Simon's brother Guy, became lord of the southern half of the Albigeois and other senior Montfortians received rents or in some cases estates.

The northern French inheritance customs, the 'coutume de Paris', were applied within the *senechausées* of Carcassonne and Béziers. This was where most land had changed hands as a result of the fighting and where the northerners remained most firmly entrenched. Outside in the County of Toulouse and Foix it did not impinge upon noble life (Timbal 1950). However, there were a considerable number of northern Frenchmen, foreign in local eyes, now holding land in the Languedoc, and further disrupting the southern aristocracy who had never, even at the height of the fighting, been unanimous supporters of the Southern cause.

## The king and the towns

The large number of towns in the Languedoc posed especial problems for the king's administration. The twelfth century had seen towns such as Toulouse and Béziers develop their own governments and treat with rulers on equal terms. Security dictated that the king should control them more thoroughly than his predecessors had done. At Toulouse the power of the town had been checked by Raimon VII, but revived as his political fortunes waned. When Alphonse of Poitiers succeeded his father-in-law he was able to pursue control of the city government unimpeded (Mundy 1954: 160). The king's seneschal came to choose the twelve consuls from a list of twenty-four presented to him by the outgoing consuls. At Nîmes, by 1240, the seneschal chose the consuls. As with the nobility, towns did not adopt a universally hostile attitude to the French during the war. Local politics were always very important and often affected the decisions taken by the consuls. After the accession of the king, with heresy increasingly unimportant, the towns were mostly disposed to think in terms of their economic advantage. The growth of opposition to the rule of the consular oligarchies by the urban poor, in the later part of the century at Agen, Albi and Montauban, made control much easier for the king since his officials were the only authority which could support the wealthy in their privileges (Armengaud et Lafont 1979: 339–40).

The rejuvenation of the economy needed peace and this at least the kings of France could provide. After 1241 Henry III of England had little opportunity to interfere in the Languedoc and in 1259 he made a permanent settlement with Louis IX (Powicke 1953: 126–7). The power of the French crown meant that the routiers were no longer a problem, so that, with outside interference reduced to a minimum, it was possible to maintain internal order. The old established towns of the Midi continued to grow as their trade and manufacturing expanded. Montpellier seems to have had a population of at least 30,000, perhaps 35,000, by the later part of the century, with places like Toulouse, Béziers and Narbonne not far behind.

The towns themselves prospered as a result of the peace which now existed. The movement towards the foundation of many new towns throughout the Languedoc pointed to the perceived wealth to be made, as well as to a rising population which could fill them (figure 25). One of the earliest of foundations was Cordes, in 1222. Planted north of the Tarn, in the northern Albigeois, which was to become a part of the territories of the counts of Toulouse, it was clearly aimed at asserting the power of the Raimondine family in that area. It provided a new focal point for trading and proved far more successful than some of its later rivals. The size of the town houses of the later thirteenth century which still survive there attests to the wealth and success of its merchants.

Many powerful groups co-operated in the foundation of towns. In alliance with Count Alphonse, the Cistercian abbey of Bonnefont founded the bastide of Carbonne in 1256 through an agreement of paréage – an agreement to share in the expense and the profits of the new town. While the abbey provided the site and much of the capital, the

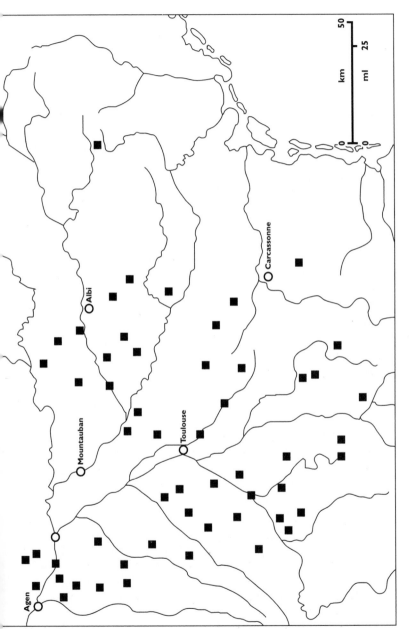

Figure 25  Bastides in the County of Toulouse and Sénéchausée of Carcassonne

count provided the legal backing which gave the new town its privileges. During the rest of the century this partnership continued with the Cistercian abbeys of Cadouin, Belleperche, Combelongue, Grandselve, Gimont, Berdoues, Nizors, Feuillant and Bonnefont all founding towns in conjunction with the seneschals of the Agenais and the Toulousain. The movement continued until 1325 and produced twenty-eight new towns in the Languedoc, mostly in the western Toulousain and the Agenais (Higounet 1950). Meddling in such an enterprise might seem to run counter to the Cistercian ideal of withdrawal from the world and from day-to-day administration, but the foundation of towns, by providing chiefly cash rents, avoided the need for close day-to-day seigniorial supervision, and may have helped to counter a crisis caused by the fall in the number of *conversi* available to work rural estates. The abbey of Gimont, whose lands lay to the west of Toulouse, founded Francheville in 1266 and St-Lys in 1280, both on land belonging to its granges and both to exploit the growing population and agricultural output of the region (Lacaze 1993: 182).

A curtain of bastide towns was founded in the Agenais during the second half of the century, some with the aid of the Cistercians and the Premonstratensians, but many others in conjunction with other lords. St-Foy-la-Grande in the Dordogne was founded in partnership with the Benedictine abbey of Conques by Alphonse in 1255. During the rest of the century and into the fourteenth century, towns were founded in a great sweep of territory, from the Dordogne almost to the Pyrenees. When Alphonse and Jeanne died in 1271, Philippe III took over the Agenais, despite its being an English fief, and continued the construction of towns (Higounet 1948: 113–31). These mostly profited the English King, since the Agenais was returned to him in 1279.

A similar group of bastides was founded along the border between the Carcassonnais and the Toulousain. Thus Mazères-sur-l'Hers was founded in 1253 by Roger IV of Foix on land belonging to the Cistercian abbey of Boulbonne. La Bastide de Bousignac, La Bastide de Lordat and Villeneuve de Pareage were founded to exploit the still largely unpopulated lands of the Ariège and the Hers, also part of Foix. Raimon VII built the new town of l'Isle and the seneschal of Toulouse, Sicard Alman built St-Sulpice where the Agout joined the Tarn in 1241. At Carcassonne the inhabitants of the *cité* after the revolt of 1240 were resettled in a new *bourg* below the city. In 1262 they were moved to another new town, on the site of the present town of Carcassonne. About forty-five bastides in all were founded (Higounet 1948–9: 359–67).

The most famous of the king's foundations was Aigues-Mortes, planted in 1241 in the marshes of the Rhone delta. The new port was

intended as a supply base for Saint Louis' crusading activities and this it
certainly was. It was also a potent symbol of the political and economic
position. The King of France at last controlled an outlet to the Mediterranean.

The new town foundations of the Languedoc were only part of the
much wider movement of foundation which occurred all over France in
the later thirteenth century. Its motivation was three-fold. Firstly it provided the founder with the prospects of increased revenues through
taxes and the possibility that the new merchants would become rich
enough to act as bankers for the founder. Secondly the townsmen could
be allies against the possibility of local noble disorder. With charters
granted by the count or the king the citizens would look to him for
political guidance, rather than to a local nobleman (Beresford 1967:
361–3). A third motive may have been to gain more effective control
over country dwellers. Not all bastides were founded in under-populated
regions. Some at least were formed by gathering scattered populations
together, rather than by attracting new settlers from elsewhere (Berthe
1990). The spread of these new settlements across the Agenais and into
the lands between Carcassonne, the Toulousain and Foix may point to
areas which were the least densely settled and exploited but it is also
apparent that it represented a re-ordering and resettling of population
under tighter control than hitherto. Some of the foundations were urban
in character, with merchants and trade, others more agricultural. All had
the intent that they would exploit the rising population more fully.

During the thirteenth century the manufacturing output of the
towns grew as the trade between the Mediterranean and northern and
western France and the north, England and Flanders, grew. Cahors,
which had always been an important banking centre, expanded its activities and its moneylenders were to be found in Gascony and England
(Lewis 1980). It is clear that there was sufficient surplus capital for it to
be invested in loans to foreign kings – a high risk venture. For a few
years, before the Straits of Gibraltar became safe for Christian sailors and
merchants, the Languedoc, either via the Rhone valley or through Carcassonne and Toulouse, provided the trade route from the Mediterranean to the Atlantic and the North, and was able to take advantage of
that situation.

## The countryside

The evidence which survives for the countryside, outside mountainous areas, suggests that, freed from the constraints imposed by
incessant warfare, the development of population and countryside followed a path very similar to that in other parts of western Europe. At

Caignac in the Lauragais, south-east of Toulouse, on lands belonging to the Knights Templar, the arable was expanded so that by the mid-thirteenth century even unsuitable stony soils were being cultivated, while woodland and waste were converted to arable. The cultivation of grain and vines predominated and capital was invested in the construction of mills, four new ones being built between 1280 and 1290, and barns to accommodate the increase in produce (Partak 1985: 6).

The expansion of cultivation was the result of a growth in population and there were consequences for everyone who was a tenant. Demesnes were reduced in size and often let as it became easier to draw increasing rents. Tenures which included labour services were common and many members of the petty nobility sold their small freeholds. Rents were high and burdensome (Partak 1985). The Cistercians of Grandselve were able to develop a well balanced agricultural regime on their granges, dominated by the rearing of animals but also producing cereals and wine. They seem to have continued to farm their lands directly, presumably because this gave the best returns in an economy where the price of agricultural goods was high; but by the end of the century they were also letting small plots of land to peasants from nearby villages, a sign of the land hunger which affected the secular world (Mousnier 1983: 25).

Tenancies involving metayage, a system of share cropping, also became more common, as landlords were able exploit the land hunger of peasants by extracting a major part of the output of holdings. In the Béziers–Carcassone area there are signs that a real crisis of overpopulation was near after the middle of the century. In 1269 the consuls of Narbonne asked the seneschal to forbid the export of grain, which he did, and the ban was renewed in 1271, when the harvest was reported as bad, and in 1272, 1274, 1289, 1304 and 1310. There is some evidence of bad weather causing poor harvests, but the need for the ban points to the increasing difficulty of supporting the growing population (Bourin-Derrau: 205–6).

## The Church

The organisation of the church was permanently influenced by the events of the Crusade. The diocesan structure needed reform if the Church was to exercise real influence in rural areas, while the growth of population, particularly in the towns, made new dioceses necessary, but it was a long while before changes were made. Not until 1295 was a new diocese carved from the southern part of the Toulouse diocese to make a new bishopric at Pamiers, essentially a bishop for Foix. In 1317 Pope

John XXII made the existing diocese of Toulouse into an archbishopric and created new sees at Rives, Montauban, from territory taken from the Cahors, Mirepoix, St-Papoul, Lombers and Lavaur (figure 26). The diocese of Albi was also divided and a new bishopric created at Castres and another bishopric was carved from the Archdiocese of Narbonne at Alet-les-Bains (*Gallia Christiana*: vol. 1, 6, 13).

The mendicant orders, the Dominicans and the Franciscans, both became powerful in the Languedoc from an early date. We have already seen that the Dominicans began in the Languedoc and that they gained a pre-eminent position as inquisitors. They established houses at Montpellier in 1220, at Narbonne in 1231 and soon after at Carcassonne and Béziers. By 1295 the number of houses in the Languedoc had reached forty-nine (Vicaire 1973). The Franciscans had a house at Montpellier by 1220, Lavaur by 1226, by which year they had also reached Toulouse, and Lodève by 1227 (Durieux 1973). By the end of the century there were actually more houses of Franciscans than Dominicans in the Languedoc (Wolff 1969: 126). Both groups settled in the towns, for it was there that they could preach to the greatest number and where they were most urgently needed to supplement the work of parish priests and other secular clergy.

The Franciscans were particularly popular because their adherence to the ideal of poverty was at first so strong. They provided a perfect exemplar of the life of Christian poverty to which the Cathar *perfecti* aspired and were thus a powerful weapon among the Catholic Church's counter-measures. The two groups filled the need for orthodox preaching which had been so great and the structures of surviving churches bear witness to this. The great church of the Jacobins in Toulouse is unlike any other building of the period in the city. This huge brick hall has a row of vast columns down its middle which obscures the view of the altar in the eastern apse. But this device, by holding up the vault, serves to make the room shorter and wider, without side-aisles, so that the preacher is audible to the congregation. Thus the urban mob could be reclaimed for the Church, or at least controlled.

Education and control of the clergy were also important to the Church. When Dominic sought new, well educated members for his order of preachers, many men came from the Italian cities, products of the new universities. During the thirteenth century there is some evidence that the standards of the parish clergy were rising, in Toulouse at least. Most of the parishes in Toulouse had church schools by the mid-century. However, the churches of the city had always been the preserve of the well to do and often provided men who later filled important administrative offices in the local church (Mundy 1990). Raimon VI was

Figure 26  The cathedral of Lavaur

obliged by the Treaty of Meaux to found a university at Toulouse by supporting Masters of Theology, Law and Grammar for ten years.

The university was first endowed in 1229, with four theologians, two canon lawyers, six liberal arts lecturers and two grammarians (the theologians were the best paid), who were recruited from Paris. The university was supervised by the bishop and by the chancellor of the Cathedral and like other universities it was intended to train the new priests and other officials now needed by the Church with its new bureaucracy. The statutes were regulated by Gregory IX in 1233, but two years before, one of the theology lecturers, Roland of Cremona, led a group which dug up and burned a recently buried priest, known to have been a heretic. Roland was forced to leave Toulouse soon after. The new university struggled with lack of resources and it was not theology, but law, which became the pre-eminent study in the thirteenth century (Wolff 1961: 110–17). At Montpellier there had long been a famous school of medicine, officially recognised in 1181, which was regulated by the legates in 1220, and a school of law from the late twelfth century also. These two disciplines provided the core from which a university finally emerged in 1289, under the control of the bishop of Maguelonne (Bories 1970).

At the level of the parish the victory over Catharism also meant a tightening of the hold of the Church over the lives of its parishioners. At least in Toulouse, a canon was promulgated which made wills void if not made in the presence of a clerk, normally the dying person's parish priest (Mansi 22: col. 198). The grip of the Church over testamentary matters was thus strengthened and testators were forced to include bequests to the Church in their wills. Even the poorest were forced to make wills, even if they had nothing to leave. There were instances of people refused the last rites and of the dead left unburied until gifts were made by the relatives of the deceased; and in some cases these relatives were excommunicated for themselves refusing to make gifts to the Church, even when they were not beneficiaries of the will. Attendance at the bed of the dying person and control of the will also helped priests to supervise the beliefs and practices of their parishioners, so that heresy could be detected (Mundy 1990: 185–7).

The intolerance of the north was also apparent in the treatment of the Jews by the new Count of Toulouse. In 1268 Alphonse imposed a tax on all the Jews in the Toulousain. All were arrested and imprisoned on the same day and the men only released when they had paid up. Meanwhile their houses were ransacked and the cash found seized by the Count's officers. Their religious books were also seized (HGL 6: 906).

## The church and the economy

Some parts of the Church were able to benefit economically from the changes in the balance of power after 1229. Cistercian abbeys with their high cash incomes and surpluses, which were not invested in church furnishings, were quick to take advantage of the situation where many members of the nobility found themselves short of money as a result of the fighting. Olivier de Termes sold some of his land which had been returned to him by Saint Louis, to the Cistercians of Fontfroide. In the middle of the century he sold them his lordships of Merconguer, Paziols, Tuchan, St-Nazaire, St-Vallière and Pouzols-Minervois. He sold 'his castle of Tuchan, his town of Paziols, with all their appurtenances, men, women, fiefs, feudatories, mills, waters, meadows, pasturages, woods, forests, lands and lordships'.

As a result the monastery accumulated a block of land around the monastery in the eastern Corbières Mountains, with outliers to west and north. In addition the abbey was able to gain extra rights of pasturage and passage throughout the region. Using this land and rights the monastery was able to reorganise its transhumance system. The sheep went from the district around the monastery westward through the Corbières and then south towards Foix and the Pyrenees. Nearer to home, monks were able to protect their flocks by forbidding the men of Tuchan, now their men, to enclose the tops of the hills, thus leaving sheep walks. At a time when population was expanding and cultivation with it, the monastery clearly used its rights as lord to choose the course which returned the greatest profit to the monastery. Without the unquestioning support of the government such a move would have been extremely difficult. The passage of large numbers of sheep was not always easily tolerated and the monastery needed official support to maintain its new rights (Grezes-Rueff 1977).

To the north, at Albi, the church began to regain control of tithes after 1210, when the region came under crusader control, and the movement continued throughout the thirteenth century. St-Cécile in Albi received the tithes of forty-three churches between 1210 and 1229. St-Salvie received seven churches before 1219 and gained a further ten in the next ten years. The abbey of Castres collected forty parish churches. The process by which churches and their tithes were granted to ecclesiastical institutions was slow but relentless and it was not until the early fourteenth century that the process was completed. Many tithes had been granted in fee by the Church, and the papacy – as well as the count and then the king – recognised the legality of such arrangements. It needed the support of the king to overcome the deep reluctance of the minor nobility, who were often the owners and for whom the transfers meant nothing but financial loss.

The canons of Albi also benefited from tithes, as did the abbeys of Villemagne, Caunes, Lagrasse, Cassan, St-Pons-de-Thomières, Ardonel, La Salvetat, and Villemur as well as St-Victor of Marseille. The Knights Templar were granted twenty-seven churches. At Agen the bishop in mid-century also succeeded in gaining restitution of tithes, but there is evidence that threats of excommunication did not always work and that he often resorted to buying them back instead (Dossat 1965).

The value of these acquisitions is shown by the increase in income of the Bishop of Albi. His income doubled between 1200 and the mid-century and by 1300 had reached 20,000 livres a year, a revenue perhaps ten times as great as the incomes of even important local noblemen. It was income on this scale which allowed the bishop to extend his influence, and ultimately his revenues also, by the foundation of twenty-six bastides (Biget 1972). It was also this increase in clerical wealth (as well as a legacy of 20,000 sous tournois in 1275 by Sicard Alman, Raimon VII's close counsellor and the owner of tolls in the Albi region), which allowed the rebuilding of the cathedral of St-Cécile at Albi. Bishop Bernard de Castanet began the project c. 1282. The building was intended from the beginning to present a fortress-like appearance to the world. It joined the bishop's fortified palace, commenced in 1265, with its own massive western tower protecting the exposed side. The south door was the only access from the town and that was protected by a drawbridge. On the north and north-east the bishop's palace and the River Tarn closed off approach (Bonde 1994: 44). The whole scheme was never completed, but nevertheless suggests a degree of alienation and suspicion between the bishop and his flock.

Other bishops also set out to rebuild their cathedrals, perhaps as a sign of new confidence in their position in society. At Toulouse, Bishop Bertrand de L'Isle-Jourdain set about rebuilding his cathedral in 1270, but got no further than the choir (Wolff 1967: 229). It was not from lack of resources, since by the end of the century the bishop had an annual income of 45,000 livres Tournois (HGL 6: 140). At Narbonne the grandiose plans of Archbishop Maurin produced the enormous choir which still stands, naveless (Bonde 1994: 44). All across the Lauragais new parish churches were built throughout the area where Catharism had been strongest, as the Church reasserted its authority.

## Conclusions

### A house divided

In the twelfth century Languedoc was an area of arrested development compared with the rest of France. As in other parts of the west of the old Frankish Empire the region went through the phase in which local noblemen built principalities, by outright conquest, by gaining for themselves control of institutions such as courts, by control of public office and by attaching men to them by the ties of marriage and of feudal obligation. The Languedoc probably experienced an extended period of warfare and instability as the nobility fought among themselves for control of the countryside (Bonnassie 1991: 120–1). The principalities which appeared in the Languedoc in the mid-twelfth century – as the result of the fighting and dynastic manoeuvring of the previous century and a half – were apparently not much different from the principalities of northern France. A prince ruled partly by force of arms and partly by consent of his subjects, many of whom were also his vassals. The south had its own peculiarities. Internally the larger territories were more loosely held together than those of the north. The ties between rulers and their nobility were less strong than in the north. Part of the reason for this was geography. Much of the region is mountainous, and, in a period when all communication and transport was on foot or on horseback, movement and control was difficult and the initiative lay with the defender on his mountain top. As in other parts of France the landscape became heavily fortified, but it is probable that castles were no more thickly planted here than elsewhere.[1] What was different in the south was the comparative lack of control over the castles exercised by rulers. It was impossible to follow a policy of reducing castles to obedience.

In the tenth and early eleventh centuries the counts were not very rich which made it difficult for them to raise large armies. The pressures which the princes could place upon their noble subjects were comparatively mild and so it was almost impossible to demand military service from vassals on a regular basis. The military bureaucracy which was such a strong feature of Normandy and England and which became increasingly effective under Philippe-Auguste in the French kingdom in the later twelfth century did not emerge in the south (Baldwin 1986: 259–94). The counts of Toulouse could not call up a feudal host and charge scutage money, and so came to rely more upon mercenary troops than their counterparts in the north. In the north, too, the system of pri-

---

[1] It is difficult to estimate accurately, but in the first half of the eleventh century the density of fortified sites in the Languedoc and in Angouleme was much the same (Parisse 1994).

mogeniture meant that the less well off noble families could offer their younger sons little but a training as a knight. In the north mercenary troops were drawn partly from this group of men who were seeking to become a part of the society in which they fought. Although the existence of so many young and landless warriors might make it easy to raise an army and might point to instability and constant warfare, the urge to settle down and join the milieu into which they had been born propelled such men into conformity and made them easier to control. An army of mercenaries recruited from northern Spain lived for wages and plunder and, when those were short lived by armed robbery.

The semi-independent nobility lived in the foothills of the Pyrenees, in the Black Mountains and in the Corbières. While acknowledging the overlordship of the Count of Toulouse or the Viscount of Béziers–Carcassonne these men retained a practical day to day independence. It was in this situation that the brilliant courts of the twelfth century emerged with their cultivation of poets and the cult of courtly love. This nobility adopted the growing twelfth-century culture of the warrior aristocracy, with its emphasis upon the military virtues of belligerence and courage in battle, but did not need to send its younger sons out into the world to seek their fortunes at the court of the ruler.

The failure by the counts of Toulouse to develop a powerful central control was also due to political failures. Other nearby rulers with somewhat similar problems did emerge as masters of their lands. The counts of Barcelona to the south had a territory which was mountainous and had even more castles in the hands of their barons, but by the mid-twelfth century they were able to issue laws and make sure that the castles were held with their authority, by castellans of their choosing (Shideler 1983: 87–113). The counts of Toulouse struggled throughout the twelfth century to exert their authority over the smaller principalities of the eastern Languedoc. Their energies were focused upon the viscounties of Béziers, Carcassonne and Narbonne, but despite nearly a century of fighting they failed to secure control. The real victor in the region was the King of Aragon, who became overlord of the minor principalities of the coast and retained family control of a large part of Provence.

The counts of Toulouse were hampered in their attempts to seize control of the coastal strip by their relations with outside powers. The struggle between the Plantagenets and the Capets to see which family would become the dominant power inside France seemed to provide the House of Raimon with opportunities for advancement by shifting alliances. But this was a dangerous game, which led to intervention in the Languedoc by both parties and diverted resources away from the prize of control of the littoral. Had a unified Languedoc emerged, the undisputed territory of the counts of Toulouse, running from Toulouse to the Rhone and from the Pyrenees to the Auvergne, then the counts might have been able to develop a state. As it was they failed and lost the opportunity to become strong enough to build a state for themselves.

The Languedoc, because of the political weakness of its rulers, retained a highly fragmented series of jurisdictions. Properties inside one jurisdiction might well belong to a rival prince. Thus the Count of Foix was the lord of the village of Preixan and its lands, only 9 km (5½ ml) from Carcassonne, and the Viscount of Carcassonne was also lord of Lavaur well within the territory of Toulouse. Jurisdiction over towns was equally confused, with the courts of viscounts and bishops vying with one another in Narbonne, Béziers and Montpellier.

### Town and country

During the eleventh and twelfth centuries the Languedoc became increasingly urbanised. The impetus towards the growth of towns came partly from the pre-existing cities, a legacy of the Roman past, and partly from the favourable situation of the Languedoc, which made it an area of transit for merchants from the north, from Spain and from the Mediterranean, but even more from the need for revenue on the part of leading rulers. The militarisation of the Languedoc stimulated the need for revenues among the nobility and the circulation of cash. Towns provided a new source of revenue, particularly for the counts of Toulouse, who seem to have lacked large rural estates from which to draw agricultural incomes. As populations rose, and settlement and cultivation grew, the towns provided a focus through which the surpluses might be turned into cash and the prince might benefit by his control of tolls and markets. The growth in the number of fairs, deliberately encouraged by the counts of Toulouse and the Viscounts of Béziers–Carcassonne meant that the manufacturing output of the Languedoc, particularly cloth, could be widely distributed into the northern and the Mediterranean markets.

The wealth of the towns helped to keep the armies of routiers in being, but the towns themselves were by no means easy to control. Toulouse, Narbonne, Béziers and Albi all sought to become independent of their rulers, at least as far as internal government was concerned and by the mid-twelfth century had developed constitutions which marked the citizens out from the country-dwellers roundabout. The people of the towns collected their own taxes and tolls, had their own rules of inheritance, judged their own wrongdoers, negotiated with other towns over trade matters and dealt with their princes as corporate bodies with

corporate policies. Again the relative political weakness of rulers, particularly the counts of Toulouse, encouraged the swift development of
town government. In particular, Toulouse learned to fend for itself in the
1150s and 1160s. By the end of the twelfth century it had a mature
political tradition and a wealthy and sophisticated patrician class of
rulers. Toulouse had come near to becoming an independent city–state
and maintained its own citizen militia. Below the great cities were some
eighty smaller towns, all seeking to emulate their great neighbours. The
towns provided a milieu where a bourgeoisie could emerge which emulated the rural aristocracy in its sophistication and wealth.

In the eleventh and twelfth centuries the countryside passed
through the rapid expansion of population and the growth of settlement
and agriculture which was common to the rest of western Europe. Those
who benefited most fully from the expanding economy were the lords
who controlled it. They included the lay-landlords, the growing church
proprietors and the new bourgeoisie and aristocracy of the towns, who
also invested in agriculture. The rural population grew very rapidly.
Although the deliberate change in the structure of rural settlement, with
the introduction of villages as the normal unit of rural settlement,
enabled the seigniorial class to extend its control over peasant surpluses,
it was difficult to dominate rural life completely. Too many peasant
alloidal owners existed and there was too little direct exploitation of
demesne cultivation for that, so that for the peasantry also, mostly personally free, there existed a degree of freedom not found elsewhere.

The Languedoc, by the mid-twelfth century, provided a unique
environment in which a wealthy culture flourished. It was marked by its
high standard of lay education; the freedom of action and of thought
open to the privileged classes in castle and town; and the open and cosmopolitan nature of the society stimulated by the wide trading links. The
failure of the counts of Toulouse to build a single state or to impose their
wills upon the Languedoc did not mean that the society which they
headed was unsuccessful or incoherent. Despite the warfare of the
twelfth century the Languedoc flourished. How else could so many cities
and towns grow so quickly? How could noblemen and peasants give so
much land to the new monastic order? A failure of control did not mean
a failure of culture or society or economy, but it did mean that the
assumption by the papacy that the ruler could command his subjects in
such a way that heretics could be destroyed or driven out was mistaken.

## Church and heretics

The Church of the twelfth century in the Languedoc was not very
different from the Church elsewhere. Both the monastic revival of the

tenth century and the new orders of the twelfth century had left their
mark. Moissac, with its hundreds of dependent churches and its priories, and houses such as Grandmont and Fontfroide with their large
estates were similar in size and importance to great regular houses found
elsewhere. The gifts of land from the laity to the Cistercians in the mid-
twelfth century were extensive, suggesting a fund of goodwill toward
the new ascetics, both from the nobility, who provided the recruits to
the choirs, and the peasantry who gave their allods and gave themselves
as *conversi*. The military orders, the Hospitallers and the Templars, were
extremely popular and had extensive holdings and representation in the
Languedoc.

It was in the organisation of its dioceses that the Church of the
Languedoc showed its weakness, with the jurisdiction of archbishops
split between Narbonne, Bourges and Auch. Here too, the weakness of
the political settlement showed. Because of the shattered nature of political power the alliance forged in the north between the princes of the
Church and the secular princes could not be established. Raimon-
Berenger, Archbishop of Narbonne, owed his continuation in office
partly to being the uncle of the King of Aragon who needed his family
connections to help him exert influence in Septimania and partly to his
dominant position inside the tiny principality of Narbonne, over which
he held extensive rights. The bishop of Toulouse and many of his other
suffragans were outside his political jurisdiction.

The counts of Toulouse, because they had failed to control Septimania, had difficulty in establishing a close relationship with the Archbishop responsible for the bulk of their lands and could not build the
sort of 'national' church which existed in England, in Normandy or in
Germany. Nor could they develop a close relationship with the hierarchy
and could not use it as an instrument of political power. Consequently,
neither did they develop the close supportive relationship which existed
elsewhere, where clerics worked in government and the prince in turn
supported the Church in its attempts to reform itself and control the
laity.

The failure of this alliance between the prince and the Church was
the reason why relations between secular rulers and the hierarchy of the
Church became so bad in the twelfth century. As the Church itself gained
confidence in its role as the leader of a moral reform of society, the local
secular rulers were seen to lag behind; hence the need for the Church in
the Languedoc to concern itself still with the Peace movement, something largely outmoded in the north. Divided from the leaders of ecclesiastical opinion by this moral gulf, the princes of the Languedoc
maintained relations with monasteries and bishops which treated them

as secular lords and often ignored their religious claims. Without that crucial support from the princes, the Church lost much of its authority when dealing with lesser noblemen and found deference to its claims for special treatment less and less normal.

It was in this social and political setting that Catharism appeared, making the Catholic Church merely *a* Church, rather than *the* Church Universal. Catharism was the most thoroughly worked through of the various heretical strands of thought which appeared in Western Christendom in the twelfth century. As we have seen, it became a widespread heresy and can be said to have been at least as successful in Northern Italy as it was in the Languedoc. In both places it gained numerous adherents and lasted as a publicly held belief system for nearly 150 years. It was in the Languedoc that it posed the most serious threat to the monopoly of the Catholic Church as the intellectual and ideological leader of society which looked to a supernatural support for its structures. The heresy, with its belief in two great spiritual forces at work in the world, offered a picture of a cosmic drama which was as compelling for many people as the orthodox view and which could be presented as closer to reality and to everyday experience. At a time when there was an earnest and widespread desire for a personal spiritual life, Catharism offered a route to salvation which did not require an elaborate superstructure of organisation.

The growing understanding of the Gospels and the life of simplicity which seemed to flow from them was offered directly to the faithful by the new church. Its relative egalitarianism appealed to a wide cross section of society, anxious to gain control of religious expression for itself. The new religion was cheap. Catharism appealed to men and women in local communities, offering them an alternative society, within which they could find meaning. In a world where life was often short, natural hazards were augmented by the brutality of daily existence in a society which justified wide differences of rank and unequal social and economic treatment by appeal to a supernatural order. Catharism provided an explanation of this state of affairs. This was the world created by Satan and therefore a world in which the social order and the lack of justice were perfectly understandable. The perennial problem of evil was solved within the existing limited understanding of the physical universe. For that reason the local society inside which most Cathars lived could form the basis for the exclusive world of the justified; living inside the everyday world, but not of it; looking forward to a perfect existence through the mortification of the flesh and the suffering in this world.

The Church which the Cathars found so objectionable was not, as has sometimes been claimed, especially corrupt or backward in the Midi. It was as vigorous as elsewhere in Europe. Catharism should not be seen as a set of beliefs which spread in default of the actions of the Church in the Midi. To imagine that would be to subscribe to the contemporary official view. Rather it should be seen as a positive choice made by people who were given a very unusual opportunity to hear a new theology and to choose for themselves as a result of the uncoupling of the powers of Church and secular authority. Those people in southern society who were concerned by spiritual matters had an unprecedented freedom to hear a variety of views on theological issues put before them in the second half of the twelfth century. From the early teachings of orthodox radicals such as Robert of Arbrissel to heretical leaders such as Henry the Petrobrusian people became accustomed to the travelling teacher. The rise of the Cathars and the Waldensians came about quite naturally in this context. People of all degrees became used to hearing the exposition of theological positions and to adopting a position themselves.

The twelfth century in the Languedoc was a period of rapid change in the economic and social structure of both town and countryside. All groups had their problems with the changes. Changes brought on by pressures from the new reforms in the Church caused discontent, either by making it difficult for men and women to find eligible marriage partners, by interference in their sexual lives or by the demand for the return of the tithes. At such times new political and religious ideas can spread rapidly as men and women seek a new paradigm by which to shape their lives and control the dislocation they suffer. The Church was also victim of its own success. The radical call to a renewal of Christian life and the extension of a Christian morality to the laity had been a great success. Many lay men and women were serious in their need for teaching and for a moral example. The personalisation of religious feeling had entered deeply into their souls. In other parts of Europe the official Church managed to channel energy into activities such as pilgrimage, the foundation and support of new monastic institutions and the construction of charities. In the Languedoc, although all these activities took place, the heresy of Catharism provided another outlet for spiritual energy which the Church could not suppress.

Catharism rapidly developed all the characteristics of a well organised Church in its own right, with bishops and deacons settled in particular locations. Its houses of *perfecti* of both sexes acted as ecclesiastical centres and provided a focus for local spiritual activity, and the appearance of graveyards belonging to the sect suggested that it was quickly building a permanent place for itself in the countryside. The *perfecti* provided the cadre of committed believers who provided the spiritual and intellectual backbone, progressing around the countryside teaching, preaching and providing the *consolamentum*. Finally, the network of homes which welcomed the preachers gave the new sect power in the community. This organisation gave the movement great strength. It was capable of collective action, of preserving the teaching of the Church and of withstanding considerable persecution over long periods.

The official Church was rightly alarmed by the developments in the Languedoc. By the time of the accession of Innocent III spiritual control of the region had been lost. The experience of preachers who found themselves in public disputations with groups of confident heretics bore witness to the fact that the Catholic Church had lost its monopoly and was having to compete for the spiritual favours of the laity. It was impossible for the medieval Church, which claimed to provide a comprehensive and complete model of the whole of the natural world, of the place of human society within that world, of the history of that society and of its future, to ignore the challenge presented to it within its own territory.

## A crusade for the French and the papacy

The calling of the Crusade was the culmination of many years of effort by the Papacy to find means to combat the spread of heresy. It was seen as a contagion afflicting the body of the Church, which left unchecked would spread to the rest of the body, with possibly fatal consequences. All kinds of remedies were tried. These included preaching but were mostly punitive and relied on the co-operation between princes and bishops to be effective. Without that aid almost everything the Church put forward was ineffective. It was impossible to condemn and silence heretical preachers and overawe their followers when they received open support from people who should have aided the Church. Raimon VI combined the lack of authority, against which his father struggled, with a dislike of the Church hierarchy. As the leaders of the Church, particularly the Pope, pressed their demands upon him, relations deteriorated until the Pope and the bishops of the Languedoc saw him as an enemy. It is probably true that Raimon VI misjudged the Pope's determination to get his way and that he was ill-served by his supporters, but it is hard to imagine that the Crusade could have been avoided. Raimon was truly caught between his own lack of authority and the determination of the Pope to stop the spread of heresy.

The vigour of the response to the call to Crusade was a measure of the depth of religious feeling among the French nobility. The Crusade in the Languedoc was easy in that it did not involve a long journey to the

Middle East. It was close enough for a warrior to campaign in the summer and return home in the winter. It promised a crusading indulgence
and the more distant prospect of loot and possibly property, but the first
crusaders were motivated chiefly by the desire to gain their indulgence,
for Simon de Montfort was left with only his household and paid troops
in the winter of 1209–10. Throughout all the early years of campaigning, the religious motivation, the desire to destroy the heretics, was
uppermost. The burning of groups of *perfecti* was a sign of this, a practical expression of the intolerance of alien groups, whether heretics, Jews
or Moslems which had grown throughout Christendom. It was only
after the *Parlement* of Pamiers at Christmas 1212 that a more permanent
seizure of land by the leaders of the Crusade became a serious possibility. The crusaders were supported in this change by the churchmen in
the Languedoc who became more intransigent as military success bol-
stered their cause.

The early years of the Crusade showed that the leaders of the southern cause were not as militarily competent as the northerners. The loss
of the battle of Muret was not due solely to misfortune. However, the
Languedoc discovered a unity in the struggle against the crusaders
which gave its defenders the will to fight on despite the reverses. What
brought the counts of Toulouse down was financial and military exhaus-
tion when the King of France was able to enter the fray; and then the
chances of succession finally handed the whole of the Languedoc to the
Kingdom of France.

For French historians the collapse of the Languedoc and its assimilation by the French kings is part of the story of the growth of the state
of France. Louis IX was made into a saint, but he was also a very shrewd
king. On the one hand he conciliated his new subjects by offering them
an honest administration and by returning, where it was expedient, to
the tradition of support for noble families and security of inheritance.
On the other hand, he saw the Languedoc as part of his wider relations
with other sovereign rulers and saw, too, that the way forward needed a
new approach to territoriality. Louis' settlement of 1258, the Treaty of
Corbeil, was the result of that new policy.

By the treaty Louis ceded to Jaime I of Aragon all his claims over the
counties in the south, Urgel, Besalu, Roussillon, Cerdagne, Empurias,
Conflant, Ausona and Girona which were part of the territory of King
Jaime as Count of Barcelona. In return the King of Aragon ceded all his
claims in the Languedoc. These were very extensive and included his
claims to suzerainty over Narbonne and Carcassonne. Only Montpellier
and Cayla were left to him (HGL 6: 859). No nobleman in the Languedoc could any longer claim to have the Count of Barcelona as his lord

and make war on that pretext. Nor did Jaime himself have any reason for laying claim to any part of the Languedoc and invading it on the pretext of helping a vassal. The Kingdom of France could be said to have a border and Saint Louis spent much money and effort rebuilding the 'Cathar castles' of the Corbières and the Razès to provide a line of frontier fortresses.

The ally of the king of France was the Church, though to be sure the Crown itself was only at first a reluctant ally. The Church regained its monopoly and in the thirteenth century also secured its position economically. This alliance of Church and State secured both territorial and ideological integrity, but at the cost of the destruction of a culture and identity.

Catharism presented the Church with a special problem. As we have seen it took a long time for the orthodox theologians to define the nature of the new belief and perhaps longer to appreciate the threat that it posed. Here was a relatively mature and coherent set of beliefs which shared so much of the orthodox Christian world view that transition to it from orthodoxy was relatively easy for many people. It required an adaptation of belief, a reframing of traditional pictures, rather than a casting aside of everything held dear. Once the nature of the threat was understood the Church began for the first time to develop a system of repression, the form of which has remained familiar ever since.

The deep roots of Catharism were attested to by the length of time it took to extirpate the heresy. The strength of the family-based, decentralised church became apparent in the second half of the thirteenth century, but the loss of support by the nobility in the countryside and tightened control over the merchant class in the towns led inevitably to exposure of the poorer believers to the attentions of the Inquisition and the loss of adherents, while a relentless pursuit of the *perfecti* destroyed the intellectual and spiritual foundations upon which the cult rested.

Heresy was finally stamped out by the newly developed engine of repression, the Inquisition, which only functioned because the lay power was prepared to see it succeed. For both Church and the new State orthodoxy and political stability could be seen to go hand in hand. The Church retained its monopoly of religious activity, its control of belief and strengthened its control of the private lives of individuals. The new French State gained the Church as an ally in strengthening control over towns and nobility.

Catharism became connected with the brilliant but chaotic world of the Languedoc and the ruin of the one meant the fall of the other. In some sense the history of the Languedoc ceased with the death of its last native Count. As his body passed down the Tarn and up the Garonne to

Toulouse people gathered along the river bank to pay their respects not only to the last of the House of Raimon but to the end of his County. The picturesque ruins of its castles and the modern trivialised 'cathare' tourist centres are built upon the hideous deaths of the faithful and the destruction of an identity which only began to be rediscovered in the nineteenth century. There are still alive today, men and women, who as children in the 1920s were beaten for speaking the Langue d'Oc in the playground.

# References

d'Abadal i de Vinyals, R., 1964, A propos la 'domination' de la maison comitale de Barcelone sur le Midi francais, *Annales du Midi*, 76: 315–45, Toulouse, Privat.

Abels, R. and Harrison, E., 1979, The participation of women in Languedocian Catharism, *Mediaeval Studies*, 41: 215–51, Toronto.

Alauzier, L., 1950, L'heritage des Trencavels, *Annales du Midi*, 62, Toulouse, Privat.

Anglade, J., 1921, *Histoire sommaire de la littérature meridionale au moyen age*, Paris, de Bocard.

Armengaud, A. et Lafont, R., (eds), 1979, *Histoire d'Occitanie*, Paris, Hachette.

Avril, J., 1984, Les dependences des abbayes (prieurés, église, chapelles): Diversité des situations et évolutions, *Les moines noires (XIII–XIVe s)*, *Cahiers de Fanjeaux*, 19, Toulouse, Privat.

Baldwin, J. W., 1986, *The government of Philippe Auguste: Foundations of French royal power in the Middle Ages*, Berkeley, University of California Press.

Baldwin, M., 1968, *Alexander III and the twelfth century*, Glen Rock, New Jersey.

Barber, M., 1990, Catharism and the Occitan nobility, in C. Harper-Bill and R. Harvey (eds), *The ideals and practice of knighthood: III Strawberry Hill Conference, 1988*, 1–19, Woodbridge, Suffolk, The Boydell Press.

Barber, M., 1994, *The new knighthood: A history of the Order of the Temple*, Cambridge, Cambridge University Press.

Bec, P., 1973, *Manuel pratique d'occitan moderne*, Paris, A. & J. Picard.

Belperron, P., 1942, *La croisade contre les Albigeois et l'union du Languedoc à la France*, Paris, Perrin.

Beresford, M., 1967, *New towns of the Middle Ages*, London, Lutterworth.

Berman, C. H., 1986, Medieval agriculture, the southern French countryside and the early Cistercians: A study of forty-three monasteries, *Transactions of the American Philosophical Society*, vol. 76, part 5, Philadelphia, The American Philosophical Society.

Berthe, M., 1990, Les territoires des bastides: Terroirs d'occupation ancienne ou terroirs de colonisation nouvelle?, *Annales du Midi*, 102: 97–108, Toulouse, Privat.

Biget, J.-L., 1971, Un procès d'inquisition à Albi en 1300, *Le credo, la morale et l'Inquisition*, *Cahiers de Fanjeaux*, 6, Toulouse, Privat.

Biget, J.-L., 1972, La restitution des dimes par les laics dans le diocese d'Albi à la fin du XIIIe siècle, *Les évèques, les clercs et le roi, 1250–1300*, *Cahiers de Fanjeaux*, 7, Toulouse, Privat.

Biget, J.-L. (ed.), 1983, *Histoire d'Albi*, Toulouse, Privat.

Biget, J.-L., 1985, L'extinction du catharisme urbain: Les points chauds de la répression, *Effacement du Catharisme (XIII–XIVe s)*, *Cahiers de Fanjeaux*, 20, Toulouse, Privat.

Biget, J.-L., 1990, La sauvété de Vieux-en-Albigeois, *Annales du Midi*, 102, 19–27,

Toulouse, Privat.

Biller, P., 1983, Medieval Waldensian abhorrence of killing pre-1400, in W. J. Sheils (ed.), The Church and War, Studies in Church History, XX, Oxford, Oxford University Press.

Biller, P., 1994, The Cathars of Languedoc and written material, in P. Biller and A. Hudson (eds.), Heresy and Literacy, 1000–1530, Cambridge, Cambridge University Press.

Bisson, T. N., 1964, Assemblies and representation in the Languedoc in the thirteenth century, Princeton, New Jersey, Princeton University Press.

Bisson, T., 1977, The organised Peace in southern France and Catalonia, ca. 1140–ca. 1233, The American Historical Review, vol. 82, no. 2, April 1977: 290–311.

Blumenkranz, B., 1972, Histoire des Juifs en France, Toulouse, Privat.

Bond, J., 1993, The Premonstratensian order: A preliminary survey of its growth and distribution in medieval Europe, in M. Carver (ed.), In search of cult: Archaeological investigations in honour of Philip Rahtz, Woodbridge, Suffolk, The Boydell Press.

Bonde, S., 1994, Fortress churches of Languedoc, Cambridge, Cambridge University Press.

Bonnassie, P., 1978, La monnaie et les échanges en Auvergne et Rouerge aux Xe et XIe siècles d'après les sources hagiographiques, Annales du Midi, 90: 275–88, Toulouse, Privat.

Bonnassie, P., 1991, From slavery to feudalism in south-western Europe, Cambridge, Cambridge University Press.

Bouquet, Dom, 1871, Recueil des historiens des Gaules et de la France, XIII, Paris.

Bories, M., 1970, Origines de l'université de Montpellier, Les universités du Languedoc au XIII siècle, Cahiers de Fanjeaux, 5: 92–107, Toulouse, Privat.

Bourin, M., 1990, Hagiotoponymie et concentration de l'habitat, Annales du Midi, 102: 35–41, Toulouse, Privat.

Bourin-Derrau, M., 1987, Villages médiévaux en Bas-Languedoc: genèse d'une sociabilité (Xe–XIVe siècles), Paris.

Bousquet, S., 1963, La fondation de Villeneuve d'Aveyron (1053) et l'expansion de l'abbaye de Moissac en Rouerge, Annales du Midi, 75: 517–42, Toulouse, Privat

Braudel, F., 1991, The identity of France; vol. ii, People and production, London, Fontana.

Brooke, C. N. L., 1970, The missionary at home: The Church in the towns, 1000–1250, in C. L. Cumming (ed.), The mission of the Church and the propagation of the Faith, Studies in Church History, vol. 6, Cambridge, Cambridge University Press.

Brundage, J. A., 1968, The votive obligations of the crusaders, The development of canonistic doctrine, Traditio, 24: 77–118, New York.

Brundage, J. A., 1993a, Carnal delight: Canonistic theories of sexuality, in Brundage, Sex, law and marriage in the Middle Ages, Aldershot, Hampshire and Brookfield, Vermont, Variorum Reprints.

Brundage, J. A., 1993b, Allas! that evere love was sinne: Sex and medieval canon law, in Brundage, Sex, law and marriage in the Middle Ages, Aldershot, Hampshire and Brookfield, Vermont, Variorum Reprints.

Caesarius of Heisterbach, Caesarius Heiserbacensis monachi ordinis Cisterciensis, Dialogus *miraculorum*, 2 vols, ed. J. Strange, Cologne, 1851, J. M. Heberle.

Caille, J., 1985, Les seigneurs de Narbonne dans le conflit Toulouse–Barcelone au XII siècle, *Annales du Midi*, 97, Toulouse, Privat.

Capelle, R. M., 1981, The representation of conflict on the imposts of Moissac, *Viator*, 12: 79–100, Berkeley, California.

Chedeville, A., 1980, De la cité à la ville, in G. Duby (ed.), *La ville mediévale des Carolingiens à la Renaissance*, Paris, Editions du Seuil.

Cheyette, F., 1976, The castles of the Trencavels: A preliminary aerial survey, in W. C. Jordan, B. McNab and T. F. Ruiz (eds), *Order and innovation in the Middle Ages: Essays in honor of Joseph R. Strayer*, Princeton, New Jersey, Princeton University Press.

Combes, J., 1958, Les foires en Languedoc au Moyen Age, *Annales, Économies, Sociétés, Civilisation*, 13: 231–59, Paris.

Cottineau, Dom L. H., 1935–7 and 1971, *Répertoire topo-bibliographique des abbayes et prieurés*, 3 vols, Macon, Protat.

Cowdrey, H. E. J., 1970, The Peace and the truce of God in the eleventh century, *Past and Present*, 46: 42–67, Oxford, Oxford University Press.

Davis, G. W., 1974, *The Inquisition at Albi 1299–1300*, New York, Octagon Books.

Debax, H, 1988, Strategies matrimoniales des comtes de Toulouse (850–1270), *Annales du Midi*, 100: 132–51, Toulouse, Privat.

Delaruelle, E., 1968, L'état actuel des études sur le Catharisme, *Cahiers de Fanjeaux*, 3, Toulouse, Privat.

Denkova, L., 1990, Les bogomiles: Ontologie du Mal et orthodoxie orientale, *Christianisme médiéval; mouvements dissidents et novateurs, Hérésis*, 13 & 14, Villegly, Aude, France, Centre René Nelli.

DeSoigne, R. R., 1976, The fairs of Nîmes, in W. C. Jordan, B. McNab and T. F. Ruiz (eds), *Order and innovation in the Middle-Ages; Essays in honor of Joseph R. Strayer*, Princeton, New Jersey, Princeton University Press.

Dossat, Y., 1944, Le clergé méridional à la veille de la croisade Albigeoise, *Revue historique et littéraire du Languedoc*, I, Albi, 1944, reprinted in Dossat, *Église et hérésie en France au XIIIe siècle*, 1982, London, Variorum Reprints.

Dossat, Y., 1959, *Les crises de l'inquisition Toulousaine au XIIIe siècle (1233–1273)*, Bordeaux, Imprimerie Bière.

Dossat, Y., 1965, Les restitution des dimes dans le diocèse d'Agen pendant l'épiscopat de Guillaume II (1247–1263), *Bulletin philogique et historique (jusqu'à 1610), année 1962*, Paris, reprinted in Dossat, *Église et hérésie en France au XIIIe siècle*, 1982, London, Variorum Reprints.

Dossat, Y., 1971, Une figure d'inquisiteur: Bernard de Caux, *Le credo, la morale et l'inquisition, Cahiers de Fanjeaux*, 6: 253–72, Toulouse, Privat.

Dossat, Y., 1980, Types exceptionnels de pèlerins: L'hérétique, le voyageur déguisé, le professionel, *Le pèlerinage, Cahiers de Fanjeaux*, 15: 207–25, Toulouse, Privat

Douais, Mgr, Bishop of Beauvais, 1900 and 1977, *Documents pour servir à l'histoire de l'inquisition dans le Languedoc*, Paris, Société de l'histoire de France.

Duby, G., 1968, *Rural economy and country life in the medieval West*, London, Edward Arnold.

Duby, G. (ed.), 1975, *Histoire de la France rurale: t. 1, La formation des campagnes française*, Paris, Editions Seuil.

Duggan, C., 1995, Papal Judges Delegate and the making of the 'New Law' in the twelfth century, in T. N. Bisson (ed.), *Cultures of power: Lordship, status and process in twelfth-century Europe*, Philadelphia, University of Pennsylvania Press.

Dunbabin, J., 1985, *France in the Making*, Oxford, Oxford University Press.

Durieux, S., 1973, Approches de l'histoire franciscaine, *Les mendiants en Pays d'Oc au XIIIe siècle, Cahiers de Fanjeaux*, 8, Toulouse, Privat.

Duvernoy, J. (ed.), 1958, *Chronique de Guillaume Pelhisson*, Toulouse, Privat.

Duvernoy, J., 1963, Les Albigeois dans la vie sociale et économiques de leur temps, *Actes du colloque de Toulouse; annales de l'institut d'études occitanes*, 1962–3: 64–72, Toulouse.

Duvernoy, J. (ed.), 1965, *Le registre d'inquisition de Jacques Fournier, Évêque de Pamiers (1318–1325)*, 3 vols, Toulouse, Privat.

Duvernoy, J. (ed. and trans.), 1976a, *Guilhem de Puylaurens, Chronique; Chronica Magistri Guillelmi de Podio Laurentii*, Paris, Editions CNRS.

Duvernoy, J., 1976b, *Le catharisme: La religion des cathares*, Toulouse, Privat.

Duvernoy, J., 1979, *Le catharisme: L'histoire des cathares*, Toulouse, Privat.

Duvernoy, J., 1985, *Le Catharisme en Languedoc, Effacement du Catharisme? (XIIIe–XIVe s.), Cahiers de Fanjeaux*, 20, Toulouse, Privat.

Duvernoy, J., 1990, Les origines du mouvement Vaudois, *Christianisme médiéval; mouvements dissidents et novateurs, Hérésis*, nos 13 & 14, Villegly, Centre René Nelli.

Duvernoy, J., 1994, *Cathares, Vaudois et Béguins, dissidents du Pays d'Oc*, Toulouse, Privat.

Evans, J., 1938, *The romanesque architecture of the Order of Cluny*, Cambridge, Cambridge University Press.

Fearns, J. (ed.), 1968, *Petri Venerabilis; contra Petrobrusianos hereticos*, Turnholt, Belgium, Brepols S.A.

Fliche, A., Thouzellier, C. and Azais, Y., 1950, *Histoire de l'église depuis les origines jusqu'à nos jours*, 10, *La Chrétienté romaine*, Paris, Bloud et Gay.

Foreville, R., 1969, Innocent III et la croisade des Albigeois, *Paix de Dieu et guerre sainte en Languedoc au XIIIe siècle, Cahiers de Fanjeaux*, 4, Toulouse, Privat.

Foreville, R. and Rousset de Pina, J., 1953, *Histoire de L'église, 9; du premier concile du Latran à l'avènement d'Innocent III*, 2ème partie, Paris, Bloud et Gay.

*Gallia Christiana in provincias distributa*, 1874, ed. Dom D. Sammarthanus and further edited Dom P. Piotin, vols 1–16, Paris.

*Gallia*, 1973, Fouilles et monuments archéologiques en France métropolitaine, tome 31 (1973), fascicule I, Paris, CNRS.

*Gallia*, 1981, Fouilles et monuments archéologiques en France métropolitaine, tome 39 (1981), fascicule I, Paris, CNRS.

Gérard, P., 1990, Origine et développement des paroisses du Bourg de Toulouse (XIIe–XIIIe siècles), *La paroisse en Languedoc (XIIIe–XIVe s.), Cahiers de Fanjeaux*, 25, Toulouse, Privat.

Gerard, P. et Magnou, E. (eds), 1965, *Cartulaire des Templiers de Douzens*, Paris, Bibliothèque Nationale.

Ghil, E. M., 1989, *L'age de parage: Essai sur le poétique et le politique en Occitanie au XIIIe siècle*, New York, Berne and Frankfurt, Columbia University Press.

Gilchrist, J., 1969, *The Church and economic activity in the middle ages*, London.

Gilles, H., 1977, Commentaires méridionaux des prescriptions canoniques sur les juifs, *Juifs et judaïsme de Languedoc, Cahiers de Fanjeaux*, 12, Toulouse, Privat.

Gimpel, J., 1988, *The medieval machine*, 2nd edn, London, Pimlico.

Goody, J., 1983, *The development of the family and marriage in Europe*, Cambridge, Cambridge University Press.

Gordon, J., 1992, *The laity and the Catholic Church in Cathar Languedoc*, unpublished Oxford D.Phil. thesis.

Gouron, A., 1958, *La réglementation des métiers en Languedoc au moyen âge*, Geneva.

Gramain, M., 1980, Castrum, structures féodales et peuplement en Biterrois au XI siècle, *Structures féodales et féodalisme dans l'occident Méditerranéen (Xe–XIIIe siècles): Bilan et perspectives de recherches*, Rome, École Française de Rome.

Grezes-Rueff, F., 1977, L'abbaye de Fontfroide et son domain foncier aux XIIe–XIIIe siècles, *Annales du Midi*, 89, Toulouse, Privat.

Griffe, E., 1936, Géographie Écclésiastique de la province de Narbonne au moyen âge, in *Annales du Midi*, 49, Toulouse, Privat.

Griffe, E., 1969, *Les débuts de l'aventure cathare en Languedoc 1140–90*, Paris, Letouzey et Ané.

Griffe, E., 1971, *Le Languedoc cathare de 1190 à 1210*, Paris, Letouzey et Ané.

Griffe, E., 1980, *Le Languedoc cathare et l'Inquisition*, Paris, Letouzey et Ané.

Guébin, P. et Maisonneuve, H., 1951, *Histoire Albigeoise de Pierre des Vaux-de-Cernay*, Paris, J. Vrin.

Hallam, E., 1980, *Capetian France, 987–1328*, London, Longman.

Hamilton, B., 1979, The Cathar Council of St Felix reconsidered, *Monastic reform, Catharism and the crusades (900–1300) (IX)*, London, Variorum Reprints.

Hamilton, B., 1981, *The medieval Inquisition*, London, Edward Arnold.

Hensel, W. and Dąbrowski, K. et al., 1965, Le village déserte de Saint-Jean-le-Froid; rapport des fouilles, *Villages désertes et histoire économique xi–xviii siècles*, Paris, École pratique des Haute Études.

Hensel, W., Nadolski, A. et al. 1965, Le village déserte de Montaigut; rapport des fouilles, *Villages désertes et histoire économique xi–xviii siècles*, Paris, École pratique des Haute Études.

Herlihy, D., 1958, Church property on the Continent, 701–1200, *Speculum*, 33: 23–41, Cambridge, Massachusetts.

HGL, Dom C. L. Devic and Dom J. Vaissette, *Histoire générale du Languedoc*, 16 vols, revised edn, 1875–1904, Paris, Privat.

Higounet, C., 1948, Bastides et frontières, *Le Moyen age*, 54: 113–131, Paris.

Higounet, C., 1948–9, La frange orientale des bastides, *Annales du Midi*, 61: 359–67, Toulouse, Privat.

Higounet, C., 1950, Cisterciens et bastides, *Le Moyen Age*, 56: 69–84, Paris.

Higounet, C., 1953, Mouvements de population dans le Midi de la France du XI au XV siecle, *Annales, Économies, Societés, Civilisation*, 8: 1–24, Paris.

Higounet, C., 1963, Les sauvetés de Moissac, *Annales du Midi*, 75: 505–16, Toulouse, Privat.

Hill, J. H. and Hill L. L., 1959, *Raymond IV de Saint-Gilles*, Toulouse, Privat.

Hill, R.T. and Bergin, T. G., 1973, *An anthology of the Provençal Troubadours, vol. 1*, 2nd edn, New Haven, Connecticut and London, Yale University Press.

Hilton, R H., 1992, *English and French towns in feudal society*, Cambridge, Cambridge University Press.

Hodges, R., 1982, *Dark age economics*, London, Duckworth.

Housley, N., 1985, Crusades against Christians: Their origins and early development, c. 1000–1216, in P. Edbury (ed.), *Crusade and settlement*, Cardiff, University of Wales Press.

Keen, M., 1984, Chivalry, New Haven, Connecticut and London, Yale University Press.

Kuttner, S. and Garcia y Garcia, A., 1964, A new eyewitness account of the Fourth Lateran Council, Traditio, 22: 115–78, New York.

Lacaze, M., 1993, Les granges de l'abbaye cistercienne de Gimont, Annales du Midi, 105: 167–82, Toulouse, Privat.

Lambert, M., 1992, Medieval heresy; Popular movements from the Gregorian reform to the Reformation, 2nd edn, Oxford, Blackwell.

Langlois, G., 1991, La formation de la seigneurie de Termes, in Hérésis, 17: 51–72, Villegly, Centre René Nelli.

Langmuir, G. I., 1984, Historiographic crucifixion, in D. R. Blumenthal (ed.), Approaches to Judaism in medieval times, Chico, California, Scholars Press.

Lavedan, P. and Hugueney, J., 1974, L'urbanisme au moyen age, Bibliotheque de la Société Française d'Archéologie, 5, Paris, Arts et Métiers Graphiques.

Le Bras, G., 1964, Histoire de L'église, 12, Institutions ecclésiatiques de la Chrétiené médiévale, Paris, Bloud et Gay.

Le Goff, J., 1979, The usurer and purgatory, in The dawn of modern banking (UCLA Conference 1977), New Haven, Connecticut and London, Yale University Press.

Le Goff, J., 1980, Histoire de la France urbaine: t. 2, la ville médiévale des Carolingiens à la Renaissance, Paris, éditions Seuil.

Lewis, A. R., 1947, The development of town government, Speculum, XXII, Cambridge, Massachusetts. Reprinted in Medieval society in southern France and Catalonia, 1984, London, Variorum Reprints.

Lewis, A. R., 1965, The development of southern French and Catalan society, 718–1050, Austin, Texas, University of Texas Press.

Lewis, A. R., 1980, Patterns of economic development in southern France, 1050–1271, Studies in Medieval and Renaissance History, new series, III, Vancouver, British Columbia. Reprinted in Lewis, Medieval society in southern France and Catalonia, 1984, London, Variorum Reprints.

Lewis, A. R., 1984, La feodalité dans le Toulousain et la France meridionale (850–1050), Medieval society in southern France and Catalonia, London, Variorum Reprints.

Lewis, R. E., (ed.), 1978, Lotario dei Segni (Pope Innocent III), De Miseria Condicionis Humane, Athens, Georgia, USA, University of Georgia Press.

Leyser, H., 1983, Hermits and the new monasticism; A study of religious communities in western Europe 1000–1150, London, Macmillan.

Limouzin-Lamothe, R., 1932, La commune de Toulouse, Toulouse, Privat.

Loeb, A., 1983, Les relations entre les trobadours et les comtes de Toulouse (1112–1229), Annales du Midi, 95, Toulouse, Privat.

Lunel, A., 1975, Juifs du Languedoc, de la Provence et des états français du Pape, Paris, Albin Michel.

Magnou, E., 1958, L'introduction de la reforme gregorienne à Toulouse (fin xi–début xii siècle), Toulouse, Privat.

Magnou-Nortier, E., 1974, La société laique et l'église dans la province ecclésiastique de Narbonne (zone cispyrénéenne) de la fin du VIIIe siècle à la fin du XIe siècle, Toulouse, Privat.

Maisonneuve, H., 1960, Études sur les origines de l'inquisition, 2nd edn, Paris.

Manselli, R., 1956, Una designazione dell'eresia catara: 'Arriana Heresis', *Bulletin dell Instituto storico italiano per il medio evo*, lxviii.

Manselli, R., 1985, La fin du catharisme en Italie, in *Effacement du Catharisme? (XIII–XIVs)*, Cahiers de Fanjeaux, 20: 101–8, Toulouse, Privat.

Mansi, J. D. (ed.), *Sacrorum conciliorum nova et amplissima collectio...*, 53 vols, Venice, Florence and Paris, 1759–1927, reprinted Graz 1961, Akademische Druck -u Verlagsanstalt.

Martin-Chabot, E., 1973–89 (ed. and trans.), *La Chanson de la croisade Albigeoise*, 3 vols (3rd edn), Paris, Les Belles Lettres.

Menard, H., 1990, Le réseau des églises dans l'ancien diocèse de Rieux: Les sanctuaires, *La paroisse en Languedoc (XIIIe–XIVe s.)*, Cahiers de Fanjeaux, 25, Toulouse, Privat.

Mollat, M., 1967, Le problème de la pauvreté au XIIe siècle, Cahiers de Fanjeaux, 2, Toulouse, Privat.

Mollat, M., 1986, *The poor in the Middle Ages*, New Haven, Connecticut and London, Yale University Press.

Montpellier, Société archéologique de, 1884–6, *Cartulaire des Guillems de Montpellier*, Montpellier.

Moore, R. I., 1974, St Bernard's Mission to the Languedoc in 1145, *Bulletin of the Institute of Historical Research*, vol. xlvii, no. 115: 1–10, London.

Moore, R. I., 1977a, Some heretical attitudes to the renewal of the church, in D.Baker (ed.), *Renaissance and renewal in Christian history: Studies in Church history*, Oxford, Blackwell.

Moore, R. I., 1977b, *The origins of European dissent*, London, Allen Lane.

Moore, R. I., 1987, *The formation of a persecuting society*, Oxford, Blackwell.

Moore, R. I., 1992, Anti-semitism and the birth of Europe, in D. Wood (ed.), *Christianity and Judaism: Studies in Church history*, 29, Oxford, Blackwell.

Moreau, M., 1988, *L'âge d'or des religieuses: Monastères féminins du Languedoc méditerranéen au moyen age*, Montpellier.

Morris, C., 1972, *The discovery of the individual 1050–1200*, London, SPCK.

Morris, C., 1989, *The papal monarchy: The western Church from 1050 to 1250*, Oxford, Oxford University Press.

Mousnier, M., 1983, Les granges de l'abbaye cistercienne de Grandselve, in *Annales du Midi*, 95: 7–27, Toulouse, Privat.

Mundy, J. H., 1954, *Liberty and political power in Toulouse, 1050–1230*, New York, Columbia University Press.

Mundy, J. H., 1966, Charity and social work in Toulouse 1100–1250, in *Traditio*, 22: 203–88, New York.

Mundy, J. H., 1981, Village, town and city in the region of Toulouse, in J. A. Raftis (ed.), *Pathways to medieval peasants; Papers in medieval studies*, 2, Toronto, Pontifical Institute of Medieval Studies.

Mundy, J. H., 1985, *The repression of Catharism at Toulouse: The royal diploma of 1279*, Toronto, Pontifical Institute of Medieval Studies.

Mundy, J. H., 1987, Le mariage et les femmes à Toulouse au temps des cathares, *Annales, Économies, Societés, Civilisation*, 42 année, no. 1.

Mundy, J. H., 1990, *Men and women at Toulouse in the age of the Cathars*, Toronto, Pontifical Institute of Medieval Studies.

Nahon, G, 1977, Condition fiscale et économique des juifs, in *Juifs et judaïsme de*

Languedoc; Cahiers de Fanjeaux, 12, Toulouse, Privat.

Narbonne, 1994, 'Narbonne au temps des seigneurs, XI–XV siècles', Exhibition of documents held at the Municipal Museum in Narbonne, July–October 1994.

Nelli, R., 1969, La vie quotidienne des cathares du Languedoc au XIIIe siècle, Paris, Hachette.

Nelson, J., 1972, Society, theodicy and the origins of heresy: Towards a Reassessment of the medieval evidence, in D. Baker (ed.), Schism, heresy and religious protest: Studies in Church history, vol. 9, Cambridge, Cambridge University Press.

Nelson, J., 1992, Charles the Bald, London, Longman.

Oblensky, D., 1948, The Bogomils: A study in Balkan neo-Manichaeism, Cambridge, Cambridge University Press

Ourliac, P., 1990, Le peuplement de la haute vallée de la Garonne vers l'an mil', Annales du Midi, 102: 121–35, Toulouse, Privat.

Ourliac, P. and Magnou, A.-M., 1984, Les paroisses de l'abbaye de Lezat, in Les moines noires (XIII–XIVe s), Cahiers de Fanjeaux, 19, Toulouse, Privat.

Pailhes, C.-L., 1984, L'abbaye de Lagrasse de 1100–1270, Les moines noires (XIII–XIVe s), Cahiers de Fanjeaux, 19, Toulouse, Privat.

Parisse, M., 1994, Atlas de la France de l'an mil, Paris, Picard Editeur.

Partak, J., 1985, Structures foncières et prélèvement seignural dans un terroir du Lauragais, Annales du Midi, 97: 5–24, Toulouse, Privat.

Pasquier, F., 1921, Cartulaire de Mirepoix, 2 vols, Toulouse, Privat.

Paterson, L. M., 1993, The world of the troubadours: Medieval Occitan society, c. 1100–c. 1300, Cambridge, Cambridge University Press.

Pawlowski, K., 1987, Villes et villages circulares du Languedoc: Un des premiers modèles de l'urbanisme médiéval?, Annales du Midi, 99: 407–27, Toulouse, Privat.

Peal, A., 1986, Olivier de Termes and the Occitan nobility in the thirteenth century, Reading Medieval Studies, xii, 109–30, Reading, Berkshire.

Petit-Dutaillis, C., 1894, Étude sur la vie et le règne de Louis VIII, Paris, Librarie Émile Bouillon.

PL, Patrologia Latinae cursus completus, series Latina, 221 vols, ed. J.-P. Migne, 1844–64, Paris.

Poly, J.-P. and Bournazel, E., 1991, The feudal transformation; 900–1200, New York and London, Holmes and Meier.

Powicke, M., 1953, The thirteenth century: 1216–1307, Oxford, Oxford University Press.

Quèhen, R. and Dieltiens, D., 1983, Les chateaux Cathares et les autres: Les cinquante chateaux des Hautes-Corbières, Montesquieu-Volvestre, published by the authors.

Racinet, P., 1988, L'expansion de Cluny sous Hugues 1er de Semur, Le gouvernement d'Hugues de Semur à Cluny; Actes du colloque scientifique international, Cluny, Ville de Cluny – Musée Ochier.

Rainerius Sacconi, Summa de Catharis et pauperibus de Lugduno, translated and printed in W. Wakefield and A. Evans, 1991, Heresies of the high Middle Ages, New York, Columbia University Press.

Ramière de Fortanier, A., 1990, Du décimaire à la paroisse: L'exemple de Prouille, in La paroisse en Languedoc (XIIIe–XIVe s.), Cahiers de Fanjeaux, 25, Toulouse, Privat.

Riley-Smith J., 1987, *The Crusades: A short history*, London, Athlone.

Riley-Smith, J., 1992, *What were the Crusades?* (2nd edn), London, Macmillan.

Rivet, A. L. F., 1988, *Gallia Narbonnensis*, London, Batsford.

Roquebert, M., 1970, *L'épopée cathare, 1198–1212, l'invasion*, Toulouse, Privat.

Roquebert, M., 1989, *Mourir a Montségur: L'épopée cathare*, vol. 4, Toulouse, Privat.

Rosenwein, B. H., 1971, Feudal war and monastic peace: Cluniac liturgy as ritual aggression, *Viator*, 2: 129–57, Berkeley, California.

Runciman, S., 1951, *A history of the Crusades*, 3 vols, London, Penguin Books.

Russell, J. C., 1962, Evolution demographique de Montpellier. *Annales du Midi*, 74: 345–60, Toulouse, Privat.

Salch, C.-L. (ed.), 1977, *L'atlas des chateaux forts en France*, Strasbourg, Éditions Publiotal.

Sayers, J. 1994, *Innocent III: Leader of Europe 1198–1216*, London and New York, Longman.

Schapiro, M., 1985, *The sculpture of Moissac*, London, Thames and Hudson.

Shideler, J., 1983, *A medieval noble Catalan family: The Montcadas, 1000–1230*, Berkeley, Los Angeles, London, University of California Press.

Shirley, J. (trans.), 1996, *The song of the Cathar wars: A history of the Albigensian crusade of William of Tudela and an anonymous successor*, Aldershot, Hampshire and Brookfield, Vermont, Scolar Press.

Siberry, E., 1985, *Criticism of crusading 1095–1247*, Oxford, Oxford University Press.

Strickland, M., 1992, Slaughter, slavery or ransom: the impact of the conquest on conduct in warfare, in C. Hicks (ed.), *England in the eleventh century, Harlaxton Medieval Studies*, vol. II, Stamford, Lincs.

Stubbs, W. (ed.), 1867, *Gesta regis Henrici secundi Benedicti abbatis*, Roll Ser. 49/1, London, Longmans.

Stubbs, W. (ed.), 1867–8, *Chronica Rogeri de Hovenden*, in *rerum Britanicarum medii aevi scriptores*, London, Longmans.

Tellenbach, G., 1993, *The Church in western Europe from the tenth to the early twelfth century*, Cambridge, Cambridge University Press.

Thorpe, . (trans. and ed.), 1974, *Gregory of Tours: History of the Franks*, London, Penguin Books.

Thouzellier, C., 1968, L'inquisitio et St-Dominique, *Annales du Midi*, 80: 121–36, Toulouse, Privat.

Thouzellier, C., 1969, *Catharisme et Valdéisme en Languedoc: À la fin du XIIe et au début du XIII siècle*, 2nd edn, Louvain and Paris, Presses Universitaires de France.

Thouzellier, C., 1970, Sur l'égalité des deux dieux dans le catharisme, *Annales du Midi*, 82: 343–7, Toulouse, Privat.

Thouzellier, C. (ed.), 1973, *Livres des deux principes*, Paris, Les editions du cerf.

Timbal, P., 1950, *L'application de la coutume de Paris au pays d'Albigeois*, Toulouse.

Topsfield, L. T., 1975, *Troubadours and love*, Cambridge, Cambridge University Press.

Valdeon, J. H., Salrach, J. and Zabalo, J., 1980, *Feudalismo y consolidacion de los pueblos Hispanicos (siglos xi–xv); vol. iv, Historia de Espana*, ed. M. T. Lara, Barcelona, Labor.

Verdon, J., 1976, Recherches sur les monastères feminins dans la France du sud aux IX–XI siècles', *Annales du Midi*, 88: 117–38, Toulouse, Privat.

Verlaguet, P.-A., 1910, *Cartulaire de l'abbaye de Silvanes*, Rodez, Commision des Archives Historique de Rouergue.

Verrassel, A., 1992, Mille églises romanes de France, Duculot, Paris.

Vicaire, M.-H., 1964, Saint Dominic and his times, trans. K. Pond, London, Darton, Longman and Todd.

Vicaire, M.-H., 1967, St Dominique et les inquisiteurs, Annales du Midi 79: 173–94.

Vicaire, M.-H., 1973, La province dominicaine de Provence 1215–1295, Les mendiants en Pays d'Oc au XIIIe siècle, Cahiers de Fanjeaux, 20, Toulouse, Privat.

Vidal, H., 1951, Le pouvoir épiscopale à Béziers 1152–1209, Montpellier.

Vielliard, J. (ed.), 1963, Le guide du pèlerin de Saint-Jacques de Compostelle, 3rd edn, Macon, Protat.

Vilar, P. (ed.), 1987, Historia de Catalunya: vol. II: El proces de feudalizacio, segles III–XII, Barcelona, Edicions 62.

Wakefield, W., 1974, Heresy, crusade and inquisition in southern France, London, Allen and Unwin.

Wakefield, W. and Evans, A. P., 1969, Heresies of the high Middle Ages, republished 1991, New York and Oxford, Columbia University Press.

Warren, W. L., 1973, Henry II, London, Eyre and Methuen.

Wolff, P., 1961, Histoire de Toulouse, 2nd edn, Toulouse, Privat.

Wolff, P., 1967, Histoire du Languedoc, Toulouse, Privat.

Wolff, P., 1969, Hérésie et croisade: Probleme de critique historique, in P. Wolff (ed.), 1969, Documents de l'histoire du Languedoc, 99–114, Toulouse, Privat.

Wolff, P., 1978, Regards sur le midi médiéval, Toulouse, Privat, 1978.

# Index